To Tom McBride,

A great businessman,

a great historian and

a great friend.

With best wishes,

[illegible]

July 30, 2010.

Norman's Uncle

V. K. WELLINGTON KOO

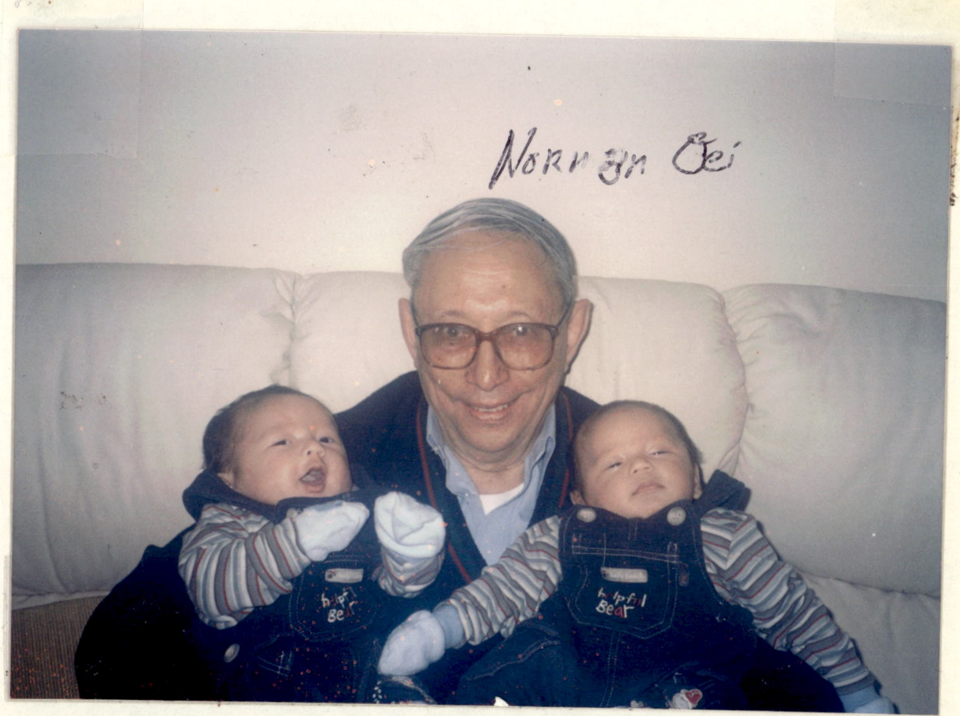

V. K. WELLINGTON KOO
A Case Study of China's Diplomat and Diplomacy of Nationalism, 1912-1966

By Pao-chin Chu

Please return:

Karen McBride
5289 Appian Way
Long Beach, CA, 90803
Ph: 562 433 4147

The Chinese University Press
Hong Kong

International Standard Book Number: 962-201-236-1

The Chinese University Press
The Chinese University of Hong Kong
SHATIN, N.T., HONG KONG

Typesetting by The Chinese University Press
Printing by Hoi Kwong Printing Co.

Contents

Foreword

Dr. V. K. Wellington Koo had an extraordinarily long and illustrious career as a diplomat, and Professor Pao-chin Chu has spent many years studying that career, which extended over fifty years in the service of China's governments, and then ten more years in international service on the International Court of Justice at the Hague. Such an illustrious career was built on the basis of intelligence, education, temperment, and skill.

Born in 1888, or by some accounts a year earlier, the young Wei-chün was given an excellent early Chinese education and later made an outstanding record in his Westernized studies at St. John's College in Shanghai. He then went, as a lad of 16, to the United States and, after a year of preparatory schooling at an academy in Ithaca, New York, he entered Columbia College in 1905. Again his academic record was outstanding, and he also distinguished himself in such extra-curricular fields as debating and as editor of the *Daily Spectator*, unusual achievements for a foreign student. Equally significant, he showed himself a natural leader among Chinese students in the United States, attracting attention of Chinese officialdom.

He had done so well in college that he could have graduated early, but he delayed his commencement till the spring of 1909 so as to graduate with his own class, in the meantime taking graduate courses and earning the M.A. degree. Studying as a graduate student in Columbia's distinguished Faculty of Political Science, he specialized in international law. Early in 1912, while still engaged in writing his doctoral dissertation on "The Status of Aliens in China," he received an invitation from China's Premier in the newly born Republican Government in Peking. His professors encouraged him to defend his dissertation as it stood, and kindly friends saw to its publication so he could leave. With his formal education behind him, Dr. Wellington Koo arrived in Peking in April 1912, to begin a government career at the age of 24. Trained in Western history, political science, and international law, he plunged into a decadent bureaucratic world left over from the last dynastic years, but a world gradually being infused by a corps of younger officials educated in Japan, Europe, and the United States.

In this environment, Dr. Koo's intelligence and Chinese breeding, his excellent education and skill in human relations aided him in the inevitable scrambles of bureaucratic politics. His career was meteoric. Professor Chu gives a clear account of his rise within the branch of government in which he became China's outstanding practitioner—foreign affairs. It was a time of imperialistic dominance of his country and of rising Chinese nationalism. China needed his talents. After less than four years in Peking, he was appointed at the age of 27, to be China's Minister to the United States and Mexico.

The central theme of Professor Chu's study is a description and analysis of the battles Dr. Koo fought to recover China's autonomy and to elevate its international position to one of equality in the family of nations. Dr. Koo dedicated his diplomatic career to these goals, and when they had been achieved at the end of the Second World War, he fought more partisan battles to preserve the international position of his Government against claims of its rival, the Government of the People's Republic of China.

Dr. Koo's official career spanned more than half a century. The present work emphasizes only certain elements of, and episodes in, that career. There are chapters devoted to Dr. Koo's efforts and failures at the Paris Peace Conference of 1919, and his achievements at the Washington Conference of 1921-22; problems resulting from the Linch'eng Incident of May 1923, when Dr. Koo was China's Foreign Minister; the negotiations toward establishment of Sino-Soviet relations in 1923 and 1924; the beginnings of the Sino-Japanese War and Dr. Koo's efforts, actually rather unavailing, to muster support for China through the League of Nations in 1937-38; and, finally, his post-war involvements in the United Nations; negotiations of the Japanese Peace Treaty of April 1952; and his efforts to preserve his Government's right to represent China in the United Nations. These were important activities with some noted accomplishments, and the telling of them is well done. Yet Dr. Koo worked on many other important problems and accomplished much that is not discussed here. He also suffered some humiliating failures—ones which probably were beyond the powers of diplomacy to achieve—such as his efforts to secure massive American aid for his Government during its disastrous civil war of 1946-50. He observed his Government's gradual loss of status in the international community as country after country transferred recognition to Peking; but he had already retired after ten years in the International Court of Justice before the Government of the Republic of China lost its seat in the United Nations.

Professor Chu's bibliographical note and his sources inspire confidence. For those subjects covered extensively in this book—that is, Dr. Koo's major diplomatic efforts up to 1938—the author commands a wide range of primary and secondary materials. If Professor Chu should undertake a second volume to deal in more detail with Dr. Koo's efforts after 1938—periods when he was China's Ambassador to wartime France and England, and then for a troubled decade as Ambassador to the United States—there is a vast amount of documentation now available in the files Dr. Koo gave to Columbia University, as well as his *Reminiscences*, done with Columbia's Chinese Oral History Project. These sources were lightly used in the final chapters of this book. Still, Professor Chu gathered some unique information through his own interviews with his subject.

We have not mentioned several interesting topics in this book, among them the influence of Chinese public opinion—that is, opinion articulated by Chinese intelligentsia and bourgeois groups in the major cities—upon the conduct of Dr. Koo's diplomacy; and the role and effectiveness during the early Republican period of that group of China's diplomats who Professor Chu calls "the Anglo-American group," made up of Sao-Ke Alfred Sze, Cheng-ting T. Wang, W. W. Yen, and Dr. Koo himself. Yet Dr. Koo's diplomatic style and accomplishments are the book's core.

"Westerners think of Koo as a Chinese, and Chinese think of him as a Westerner," according to Professor Chu. But he sees him as the epitome of Chang Chih-tung's famous motto—"Chinese learning for essential principles, Western learning for practical application."

C. Martin Wilbur
George Sansom Professor Emeritus of History
Columbia University

Wellington Koo married Norman's father's older sister

Foreword

It is a pleasure to introduce Dr. P. C. Chu's in depth study of China's most famous "international person" of the period of the two World Wars, Dr. V. K. Wellington Koo.

As indicated in the conclusion of this study, Dr. Koo devoted the major part of his diplomatic career to trying to find ways to bring China into the modern community of nations as an equal. The times were not propitious. He entered on his career at a time when China was at one of her lowest points in her long history, saddled with unequal treaties imposed by the West and Japan, with the old monarchy dead but no really stable new government in sight to replace it.

In the situation Koo leaned heavily, undoubtedly too heavily, on the Anglo-American style of diplomacy and on Anglo-American friendship for China. He was at best inadequate and often completely inept in his views of and dealings with the Soviet Union and Japan, two neighbors which can hardly be overlooked in any long range realistic view of China's international relations. However, China's needs were so great and her situation so dismal that it could be argued that Koo did remarkably well in the circumstances of the time. Dr. Chu gives him full credit for this, while at the same time indicating awareness of the deficiencies of Koo, both as a diplomat and as a man. (He certainly had his shortcomings as a husband!)

Dr. Chu's analysis, like Dr. Koo's career, is a fascinating blend of the Chinese and the Western style. Confucius would be proud of the painstaking attention to historical detail and to the lessons to be derived therefrom. The Chinese bibliography is enormous. At the same time Dr. Chu has combed the Western literature on his subject assiduously and has had the added advantage of personal interviews and correspondence with the aged but by no means senile Dr. Koo and use of his special collection and reminiscences.

Obviously this has been a labor of love as well as hard work by Dr. Chu and if it is not the definitive study of Wellington Koo's long and distinguished career, it will certainly require a huge amount of study and effort to improve on it. Dr. Chu is the author of an article related to this study entitled, "From the Paris Peace Conference to the Manchurian Incident: The Beginnings of

China's Diplomacy of Resistance Against Japan" in Alvin D. Coox and Hilary Conroy, *China and Japan: Search for Balance since World War I* (Santa Barbara, Cal.: ABC-Clio Press, 1978), pp. 61-82.

Hilary Conroy
University of Pennsylvania

Preface

This is the first scholarly study of the life and outstanding achievements of Dr. V. K. Wellington Koo, the brilliant statesman who, as regular delegate, represented China at the Paris Peace Conference after the World War I and the San Francisco Conference at the end of the World War II. While this study concerns the entire career of Koo since his childhood, it focuses on selected cases of significant international affairs, and not on every case in which Koo was involved in his half-century-long career of diplomacy. In essence, this work is designed as a case study on modern China's nationalistic diplomacy.

It is my pleasure and honor to record my gratitude to those who have at various points contributed to the project. Professor Hilary Conroy of the University of Pennsylvania initially inspired and directed this work, and Professor W. Allen Rickett of the University of Pennsylvania rendered indispensable professional assistance. Dr. Kaiming Ch'iu and the Harvard-Yenching Institute, Dr. T. K. Tong and the East Asian Library of Columbia University, and Mr. David Tseng and the East Asian Collection of Stanford University rendered extensive services far beyond their professional duties. Many of my colleagues, particularly Dr. Alvin Coox and Dr. Stanley Pincetl, of San Diego State University, have read chapters and offered their professional help. Professor C. Martin Wilbur of Columbia University was generous enough to allow the author to use some of the then restricted materials from the Wellington Koo Collection and to write a Foreword for the work. Many thanks must, of course, go to those members of my family who have sustained me over the long period the book has been in preparation. Needless to say, the author assumes all responsibility for any errors, factual or literary.

Pao-chin Chu

CHAPTER I

Origins of V. K. Wellington Koo's Diplomacy

THE SIGNIFICANCE OF THIS STUDY

Numerous biographical studies have been published and many academic projects are being undertaken concerning individual revolutionaries, intellectuals, warlords, and Communist leaders of Republican China.[1] Surprisingly, no significant study has been done, either in Chinese or in other languages, on any of the professional diplomats, such as Dr. V. K. Wellington Koo (Ku Wei-chün), Dr. Sao-Ke Alfred Sze (Shih Chao-chi), Dr. Chengting T. Wang (Wang Cheng-t'ing), and Dr. W. W. Yen (Yen Hui-ch'ing), throughout the entire span of modern China's history from the Treaty of Nanking in 1842 to the present. It is even more regrettable that many memoirs written by Chinese diplomats of the Republican period end before the death of President Yüan Shih-k'ai in 1916.[2] Besides the possibility of persecution by the ruling authorities, the reason for this may lie in a comment written by Dr. Koo in response to questions from this writer:

[1] Individual studies in English on Chinese revolutionaries include Lyon Sharman, *Sun Yat-sen: His Life and Its Meaning*, Chün-tu Hsüeh, *Huang Hsing and the Chinese Revolution*; on Chinese intellectuals, Joseph R. Levenson, *Liang Ch'i-ch'ao and the Mind of Modern China*, Huang Sung-k'ang, *Lu Hsün and the New Culture Movement of Modern China*; on Chinese warlords, Donald G. Gillin, *Portrait of a Warlord: Yen Hsi-shan in Shansi Province, 1911-1949*, James E. Sheridan, *Chinese Warlord: The Career of Feng Yü-hsiang*; on Chinese Communist leaders, Jerome Ch'en, *Mao and the Chinese Revolution*, Maurice Meisner, *Li Ta-ch'ao and the Origin of Chinese Marxism.*

[2] Sao-Ke Alfred Sze, *Shih Chao-chi tsao-nien hui-i lu* (Reminiscences of His Early Years as Told to Anming Fu). This interesting and valuable work ends in 1914, and therefore, does not cover any of Sze's important assignments to the international conferences. Hsü Shih-ying, *Hsü Shih-ying hui-i lu* (Memoir of Hsü Shih-ying). This work ends in 1911 when the Ch'ing dynasty fell and the Republic of China was established, and therefore does not cover any of his assignments to foreign posts either, particularly his assignment to Tokyo at the time of the Lukouchiao Incident on July 7, 1937. In 1974, a very useful autobiography by W. W. Yen under the title *East-West Kaleidoscope 1877-1944* was published by his family through the St. John's University Press in 1974.

> My hesitation arises from the fact that many of my erstwhile official colleagues or interlocuters are still living and I would not want to lend myself possibly to their embarrassment and cause controversies, though I quite realize that history relies only on facts and academic impartiality is a guarantee of truth.[3]

Nor has there been published any satisfactory study concerning the diplomacy of the entire period of Republican China. Yet it was during that period that China recovered from the Powers sovereign rights such as tariff autonomy and the abolition of extraterritoriality. Robert R. Pollard's *China's Foreign Relations, 1917-1931* is a comprehensive and systematic study of China's foreign relations for the period it covers. However, this work was published in 1933, more than a generation ago, and only a few popular English newspapers and periodicals such as the *North China Herald* and *China Year Book* were used. Another work is Professor Akira Iriye's *After Imperialism: The Search for a New Order in the Far East*, an extensive and scholarly study of Far Eastern international relations from the time of the Washington Disarmament Conference in 1921-1922 to the Manchurian Crisis in 1931. This work was mainly based on English and Japanese materials and it reflects the Japanese point of view. The studies of both Pollard and Iriye deal with diplomatic matters, but neither examines the diplomats. Furthermore, many significant questions remain unresolved. Perhaps the reason why scholars, both Chinese and foreign, have been reluctant to spend their effort and time on the study of the diplomats and diplomacy of Republican China is because this period is so very complicated.[4]

But studies of professional diplomats of Republican China are badly needed, and one on Dr. V. K. Wellington Koo is particularly urgent. In every sense Dr. Koo was a model of what shall be referred to as the "Anglo-American group," and this Anglo-American group was in control of China's foreign policy for almost the entire span of the Republican governments, be it a warlord government in Peking or the Nationalist Government in Nanking and Taiwan. There were no Republican Chinese other than Dr. Koo whose diplomacy played a leading role in almost every major confrontation with the powers throughout the period from 1912 to 1966—more than half a century. There have been few diplomats in the twentieth century whose diplomatic life could match that of Dr. Koo who participated as a leading figure in such

[3]Letter from V. K. Wellington Koo to Chu Pao-chin, May 9, 1966, The Hague.

[4]Ch'en Hsi-chang, *Pei-yang ts'ang-sang shih-hua* (Story of Great Changes of the Peiyang Government), pp. ii–iii, 499-540. Within a short period of seven years from January 1, 1920 to June 3, 1928, there were eight changes of presidents of the Peking Government, three acting presidents, thirty-two changes of cabinet, fifty-nine changes of premier or acting premiers. Tuan Ch'i-jui, head of An-fu Clique, was premier five times and Chu Ch'i-ch'ien, many times Minister of Communications, was acting premier for only two days.

significant international affairs as the Paris Peace Conference after World War I, the Conference on the Limitation of Armaments at Washington in the early 1920s, and the founding of the United Nations at the end of World War II. Dr. Koo's resourcefulness and energy surpassed any one of them.

Dr. Koo was, furthermore, perhaps the most controversial figure among the leading Chinese diplomats. There is reason to believe that foreigners think of Koo as a Chinese, and Chinese think of Koo as a foreigner. Was he a foreigner or a Chinese? What kind of character and thought did he possess? What influence did family, educational background, and social environment have on his character and philosophy? Was he a traditional Confucian or an Americanized Chinese? Was he a patriotic nationalist attempting to serve the cause of China's political independence and territorial integrity or a corrupted opportunist, greedy for power and reputation? Was he an idealistic revolutionary trying to liberate China from the yoke of unequal treaties or a conventional diplomat struggling with righteousness and international law at the bargaining table?

In addition, little is known of the working relationships of the Anglo-American group itself. How did members of the group coordinate with one another on the international front and react toward the government in Peking or Nanking under the control of one or another warlord or Nationalist faction? How much did they contribute to decisions of the warlords or Nationalist factions in China? To what extent did they influence the international Anglo-American group abroad? Finally, how much did their coordination and competition affect their policies and accomplishments for China?

A half century provides an appropriate interval for a meaningful evaluation of the group's policies and achievements, since most of the materials from private and official sources are now open for investigation and the effects of their decisions can be known. Were their policies basically correct? Were they successful in attaining their goals? How and why did they arrive at these decisions and policies? Were their approaches sound under the circumstances? Were the strategies partisan and inflexible and thus harmful in the long run to the peace and prosperity of China and the world in general and Sino-American relations in particular?

TRADITIONAL FAMILY AND LEARNING—CONFUCIAN PRINCIPLES AND VIRTUES

Dr. V. K. Wellington Koo's development was influenced by his family background and the learning of traditional China, his Western education and experiences in the United States, and the social-political environment of nationalism in defense of China's political sovereignty and territorial integrity.

Traditional Chinese family and Confucian principles and virtues built the fundamental character and thought of Koo. He was born into a prosperous gentry-merchant family in Shanghai,[5] on January 29, 1888, or the seventeenth day of the twelfth Moon according to the Chinese lunar calendar. His Chinese given name was Wei-chün, and his courtesy name Shao-ch'uan. He has been known in foreign circles by his English name, Vi Kyuin Wellington Koo, or in its abbreviated form, V. K. Wellington Koo.[6]

At the beginning of the Ch'ing dynasty, during the latter part of the seventeenth century, the Koo family moved from Hunan Province on the middle Yangtze River valley down to the lower Yangtze delta and finally settled in Chia-ting in Kiangsu Province. Chia-ting was then a prosperous district about one hour's journey up the Yangtze River from Shanghai. Many members of the Koo family acquired the ***hsiu-ts'ai*** and the ***chü-jen*** degrees through civil examinations, and some served the government as officials. During the Taiping Movement in the 1850s, the grandmother of Dr. Koo fled to Shanghai with her two infant children, a boy born in 1854, the future father of Wellington Koo, and a girl even younger.[7]

After the relocation of the Koo family in Shanghai, the grandmother supported her children by needlework. At thirteen the boy, named Koo Jung with the courtesy name Ch'ing-ch'uan, began to serve as an apprentice in a customs brokerage house during the day and studied the Confucian Classics at a private school at night. When Koo Jung was sixteen, he married Chiang Fu-an, the future mother of Wellington. Koo Jung so prospered that he opened his own Shen Yü Hang, a hardware store, on Foochow Road in Shanghai, and he became the leading hardware merchant and one of the gentry-merchants in Shanghai.[8] Like many successful merchants, Koo Jung turned toward a career in public service and held many important posts, including that of President of the Bank of Communications. He passed away in 1917 at the age of sixty-three. Koo Jung had three sons and two daughters, who grew up in the Chinese section of Shanghai and later moved into a fine house in the International Settlement. Chiang Fu-an was a capable lady who, with the tiny bound feet usual to women of quality in her generation, attended to household details and firmly ruled a drove of girl attendants and servants. She knew little of

[5] According to my interviews with Dr. Koo and the autobiography of Koo Hui-lan, Dr. Koo was born in 1888. Different sources including Howard L. Boorman's *Biographical Dictionary of Republican China*, indicate that he might have been born in 1887.

[6] Interview with Dr. Koo, August 11, 1967.

[7] *Ibid.*

[8] V. K. Wellington Koo, *Reminiscences of Wellington Koo*, I. Childhood and Education, pp. 1-13. (Hereinafter referred to as Koo, *Reminiscences.*)

the world and spent her summers in Chia-ting, where the Koo family still owned property.[9]

Young Koo, like his two elder brothers, was reared in the finest Chinese tradition. In 1891, at the age of five, he was sent to the school of Master Chu, a scholar with a *hsiu-ts'ai* degree but who had failed to pass the higher examinations. Chu's private school was of the old style and was situated in an ancestral temple. Like other beginners in traditional Chinese schools, young Koo started his studies with the *Trimetrical Classic* and the *Book of Family Names* and gradually progressed to the Confucian Classics. For seven years, Koo studied there, cultivating himself in the traditional Chinese spirit and principles until 1898.[10]

Koo's traditional Chinese family and his long cultivation in Confucian literature and principles during his formative years laid the foundation of his character and emphasized such qualities as loyalty, filial piety, and diligence. That the standards of Confucian virtue governed his concept of duty toward his country was beyond even the doubt of his political foes. His obedience to his parents and eldest brother was shown in his first marriage in 1908 to a girl whom he had never met until his wedding day.[11] His traditional background may be a partial solution to the puzzle that in the dangerous cross-currents of the conduct of the Peking Government, cabinets might come and go, but Wellington Koo usually survived. It perhaps also explain why Koo, although he undertook many years of Western education in China and abroad, remained a true Confucian who still had very high respect for religions and even conducted a Bible class but never became a disciple of any church.[12]

WESTERN TRAINING——ANGLO-AMERICAN DIPLOMACY

When Koo was twelve, he started his Western training by becoming a student of the Chung-hsi shu-yüan or the Anglo-Chinese Junior College on Ts'ang-shan Road in Shanghai. Koo was first exposed to the various disciplines of Western learning, including English, mathematics, physics, geography, and sports. Although typhoid fever took him out of school after he had been there only six months between 1899 and 1900, he won a first prize for his excellent

[9]Koo Hui-lan, *Hui-lan Koo: An Autobiography as Told to Mary Van Rensselaer Thayer*, p. 118. (Hereinafter referred to as Koo Hui-lan, *Autobiography*.)

Koo Hui-lan with Isabella Taves, *No Feast Lasts Forever*, pp. 118-19. (Hereinafter referred to as Koo Hui-lan, *No Feast Lasts Forever*.)

[10]Interview with Dr. Koo, August 11, 1967.

[11]Koo Hui-lan, *Autobiography*, p. 118. Koo's first marriage was to a daughter of a physician named Chang. They were divorced three years later in 1911 and she returned from Philadelphia to Shanghai alone.

[12]Interview with Dr. Koo, August 11, 1967.

performance.[13] Two months later, after he had recovered, he attended the Yü-ts'ai hsüeh-hsiao or Talent-Fostering School in Shanghai between 1900 and 1901.[14] In January of 1901 young Koo was enrolled at St. John's College, an American missionary school in Shanghai later renamed St. John's University, from which many prominent diplomats such as Dr. Sao-Ke Alfred Sze and Dr. W. W. Yen graduated. The atmosphere at St. John's was puritanical, and there were few diversions to offset the poor food and cold rooms during the winter. Discipline was so spartan that his brother was dismissed when one of the trustees caught him reading English books in the Chinese classes.[15] But Koo stayed until 1904 when he was sixteen. While at St. John's, Koo was outstanding in both academic pursuits and student activities, including the editorship of the student paper, ***Dragon.***[16]

In 1903, Dr. Sao-Ke Alfred Sze, Superintendent of Hupei Students in America, accompanied Professor Jeremiah W. Jenks to China to study monetary reform. On his way back to the United States in August of 1904, Sze took the second group of Hupei students on government scholarships to America. Koo was then sent by his father to join this group.[17] His father was unperturbed as he bid his youngest boy farewell, and prophesied reassuringly to his wife, "We need never worry about this son."[18] After a year of preparation at the Cook Academy in Ithaca, New York, between 1904 and 1905, Koo entered Columbia University. There he studied liberal arts from 1905 to 1908 and political science from 1908 to 1912. By refusing to pay the diploma fee, he delayed receiving his B.A. degree until the next year, 1909. He received his M.A. degree in 1909 and his Ph.D. in 1912.[19]

His dissertation was entitled *The Status of Aliens in China* and was written under the direction of Professor John Bassett Moore, Hamilton Fish Professor of International Law and Diplomacy. In the preface, Dr. Koo gave his reasons for writing this treatise:

> Commerce, religion, travel and other interests are drawing increasing numbers of foreigners into China, and the question of their precise status, while residing or being within her territory, becomes today not only one of enhanced interests, but one of growing practical importance. The multifarious and sometimes complex problems which arise out of their intercourse with the Chinese people depend for their prompt solution primarily upon an accurate knowledge of the rights, privileges and immunities which they are entitled to enjoy under laws and treaties,

[13] Koo, *Reminiscences*, I. Childhood and Education, pp. 19-30.
[14] A. R. Burt, J. B. Powell, and Carl Crow, *Biographies of Prominent Chinese*, p. 53.
[15] Interview with Dr. Koo, August 11, 1967.
[16] Koo Hui-lan, *Autobiography*, p. 118.
[17] Sao-Ke Alfred Sze, *Shih Chao-chi tsao-nien hui-i lu*, pp. 38-39.
[18] Koo Hui-lan, *Autobiography*, p. 118.
[19] A. R. Burt *et al.*, *Biographies of Prominent Chinese*, p. 53.

> and of the limitations and restrictions, arising from the same source of sanction, upon such rights, privileges and immunities.[20]

It was concerned mainly with the origin, protection, extent, and limitations of extraterritorial jurisdiction of aliens in China during the conventional period since 1848. Published in 1912, it was the first academic work on this subject, appearing eight years earlier than W. Willoughby's popular work, *Foreign Rights and Interests in China.*[21]

At Columbia, Koo was not only an outstanding student academically but was also involved in many kinds of student activities. He was elected to the Nacoms, The Blue Pencil, and Delta Upsilon Rho Societies in 1911. Furthermore, he was the recipient of the Philolescean Literary Prize and the Columbia-Cornell Debating Medal and was elected a member of the "Varsity" debating team for 1906-1907. Koo also served as editor of the *Columbia Daily Spectator* and manager of *The Columbia Monthly.*[22] Today he is perhaps the oldest member with longest membership in the American Society of International Law.

After attending a YMCA convention in Northfield, Massachusetts, Koo deeply felt the urgent need for the unity of Chinese students in America. He organized the Chinese Students Alliance in America and the Chinese Students Association of the Eastern States. Chinese students in various places and schools were urged to follow his example. Soon the Chinese Students Association of the Middlewestern States and the Chinese Students Association of the Western States were formed. The Chinese Students Association in All America was organized at a summer conference lasting ten days. Koo served as the editor of the *Chinese Students' Monthly* and the *Chinese Students' Annual.*[23]

His many years of study and practice in English and various disciplines of knowledge in China and America made him an outstanding orator in English as well as in Chinese. His training in Western international law and diplomacy under the direction of such leading scholars as Professor John Bassett Moore equipped him with the fundamental theory and practice of modern diplomacy. He also mastered Anglo-American bargaining arts and acquired a realistic approach to international negotiations through conventional means. It is little wonder that Dr. Koo, the youngest delegate representing a weak and split China at the Paris Peace Conference, astounded the statesmen of the world overnight. It is also significant that his eloquent English and expertise in

[20]V. K. Wellington Koo, *The Status of Aliens in China.*

[21]W. Willoughby, *Foreign Rights and Interests in China*. The original edition was published in 1920.

[22]A. R. Burt *et al., Biographies of Prominent Chinese*, p. 53.

[23]Interview with Dr. Koo, August 11, 1967.

international law and diplomacy made him indispensable to almost every Chinese Regime, be it a warlord government in Peking or the Nationalist Government in Nanking. All these governments had to remain in the Anglo-American orbit, or at least maintain an amicable relationship with the Western powers in the international arena, and Dr. Koo became the ideal instrument for such a task. It is obvious to the careful observer that all the posts Dr. Koo occupied were centers of the Anglo-American group, be it London or Washington, or a post near the center of the Anglo-American-led world organizations, be it the League of Nations or the United Nations.

NATIONALISTIC SOCIAL ENVIRONMENTS— ABOLISHING THE UNEQUAL TREATIES

Dr. Koo was born and grew up in China where nascent nationalism and patriotism were struggling against the decaying Manchu dynasty and imperialist powers. Koo was born only a few years before China's crushing defeat in the First Sino-Japanese War and the signing of the Treaty of Shimonoseki in 1895. When he was about ten, China was forced to "lease" Liaotung to Russia, Kiaochow to Germany, Kwang-chow Wan to France, and Weihaiwei to the British Empire. The partition of "the sick man's" belongings was only a question of time. In the same era, Dr. Sun Yat-sen had conducted his first uprising at Canton, and the bloody ending of the Hundred Days Reform extinguished the hopes of the patriotic intellectuals for mild reform under a constitutional monarchy and drove them into the arms of the violent nationalist revolution. The disaster of the Boxer Movement greatly influenced the mind of the fourteen-year-old Koo. Chinese intellectuals, whose nationalism had been submerged in the lesser loyalties of province, guild, and clan, arose in a fury of patriotism. Thousands of young men vowed to dedicate their lives to China's salvation, and they left home to study in Europe, Japan, and America in order to absorb the Occidental ideas and ways necessary for China's modernization. Koo was one of them.[24]

Perhaps in no other city in China was the impact of the unequal treaties more obvious and deeply felt than in Shanghai. The Shanghai Foreign Settlements existed as states within a state. Extraterritoriality made all the foreigners a class of human beings superior to the indigenous population. The right of inland navigation put all the Chinese in Shanghai constantly under the threat of the guns on the foreign warships flying their colors on the Whangpu River. The foreign garrisons placed every inhabitant at the mercy of

[24]Koo Hui-lan, *Autobiography*, p. 117.

the bayonets of foreign marines. The domination of foreigners over the Chinese Maritime Customs, Post Office, and most of the huge plants and corporations reduced most Shanghainese to the status of economic serfs. All this was too clear for thousands of young and awakened students to endure it with equanimity.

Koo's personal experiences during childhood also contributed greatly to his devotion to the courses of national salvation and the abolition of the unequal treaties. For example, while Koo was a student at the Anglo-Chinese Junior College during 1899, he chose to try out a new bicycle near the Shanghai race course one Saturday afternoon. A British boy of his age was also riding a bicycle ahead of him. Later that boy moved to a cement sidewalk and Koo followed. Suddenly an Indian policeman appeared. Although he allowed the English boy to pass, he stopped Koo. Soon he was handed over to a Chinese policeman who took him to the police station. Reacting to this unequal treatment, Koo protested to the police officer: "I don't know the rule, I only followed that English boy." All explanations and protests were in vain and he was fined five *yüan.* He returned to his sister's house and requested the sum to ransom his bicycle from the police station.[25]

After the Nationalist Revolution in 1911 and the establishment of a republic, hundreds of students rushed home from abroad, eager to employ their newly acquired knowledge in improving China. In mid-February 1912, Koo had hardly finished his dissertation when he received a telegram from T'ang Shao-i, Premier of the new Chinese Republic, summoning him back to serve the Government. Koo had first met the Premier when T'ang invited forty Chinese students to stay with him while he visited Washington on behalf of the Ch'ing dynasty in 1908. As President of the Chinese Students Association in America, Koo apparently impressed T'ang so profoundly that T'ang invited him for further personal conversation the next January.[26]

With the encouragement of Professor Moore, Koo left for China. In April 1912, he arrived in Peking via the Trans-Siberian Railway, and Premier T'ang took him immediately to see President Yüan Shih-k'ai. Koo was appointed as English secretary to the President and, concurrently, one of the eight secretaries of the Cabinet.[27] While Koo was en route to China, the faculty of Political Science of Columbia University edited his dissertation, added a conclusion, and had it published.[28]

After a dispute with President Yüan concerning the appointment of a Military Governor of Chihli, Premier T'ang resigned, and Koo followed him to

[25]Interview with Dr. Koo, November 26, 1966.

[26]Koo, *Reminiscences*, I. Childhood and Education, pp. 107-20, 129-35.

[27]Koo, *Reminiscences*, II. First Decade as Diplomat, Spring 1912. A, 1-2.

[28]V. K. Wellington Koo, *The Status of Aliens in China*, pp. 7-8.

Tientsin for a short time. In August 1912, he was appointed as the English secretary to Foreign Minister W. W. Yen and returned to Peking to begin a brilliant diplomatic career spanning over half a century. In the following year, while in Shanghai, Koo married T'ang's eldest daughter, whom he first met when T'ang assigned him to accompany her and her sisters to see the Temple of Heaven in Peking in 1912.[29] In October 1913, he was promoted to be a councilor to assist in the negotiations with Minister Jordan of the British Empire concerning a provisional agreement in regard to Tibet.[30] Foreign Minister Lou Tseng-tsiang and Vice-Foreign Minister Ts'ao Ju-lin brought Koo Japan's ultimatum on the Twenty-One Demands while he was a patient at the German hospital in Peking. With the permission of the German Doctor Klieg, Koo worked all night to draft the English answer.[31]

In July 1915, Vice-Foreign Minister Ts'ao recommended Koo, only twenty-seven years of age, for the post of Chinese Minister to Mexico. Three months later while en route to this post, he was reassigned to be Minister to the United States and Cuba. Because of his distinguished performance as a diplomat, Wellington Koo received his first Honorary degree, a LL.D., from Yale University in 1916. Tragedy, however, followed this success. In late 1918, his wife died of Spanish fever in Washington, leaving behind a boy and a girl; yet when the European War came to an end, Dr. Koo accepted an appointment to serve as one of the Chinese delegates to the Paris Peace Conference.[32]

An unofficial test of Koo's diplomatic skills emerged after his arrival in Europe, and he was certainly successful in combining his already admirable position with wealth by marriage. Huang Hui-lan, daughter to Oei Tiong Ham (Huang Tsung-han), a multimillionaire and sugar king of Indonesia, was on a European tour while the Paris Peace Conference was in session. After a banquet with Dr. Koo as the guest of honor, she "was skillfully separated from the others and maneuvered into His Excellency's new high-powered French car." As the days passed she was to be "tremendously flattered by the attentions Dr. Koo showered on her." Dr. Chengting T. Wang employed his famous oratorical powers to praise Koo in glowing terms. Madame Wei Tao-ming, wife of the Chinese ambassador to the United States during World War II, was even more persuassive, saying that:

> It was the solemn duty of every Chinese man and woman to work for his or her country and that you and your fine education and material advantages could do a great deal for China. It would be difficult for a woman to work alone, and

---

[29]Interview with Dr. Koo, August 11, 1967.

[30]John V. A. MacMurray, "Agreement in Regard to Tibet," *Treaties and Agreements with and conerning China, 1894-1919*, I:581-82 (summary only).

[31]Interview with Dr. Koo, November 19, 1966.

[32]A. R. Burt *et al.*, *Biographies of Prominent Chinese*, p. 53.

> you would prove of much greater value if you combined forces with brilliant Dr. Koo.[33]

Koo's "extremely good looks," his wisdom, and his promising career made the courtship very short. On October 10, the engagement was announced and was followed by an official ball attended by all the dignitaries of the various delegations of the Peace Conference.

On the eve of the wedding, Koo was "working, surrounded by four secretaries with notebooks, dictating memos and instructions." The bride-to-be, entering the living room of the suite, was hardly noticed. It was then she discovered that they were going to Geneva on the night train after the marriage at the Chinese legation in Brussels on November 11, 1920. This journey was imperative because Dr. Koo headed the Chinese Delegation at the opening ceremony of the assembly of the League of Nations.[34] The engagement and marriage created a dramatic effect at the Paris Peace Conference as well as at the League of Nations.

As we saw, Westerners think of Koo as a Chinese, and Chinese think of him as a Westerner. The Westerners and the Chinese are both right and wrong in the sense that they only discern the part of Koo which is different from themselves. The Westerners only perceive his characteristics and principles of traditional Chinese culture, while the Chinese are only impressed by his Western manners, his English eloquence, and his skill at Anglo-American diplomatic practices. As a matter of fact, Koo represents the model for the main stream of the political philosophy of the late Ch'ing reformers summed up by Governor-General Chang Chih-tung in the 1890s: "Chinese learning as the essential principles, Western learning for the practical applications."[35] The prevailing nationalism added to his patriotism, his personal integrity, and his lasting devotion to the goal of liberation of China from the bonds of the unequal treaties and the elevation of the Chinese people to the position of equality with other peoples in the community of nations.

[33]Koo Hui-lan, *Autobiography*, pp. 105-7.

[34]Koo Hui-lan, *No Feast Lasts Forever*, pp. 118-21.

[35]Chang Chih-tung, *Chang Wen-hsiang-kung ch'üan-chi* (The Complete Works of Chang Chih-tung). In a monograph of 1898 entitled "Exhortation to Learning," Chang Chih-tung, Governor-General of Hunan and Hupei provinces, illustrated his educational philosophy and the specific measures to realize it. See "Ch'üan-hsüeh p'ien" in *chüan* 202-3.

> you would prove of much greater value if you combined forces with brilliant Dr. Koo.[53]

Koo's "extremely good looks," his wisdom, and his promising career made the courtship very short. On October 10, the engagement was announced and was followed by an official ball attended by all the dignitaries of the various delegations of the Peace Conference.

On the eve of the wedding, Koo was "working, surrounded by four secretaries with notebooks, dictating memos and instructions." The bride-to-be "entering the living room of the suite was hardly noticed. It was then she discovered that they were going to Geneva on the night train after the marriage at the Chinese Legation in Brussels on November 11, 1920. This journey was imperative because Dr. Koo headed the Chinese Delegation at the opening ceremony of the assembly of the League of Nations.[54] The engagement and marriage created a dramatic effect at the Paris Peace Conference as well as at the League of Nations.

As we saw, Westerners think of Koo as a Chinese, and Chinese think of him as a Westerner. The Westerners and the Chinese are both right and wrong in the sense that they only discern the part of Koo which is different from themselves. The Westerners only perceive his characteristics and principles of traditional Chinese culture, while the Chinese are only impressed by his Western manners, his English eloquence, and his skill at Anglo-American diplomatic practices. As a matter of fact, Koo represents the model for the main stream of the political philosophy of the late Ch'ing reformers summed up by Governor-General Chang Chih-tung in the 1890s: "Chinese learning for the essential principles, Western learning for the practical applications."[55] The prevailing nationalism adapted to his patriotism, his personal integrity, and his lasting devotion to the goal of liberation of China from the bonds of the unequal treaties and the elevation of the Chinese people to the position of equality with other peoples in the community of nations.

[53] Koo Hui-lan, *Autobiography*, pp. 105-7.

[54] Koo Hui-lan, *No Feast Lasts Forever*, pp. 118-21.

[55] Chang Chih-tung, *Chang Wen-hsiang-kung Ch'üan-chi* (The Complete Works of Chang Chih-tung). In a monograph of 1898 entitled "Exhortation to Learning," Chang Chih-tung, Governor-General of Hunan and Hupei provinces, illustrated an educational philosophy and the specific measures to realize it. See "Ch'üan-hsüeh p'ien" in *ibid.*, 202-3.

CHAPTER II

Koo and the Paris Peace Conference, 1919–1920

GOVERNMENT, POLICY, AND THE DIPLOMATS

The policy of the Peking Government toward the war in Europe split the government into a "reserved faction" and a "realistic faction." President Li Yüan-hung, who succeeded Yüan Shih-k'ai after Yüan's ill-fated Monarchical Movement and death, and the veteran Foreign Minister, Wu T'ing-fang, were strongly in favor of a neutralist position. Nevertheless, Premier Tuan Ch'i-jui, the powerful leader of the Peiyang Army, and the members of his Committee on Foreign Affairs, including the veteran diplomat, Lou Tseng-tsiang, and the financier, Ts'ao Ju-lin, strongly favored immediate participation in the war on the Allies' side. A formal proposal of the Committee was submitted to the Government for consideration.[1]

Eventually the "realists" prevailed for a number of reasons: (1) the superior British Navy would keep Great Britain secure from the attacks of Germany until a turn of the international situation; (2) sooner or later, the United States would come to the aid of the British Empire, and Germany, although strong in its army and superior in armament, could not match the combined strength of the British Empire and the United States; (3) well experienced in international affairs, Japan must be fairly certain of the eventual defeat of Germany as she joined the war on the Allies' side; (4) Japan, which had already seized Tsingtao, would have a greater voice than China in the future peace conference concerning the Far East if China were to remain neutral; and (5) a war against an outside power would, perhaps, unify the Canton and Peking Governments. Refusing to affix the seal of the President to Premier Tuan's Declaration of War against Germany, President Li accepted the latter's resignation. Li Ching-hsi was authorized to organize a new cabinet, which was only to be destroyed by the dramatic restoration of the late Ch'ing by the queued General Chang Hsün.[2] When Tuan again became premier after the demise of the week-old monarchical restoration, the Peking Government

[1] Ts'ao Ju-lin, *I-sheng chih hui-i*, pp. 160–61.

[2] Kao Yin-tsu, *Chung-hua ming-kuo ta-shih chi*, pp. 45-46. The restoration of the late Ch'ing lasted one week, July 1-7, 1917.

declared war against Germany and Austria on August 14, 1917.

When the armistice finally brought the World War to an end, China, as a victorious power, immediately faced the problem of representation to the Paris Peace Conference. At a meeting of the Administration Council of the Nationalist Military Government on December 13, 1918, the rival government in Canton, recently strengthened by the so-called legitimate National Assembly, had elected Wu T'ing-fang, Sun Yat-sen, Chengting T. Wang, Wang Chao-ming (Wang Ching-wei), and Wu Ch'ao-shu to represent China at the Paris Peace Conference.[3] Having failed to achieve the recognition of the Powers, the Canton Government dispatched Wu T'ing-fang to Shanghai to offer the Peking Government a compromise formulation under which the North would name three delegates, and the South would name two. Both would approve the entire delegation, and the credentials would be provided by the Peking Government.[4] Realizing the significance of a united front between the North and the South for a diplomatic war championing China's lost rights, the Peking Government added Chengting T. Wang, who had already been sent to Washington by Canton to lobby for Southern representation for China, as the fifth delegate to the list which also included Lou Tseng-tsiang, Minister of Foreign Affairs; Sao-Ke Alfred Sze, Minister in London; V. K. Wellington Koo, Minister in Washington; and Suntchou Wei (Wei Ch'en-tsu), Minister in Brussels.[5] Aggravated by what it considered to be such high-handedness, the Canton Government refused to sanction Chengting T. Wang as its official delegate and sent its own delegate, Wu Ch'ao-shu, to Paris. Wu left Hong Kong on February 4, 1919 for Paris. However, he never worked his way into the Conference.[6]

A preparatory conference was held by President Hsü Shih-ch'ang, who had succeeded Feng Kuo-chang as President of the Peking Government on October 10, 1918. All major members of the cabinet attended, including Tuan Ch'i-jui, the head of the An-fu Clique in power and the Commissioner of the War Participation Army, and Ts'ao Ju-lin, Minister of Communications. Tuan, the chief beneficiary of the Nishihara Loans and supporter of the Sino-Japanese Military Alliance, stated that:

[3]The American Consul (Albert W. Pontius) to the American Minister (Paul S. Reinsch), Canton, December 14, 1918. *National Archives Microfilm Publications Microcopy No. 329, Records of the Department of State Relating to Internal Affairs of China, 1910-1929.* Reel No. 20. (Hereinafter referred to as *Internal Affairs of China, 1910-1929.*)

[4]The American Consulate-General (Thomas Sammons) to the American Minister (Paul S. Reinsch), Shanghai, December 27, 1918. *Internal Affairs of China, 1910-1929.*

[5]Wunsz King, *China at the Paris Peace Conference in 1919*, pp. 4-5. Koo, *Reminiscences*, II. First Decade as Diplomat, B, L, 5, 7, 8.

[6]The American Consul (Albert W. Pontius) to the American Minister (Paul S. Reinsch), Canton, January 22, 1919. *Internal Affairs of China, 1910-1929.*

> China joined the allies at a very late date and only in name, therefore, our claims should be accordingly confined to a few items, such as restoration of the German and Austrian concessions; abrogation of Articles VII and IX of the note of December 22, 1900, and of the protocol of September 7, 1901, permitting the signatory Powers to keep permanent guards for their legations, and to station troops between the capital and the sea; and the restoration of tariff autonomy. As for the Shantung problem, Japan has repeatedly declared that she would agree to the reversion to China of the interests she has taken over from Germany.[7]

Tuan continued, "It is fairly certain that she will not break the promise. The Shantung problem should be dealt with when the matter is brought up by Japan."[8]

Everyone present agreed, and no definite decision on Shantung was made at that meeting. The designated representatives of China abroad were informed accordingly. Lou Tseng-tsiang, the chief delegate, and Suntchou Wei started their trip to Paris via Japan and the United States.[9]

Upon receiving instructions from Peking concerning the Peace Conference, Dr. V. K. Wellington Koo visited Robert Lansing, Secretary of State, on November 15 and briefly outlined the proposals which the Chinese Government intended to present at the Peace Conference. These proposals were later incorporated into the Informal Memorandum of November 25 and were conveyed to Mr. Lansing.[10] They were divided into three groups embodying the principles of (1) territorial integrity, (2) preservation of sovereign rights, and (3) economic and fiscal independence.

The proposal of territorial integrity embraced the abrogation of foreign "concessions" and "settlements," within which the foreign powers claimed and exercised exclusive rights of police, taxation, public domain, and the like, independent of the Chinese Government. This proposal also requested the full restoration to Chinese jurisdiction of the "leased" territories of Kiaochow (Chiao-chou) Wan, Port Arthur (Lü-shun), Talien Wan, Kwangchow (Kuang-chou) Wan, and Kowloon—all extorted from China either by threat or by actual force on slight provocation in order to create a balance of power between rival foreign aspirants to power and advantage.

The proposal of preservation of sovereign rights called for the abrogation

[7]The problem under discussion can be termed as the problem of Tsingtao, the city, or the problem of Kiaochow, the leased territory, or the problem of Shantung, the province where the leased Kiaochow Wan is situated.

[8]Ts'ao Ju-lin, *I-sheng chih hui-i*, p. 188.

[9]Lo Kuang, *Lu Cheng-hsiang chuan*, pp. 110-11.

[10]The Chinese Minister (V. K. Wellington Koo) to the Secretary of State (Robert Lansing), Washington, November 25, 1918 and Memorandum; V. K. Wellington Koo, *Wunsz King Collection of V. K. Wellington Koo Papers*, No. 10, pp. 2-7, (Hereinafter referred to as Koo, *Wunsz King Collection.*)

of the permanent guards for the legations, the stationing of foreign troops between the capital and the sea, and extraterritoriality.

The proposal on economic and fiscal independence was focused mainly on the restoration of China's freedom in the regulation and administration of tariffs.[11]

The next afternoon on November 26, 1918, Koo had an interview with President Wilson at the White House. Koo stated to the President that:

> China would hope to present certain proposals at the peace conference concerning her territorial integrity, the preservation of her sovereign rights, and her fiscal and economic independence . . . merely to restore to her some of the things which, in the view of the Chinese people, had been wrongly taken from her. So the people of China were all looking to the President and the great country which he represented for help in the realization of their just claims and aspirations.[12]

The President answered that "he would gladly do his best to support China at the peace conference. He said that there was difficulty in the case of China, i.e., there were many secret agreements between the subjects of China and other powers." The President told Koo that he was going to have a preliminary conference with the premiers of Great Britain, France, and Italy on the essentials of peace and assured Koo that "there would be nothing for China to fear from the discussion at this conference."[13]

In reply, Koo endorsed Wilson's Fourteen Points[14] by saying that China "would most heartily support his plans and his principles," and expressed the hope that the President "would see to it that the Fourteen Principles would be made applicable to the Far East, as well as to other parts of the world." The President stated that they would probably be more difficult to apply to the Far East. In conformity with Koo's instructions, the Shantung problem specifically was not raised.

By the end of 1918, most of the Chinese as well as the majority of delegates from other countries were in Paris. In January 1919, Dr. Koo also arrived in Paris. Before the beginning of the conference, Dr. Koo and Alfred Sze

[11]Koo, *Wunsz King Collection*, pp. 6-7.

[12]Koo, *Wunsz King Collection*, No. 2, pp. 8-9. Koo's memorandum of a conversation at an audience with President Wilson at the White House, November 26, 1918.

[13]Koo, *Wunsz King Collection*, No. 2, pp. 8-9.

[14]Herbert Hoover, *The Ordeal of Woodrow Wilson*, pp. 23-27. The Fourteen Points were developed from a series of President Wilson's addresses such as: (a) Presidential address to Congress on Five Demands and the Four Principles, February 11, 1918; (b) Presidential address on the basis of peace at Mount Vernon on Four Ends, July 4, 1918; (c) Presidential address in New York concerning the basis of peace on Five Particulars, September 27, 1918; (d) Presidential address at Manchester, England, on Abolition of the Balance of Power, December 30, 1918; and (e) Presidential address at Rome on Abolition of the Balance of Power, January 3, 1919.

interviewed Secretary Lansing on December 18, 1918. When questioned about his views concerning the Chinese questions, the Secretary said that:

> . . . the United States had no interests of its own to serve but to readjust the conflicting interests of the different powers by concessions and compromise . . . . Consequently, the United States might find it necessary to modify its views relating to Chinese questions after consultation with the other governments, although he favored tariff autonomy for China.[15]

No particular question was raised between Dr. Koo and Colonel E. M. House at a conversation held the same day at the Hotel Crillon. The Colonel, however, did convey the deep sympathy of the President and himself for China.[16] On January 22, 1919, both Koo and Wang attended a dinner with Ronald Macleay of the British Delegation sponsored by Alfred Sze. Macleay gave the impression that because of the valuable help the Japanese Navy had given to England at a very crucial period and on account of their existing alliance, Great Britain could not do much with respect to raising the issue of Shantung.[17] The British attitude as seen by Macleay was equally negative toward the restoration of tariff autonomy, the abrogation of foreign post offices, and the nullification of unequal treaties and extraterritoriality.

The Chinese Delegation at the Paris Peace Conference was split from the beginning. Contrary to the information of the State Department that co-operation between the representatives of North and South China at the Paris Peace Conference was most cordial and effective,[18] the relationships among the five delegates from China were tense all the time. Besides the understandable suspicion of the Peking Government toward Chengting T. Wang, who, although appointed by them as a delegate, nevertheless represented the revolutionary Military Government in the South, the delegates from the North were also involved in questions of seniority.[19] On the arrival of the Chinese Delegation in Paris, the sequence of the Chinese Delegation was as follows: Lou Tseng-tsiang, Foreign Minister and head of the Delegation, Chengting T. Wang, Sao-Ke Alfred Sze, V. K. Wellington Koo, and Suntchou Wei. With the exception of Wang, this order was determined according to

[15] Koo, *Wunsz King Collection*, No. 3, p. 10. Koo's Memorandum of a conversation between Robert Lansing and Hoo Wei-teh (Hu Wei-te), S. K. Alfred Sze, and V. K. Wellington Koo, December 18, 1918.

[16] Koo, *Wunsz King Collection*, No. 4, p. 11, Koo's Conversation with Colonel E. M. House at Hotel Crillon, Paris, December 18, 1918.

[17] Koo, *Wunsz King Collection*, No. 5, pp. 12-14. Alfred Sze's Memorandum on Dinner with Ronald Macleay, Paris, January 22, 1919.

[18] Dispatch from the State Department to the American Legation in Peking, February 1, 1919. *Internal Affairs of China, 1910-1929*, 893.00.

[19] Letters from V. K. Wellington Koo to Chu Pao-chin, New York, May 19 and June 16, 1969.

seniority in the diplomatic service and current ranks and posts. As the authority of President Wilson at the Conference became more obvious to the Peking Government and the health of Foreign Minister Lou deteriorated, the role of the Chinese Minister to Washington, Dr. Koo, increased.[20] Instructions that Koo should take charge over both Wang and Sze finally reached Paris from Peking. Against the wishes of Koo, Sze, and Wang, Lou Tseng-tsiang subsequently notified the Secretariat. Disheartened, Sze, who was very much Koo's senior, became almost inactive, and China's links to the court of St. James deteriorated. A significant foundation for the failure of the Chinese Delegation's mission was laid. A seed of discord was also sown between Koo and Wang for years to come; it eventually bore the fruit in the negotiations for restoration of Sino-Russian relations.

THE COUNCIL OF TEN AND THE PROBLEM OF SHANTUNG

The Chinese Delegation was invited to present its views on the problem of Shantung on three different occasions: the two consecutive sessions of the Council of Ten on January 27 and 28 and the session of the Council of Four on April 22, 1919. In the morning of January 27, 1919, the five Powers decided to bring the case of Shantung up for discussion that afternoon. Japan urged that China be excluded from representation but, at the insistence of President Wilson and Secretary Lansing, the Chinese Delegation was invited to participate.[21]

The Chinese Delegation decided that Koo and Wang, the latter representing the South, should be present. Koo and Wang went to see Secretary Lansing approximately one hour before the meeting. Koo said that the invitation was so sudden he had not had an opportunity to look over the documents and refresh his memory. He asked, therefore, if it would be proper to allow the Chinese Delegation an interval before presenting their case to the Council. Secretary Lansing said that such a request would be quite proper. He thought that a grace period of twenty-four hours would be granted.[22] Lansing also emphatically assured the Chinese delegates that America would do her best for China, although he was somewhat apprehensive about the attitudes of Great Britain,

[20] Koo, *Reminiscences*, II. First Decade as Diplomat, C, 1-3. In 1911 while Koo was still a student at Columbia University, Alfred Sze was appointed as Chinese Minister to the United States. Sao-Ke Alfred Sze, *Shih Chao-chi tsao-nien hui-i lu*, pp. 39, 89.

[21] Koo, *Wunsz King Collection*, No. 6, p. 15. Koo's Memorandum of an Interview with Secretary Robert Lansing, at Hotel Crillon, January 27, 1919 (time: 2:30 p.m.).

[22] Wunsz King, *China at the Paris Peace Conference in 1919*, pp. 4-5. Koo, *Reminiscences*, II. First Decade as Diplomat, C, 4-5.

France, and Italy.

When Clemenceau declared the meeting of the Council of Ten opened on the afternoon of January 27, he called on the Japanese representative to state the views of his government. Baron Makino then read a prepared statement:

> The Japanese Government feels justified in claiming from the German Government the unconditional cession of (a) the leased territory of Kiaochow together with the railways, and other rights possessed by Germany in respect of Shantung province; (b) German Pacific Islands north of the Equator . . . in view of the extent of their effort and achievements in destroying German bases in the Extreme Orient and the South Seas, and in safeguarding the important routes on the Pacific and Indian Oceans and the Mediterranean waters . . . the Japanese Government feels confident that the claim above advanced would be regarded as only just and fair.[23]

At Koo's request, a decision was reserved to allow the Chinese Delegation an interval before presenting their case to the Council.

Japan's position was very strong after the war—economically, militarily, and legally. She had been hurt less and had profited more by the war than most. With Russia and Germany removed from the stage in North China, Japan became the supreme power in the Far East, and this position was further strengthened by the renewed Anglo-Japanese Alliance. Her legal position was also strengthened by the secret agreements of 1917 with Great Britain and France which approved her claims to German rights in Shantung and the Pacific Islands north of the Equator. Japan's secret treaty with China in 1915, as a result of the Twenty-One Demands, also provided Japan with a right to claim all privileges and interests possessed by Germany.[24] The secret treaty with China in 1918, as a result of a 20,000,000 yen loan, granted Japan the rights to station troops in Shantung and construct the Kaomi-Hsuchow and Tsinan-Shunteh Railways and provided for Sino-Japanese management over the Kiaochow-Tsinan Railway and Japanese instructors for the Kiaochow-Tsinan Railway police.[25]

Immediately after the meeting, Dr. Koo and Lou Tseng-tsiang had an interview with President Wilson at Murat Mansion. The President did not hide his feelings: "he had listened not only with surprise but with distress to the claims made by Baron Makino in such plain terms to the Pacific Islands north of the

[23] Koo, *Wunsz King Collection*, No. 7, pp. 16-18. Secretary's Note (British) of a conversation held in M. Pichon's room at Quai d'Orsay, Paris, on Monday, January 27, 1919.

[24] Memorandums of the Chinese Delegation Submitted at the Paris Peace Conference, No. 1, Annex No. 12—Twenty-One Demands, *Wai-chiao kung-pao*, No. 5, November 1921. Documents, pp. 1-2.

[25] Memorandum of the Chinese Delegation Submitted at the Paris Peace Conference, No. 1, Annex No. 17—Draft Contract on Kaomi-Hsuchow Railway and the Tsinan-Shunteh Railway between China and Japan, *Wai-chiao kung-pao*, No. 6, December 1921. Documents, pp. 1-3.

Equator and the leased territory of Kiaochow in Shantung."[26] Koo and his Chinese colleagues, painfully aware of what Japan had already done in Korea, Liaotung, and Manchuria, said they had no confidence whatever in Japanese policies and feared being left at the mercy of Japan. He reported to the President China's decision to propose a direct restitution by Germany of her leased territory, the Kiaochow-Tsinan Railway, and her rights in Shantung to China, and he explained the reasons. Asked if he thought it would be advisable to put the question of Shantung in this way, President Wilson stated that it would be perfectly legitimate and advisable for China to speak just as plainly about her desires as Baron Makino did on behalf of Japan. When Koo expressed the hope that President Wilson might see fit to say something on behalf of China when the question of Shantung should be brought up at the conference, Wilson assured Lou and Koo that "he felt deeply sympathetic for China and would do his best to help her."[27]

Next morning at the Villa Majestic, Clemenceau opened the Council to the Chinese delegates for discussion of the question of the German possessions in the Far East. Koo asked for the restoration to China of the leased territory of Kiaochow, the railway in Shantung, and all rights Germany possessed in that province before the war. He stated:

> The territories in question were an integral part of China. They were a part of a Province containing 36 million inhabitants, Chinese in race, language, and religion. The history of the lease to Germany was doubtless familiar to all. The lease had been wrung out of China by force .... On the principles of nationality and of territorial integrity, principles accepted by the Conference, China had a right to the restoration of those territories .... If the Congress were to transfer these territories to any other Power, it would, in the eyes of the Chinese Delegation, be adding one wrong to another.
>
> The Shantung Province, in which Kiaochow and the railway to Tsinanfu were situated, was the cradle of Chinese civilization, the birthplace of Confucius and Mencius and a Holy Land for the Chinese .... Economically, it was a densely populated country, with 36 million people in an area only 35,000 square miles. The density of the population produced an intense competition and rendered the country quite unsuitable for colonization .... Strategically, Kiaochow commanded one of the main gateways of North China. It controlled one of the shortest approaches from the sea to Peking, namely the railway to Tsinanfu, which at its junction with the railway from Tientsin, led straight to the capital .... (Japan already dominated Manchuria and its railway leading to Peking from the North. With Shantung and its railway, Japan would be in a pincers-like position pointing to Peking.)
>
> China was fully cognizant of the services rendered to her by the heroic army and

[26] Koo, *Wunsz King Collection*, No. 8, p. 19. Koo's Memorandum of an interview with President Wilson at Murat Mansion (with Minister Lou Tseng-tsiang), January 27, 1919.

[27] *Ibid.*, p. 20.

> navy of Japan in rooting out German power from Shantung . . . . China appreciated these services all the more because her people in Shantung had also suffered and sacrificed in connection with the military operation for the capture of Kiaochow . . . . But, grateful as they were, the Chinese Delegation felt that they would be false to their duty to China and to the world if they did not object to paying their debts of gratitude by selling the birthright of their countrymen, and thereby sowing the seeds of discord for the future . . . .[28]

Then Baron Makino of Japan reiterated his previous note and reminded the Council that Japan had been in actual possession of the territory under consideration by conquest from Germany. Agreement had also been reached with regard to the leased railways. Baron Makino held that before Japan could dispose of the territory to a third party, it would be necessary for Japan to obtain the right of free disposal from Germany. Dr. Koo argued that the treaties and notes made in consequence of the negotiations on the Twenty-One Demands in 1915 had been agreed upon by the Chinese Government only after an ultimatum from Japan.[29] They were at best only provisional and temporary arrangements subject to the final review of the Conference because they were questions arising from the war. Furthermore, "even if the treaties and notes had been entirely valid, the fact of China's declaration of war on Germany had altered the situation in such a way that on the principle of *rebus sic stantibus* they could not be enforced today."[30] Moreover, in her declaration of war against Germany, China expressly stated that "all treaties and conventions concluded between China and Germany should be considered as nullified by the state of war between them." Koo continued that "even if the lease had not been terminated by China's declaration of war, Germany would be incompetent to transfer it to any other Power than China because of an express provision therein against transfer to another Power." Koo asked for direct restitution, for it was always easier to take one step than two if it led to the same place.[31] The meeting was adjourned without decision.

"He simply overwhelmed the Japanese with his argument," Secretary Lansing recorded in his notes after Koo had spoken. "In fact it made such an impression on the Japanese themselves, that one of the delegates called upon me the following day and attempted to offset the effect by declaring that the United States would be blamed if Kiaochow was returned to China."[32] Wunsz King, Koo's secretary at the Paris Peace Conference, also recorded that "Koo

[28]Koo, *Wunsz King Collection*, No. 9, pp. 21-22. Secretary's Notes (British) of a Conversation held in M. Pichon's room at the Quai d'Orsay, Paris, January 28, 1919, at eleven hours.

[29]*Ibid.*, p. 24.

[30]C. Hill, *The Doctrine of Rebus Sic Stantibus in International Law.*

[31]Ray Stannard Baker, *Woodrow Wilson and World Settlement*, I:231.

[32]Robert Lansing, *The Peace Negotiations: A Personal Narrative*, p. 253.

was dignified and agreeable in manner, skillful in choice of words, cogent and forceful in argument, firm in tone, though at the beginning a bit trembling in voice."[33] For China, it was the beginning of a new era in her diplomatic history launched by the first Chinese plenipotentiary speaking for his country in a significant international conference. A memorandum summarizing his argument was presented to the Council of Ten by Koo next day.

THE BIG THREE AND THE DECISION

On March 24, Koo utilized an opportunity to introduce Liang Ch'i-ch'ao, the famous reformer of the Hundred Days Reforms, and Carson Chang (Chia-sen or Chün-mai), founder of the Chinese National Socialist Party, to President Wilson as a means of gaining an interview with the President at the Place des Etats-Unis. Answering Wilson's question why Japan wanted to keep the railway and return Kiaochow to China, Koo stated:

> ... that must be one of Japan's reasons in asking for the surrender to herself. One of these conditions as provided in the Shantung treaty made in consequence of the 21 Demands would be that Japan should be allowed to set up an exclusive Japanese settlement in the best part of the leased territory .... If Japan was to have the railway and exclusive settlement in the best part of the leased territory, it would mean the returning of the shadow to China, while leaving the substance to Japan.[34]

Koo also informed the President that China would place more emphasis on the restoration of the railway because the line traversed the whole province of Shantung and controlled the gateway to Peking.

A few days later, on April 2, Koo interviewed Colonel Edward House and informed the man closest to the President that a group of influential Chinese statesmen had from the beginning "favored direct negotiations with Japan on the ground that the Occident could not be relied upon for effective support ...."[35] If China should not receive satisfaction from the Western powers, Koo expressed his fear that "the reaction from such an outcome should make the Chinese people feel that their hope lay in the direction of close cooperation with Japan." Koo also urged that if the United States would stand firm in support of China, the three other big Powers would fall in line eventually, for they could reasonably claim that:

[33]Wunsz King, *China at the Paris Peace Conference in 1919*, pp. 10-11.

[34]Koo, *Wunsz King Collection*, No. 10, pp. 25-26. Koo's Memorandum of an Audience with President Wilson. Liang Ch'i-ch'ao and Carson Chang were present at 11 Place des Etats-Unis, March 24, 1919, 2:00 p.m.

[35]Koo, *Wunsz King Collection*, No. 11, p. 28. Koo's Interview with Colonel House, April 2, 1919.

> . . . the secret engagements which they had undertaken in 1917 binding themselves to support Japan's claim in regard to Shantung were no longer applicable. These dealt with questions which had arisen out of the war and were made before the United States or China joined the Allies in the war against the Central Powers.[36]

Furthermore, Koo contended that President Wilson's Fourteen Points, which all of them had accepted, would in spirit have nullified those engagements.

As the end of the Paris Peace Conference drew near, the Chinese delegates became increasingly anxious about the settlement of the Shantung question. At an interview with Lansing on April 4, 1919,[37] Koo proposed that the Shantung question should be settled by the Council of the Four Chiefs of State before the opening of negotiations with the Germans for peace, thereby implying that Japan would not be represented at the Council. Koo also advanced his argument that "to leave Japan in Shantung would mean to allow her to build up an influence capable of dominating North China." Such an eventuality would not only prejudice the future of China but also jeopardize the interests of foreign countries. Lansing assured Koo that he was fully in sympathy with China, and he expressed his willingness to speak to the President about it. Four days later Koo followed his conversation with Secretary Lansing by presenting Lansing with a lengthy aide-memoire[38] outlining all the arguments previously presented to the Council and members of the American Delegation.

Having failed to induce the Japanese to accept Wilson's proposal that the Five Powers act as trustees of the former German rights in Shantung in the morning session of April 22, the Big Three called upon the Chinese Delegation in the afternoon of the same day and tried to induce it to give up China's claim on Shantung. Lou Tseng-tsiang and Dr. Koo were selected to represent China. President Wilson opened the meeting by apologizing for his failure to champion China and blamed it on the many secret treaties concluded between China and Japan and between Japan and Great Britain and France.[39] In the Notes between China and Japan concluded before China had entered the war,

[36]Koo meant the pro-Japanese faction in Peking including Ts'ao Ju-lin, Lu Tsung-yü, and Chang Tsung-hsiang, negotiators of the Nishihara Loans and the Sino-Japanese Agreements on the Kaomi-Hsuchow Railway and the Tsinan-Shunteh Railways. Ts'ao Ju-lin, *I-sheng chih hui-i*, p. 194.

[37]Koo, *Wunsz King Collection*, No. 12, pp. 31-32. Koo's interview with Lansing at Hotel Crillon, Paris, April 4, 1919, at 11:30 a.m.

[38]Koo, *Wunsz King Collection*, No. 13, pp. 33-35. Koo's Aide-Memoire to Secretary Lansing, 5 rue Charles Lamoureux, Paris, April 8, 1919.

[39]The Council of Four: Notes of Meeting Which Took Place at President Wilson's House, Place des Etats-Unis, Paris, on Tuesday, April 22, 1919, at 4:30 p.m. *Papers Relating to the Foreign Relations of the United States: The Paris Peace Conference, 1919*, V:138-40.

Japan had obtained full authority to dispose of the rights in Shantung and China; in reply, China stated she had taken note of it. In the exchange of Notes between China and Japan concluded on September 24, 1918 after China had entered the war, the Chinese Minister at Tokyo stated that "the Chinese Government was pleased to agree to the above-mentioned articles proposed by the Japanese Government," particularly those concerning the article granting Japanese the right to control the railway police with Japanese personnel.[40] Koo explained in detail the circumstances surrounding China's acceptance of the Twenty-One Demands in 1915 and the exchange of notes on September 24, 1918. He argued that the former came only in the face of Japan's ultimatum and that the latter was an attempt to induce Japan to remove her troops and civil administration from Shantung.

Disinterested in China's difficulty and reluctant to spend any more time on the problem of Shantung, Lloyd George suddenly asked Koo: "Which would China prefer—to allow Japan to succeed to the German rights in Shantung as stated in the treaty between China and Germany, or to recognize Japan's position in Shantung as stipulated in treaties between China and Japan?"[41] Koo hesitated and answered that both conditions were unacceptable. When Lloyd George again pressed for an answer, Koo, after consulting the Chinese Foreign Minister Lou, stated that "for the sake of mere comparison of the German treaty and that of the Japanese . . . if we take everything into consideration, it looks as if the German rights in Shantung are more limited."[42] He further stated China was now asking for the direct restoration of Kiaochow to China as an act which would help maintain permanent peace in the Far East.

Lloyd George asserted that Great Britain had to keep her present engagement with Japan, but he did say that he would ask his experts to examine the two positions, German or Japanese, as to which would be more advantageous to China. Clemenceau said that "he was in accord with every word of Lloyd George. Whatever he said had also expressed his [Clemenceau's] view."[43]

[40] Memorandums of China Presented at the Paris Peace Conference, No. 1, Annex 18. Notes exchanged between the Chinese Minister at Tokyo and the Foreign Office of Japan concerning problems of Shantung, September 24, 1918, *Wai-chiao kung-pao*, No. 6, December 1921. Documents, pp. 4-5.

[41] Lloyd George was obviously not interested in the problem of Shantung. In his two-volume memoirs no problem of Shantung was mentioned. David Lloyd George, *Memoirs of the Peace Conference.*

[42] The Council of Four: Notes of a Meeting Which Took Place at President Wilson's House, Place des Etats-Unis, Paris, on Tuesday, April 22, 1919, at 4:30 p.m. *Papers Relating to the Foreign Relations of the United States: The Paris Peace Conference, 1919*, V:142-43.

[43] Koo, *Wunsz King Collection*, No. 15, pp. 43-45. Secretary's Report of the Secret Session of the Council of Three, at 11 Place des Etats-Unis, April 22, 1919.

President Wilson said that Japan had promised the return of Kiaochow to China and actual partnership with China in the control of the Shantung railway. What they were trying to do was to make the best of a bad business. He concluded that it would be better to live up to a bad treaty than to tear it apart. Furthermore, the President believed that with the establishment of the League of Nations, the Powers would have a right to intervene on China's behalf. It was clear that China's cause was lost.

Perhaps President Wilson had made up his mind after the Japanese Delegation pressed him with an ultimatum on April 22 stating that it had been explicitly instructed not to sign the treaty if the Shantung question was settled in China's favor.[44] However, Secretary Lansing did not conclude that "a bargain had been struck by which the Japanese agreed to sign the Covenant in exchange for admission of their claims" until Baron Makino declared that he would not press for his proposed amendment to the Covenant on "racial equality" on April 28.[45] With Italy's absence and Belgium's defection, the President finally retreated on two conditions: Shantung was to be ceded to Japan in the Treaty, but Japan was to make a separate declaration with the other powers reaffirming her promise to return Shantung to China. Japan's draft of clauses ultimately became Articles 156, 157, and 158 of the Treaty.[46] A separate declaration was also given on April 30 by Japan.

In reply to questions by President Wilson, the Japanese Delegation declared that:

> The policy of Japan is to hand back the Shantung Peninsula in full sovereignty to China retaining only the economic privileges granted to Germany and the right to establish a settlement under the usual conditions at Tsingtao. The owners of the Railway will use special Police only to ensure security for traffic. They will be used for no other purpose. The Police Force will be composed of Chinese, and such Japanese instructors as the Directors of the Railway may select will be appointed by the Chinese Government.[47]

Ray S. Baker tried to justify President Wilson's decision:

> At that moment three things seemed of extreme importance if anything was to be saved out of the wreckage of the world. The first was a speedy peace, so that men everywhere might return to the work of production and reconstruction and

[44]Baker, *Woodrow Wilson and World Settlement*, II:241, 260-61.

[45]Lansing, *The Peace Negotiations, A Personal Narrative*, pp. 255-56.

[46]The Treaty of Peace between the Allied and Associated Powers and Germany, signed at Versailles, June 28, 1919. *Papers Relating to the Foreign Relation of the United States: The Paris Peace Conference, 1919*, XIII:258-301.

[47]Council of Four: Notes of a Meeting Held at President Wilson's House in the Place des Etats-Unis, Paris, on Wednesday, April 30, 1919, at 12:30 p.m. *Papers Relating to the Foreign Relations of the United States: The Paris Peace Conference, 1919*, V:363-67.

> the avenues of trade everywhere be opened. Peace and work. The second was of supreme importance—keeping the great Allies firmly welded together to steady a world which was threatened with anarchy. It was absolutely necessary to keep a going concern in the world. The third was to perpetuate this world organization in a League of Nations: this the most important of all .... If the Conference were broken up, or even if Italy remained out, and Japan went out, these things would be impossible .... If the President had risked everything in standing for the Chinese demands, and had broken up the Conference upon that issue, it would not have put Japan either politically or economically out of China. Neither our people nor the British would go to war with Japan solely to keep her out of Shantung ....[48]

Baker also recorded the words President Wilson used next morning when he went to see him:

> I was with the President at 6:30 as usual and he went over the whole ground (of the Japanese settlement) with me at length. He said he had been unable to sleep the night before for thinking of it. Anything he might do was wrong .... The only hope was to unite the world together, get the League of Nations with Japan in it and then try to secure justice for the Chinese not only as regarding Japan but England, France, Russia, all of whom had concessions in China. If Japan went home there was the danger of a Japanese-Russian-German alliance, and a return to the old "balance of power" system in the world, on a greater scale than ever before. He knew his decision would be unpopular in America, that the Chinese would be bitterly disappointed, that the Japanese would feel triumphant, that he would be accused of violating his own principles, but nevertheless, he must work for world order and organization against anarchy and a return to the old militarism.[49]

Nevertheless, it was a surrender of the principle of self-determination, a transfer of millions of Chinese from one foreign master to another. This was another of those secret arrangements which riddled the Fourteen Points, Lansing admitted to himself in his diary. He further recorded that the "President fully believed that the League of Nations was in jeopardy and that to save it he was compelled to subordinate every other consideration. The result was that China was offered up as a sacrifice to propitiate the threatening Moloch of Japan."[50]

THE STRUGGLE FOR SIGNING WITH CONDITIONS

The Chinese Delegation was bitterly disappointed when Baker, at the President's request, informed them on the night of April 30 of the adverse

[48] Baker, *What Wilson Did at Paris*, pp. 103-6.
[49] Baker, *Woodrow Wilson and World Settlement*, p. 266.
[50] Lansing, *The Peace Negotiations, A Personal Narrative*, pp. 256, 262.

decision. Earlier, Koo had presented President Wilson with a memorandum on April 24, two days after his confrontation with the Big Three.[51] Besides a summary of the views of the Chinese delegates, he argued that Japan should engage to effect the restoration to China within one year after the signature of the Treaty and stated that China would agree to make a pecuniary compensation to Japan for the military expenses incurred in the capture of Tsingtao, open the whole of Kiaochow Wan as a commercial port, and provide a special quarter for the residence of citizens of the Treaty Powers. Failing to receive any response, Koo sent the President another note on May 3. Again there was no answer. Consequently, at the plenary session on May 6, Lou Tseng-tsiang and Chengting T. Wang, representing the Chinese Delegation formally registered China's reservation to have freedom of action with reference to the Shantung question.[52]

Furthermore, Koo contacted Colonel House[53] and Secretary Lansing on May 22 and 29 respectively to announce China's intent to sign the Treaty with reservations. Both Lansing and James B. Scott assured Koo that China had laid a foundation for signing the treaty under reservation and that China's signature to the treaty would be in full except for the Shantung provisions.[54] However, the Chinese Delegation was told abruptly on June 24 by Mr. Dutasta, Secretary General of the Conference, that Clemenceau, on behalf of the Supreme Council, expressed the opinion that "it was impossible for China to sign the treaty with a reservation: that China must either sign it in full, or not at all." Dutasta did not want to establish a precedent because both Germany and Roumania had also asked to sign with reservations. To this, Koo said that "he would feel sorry if the Conference should deem it proper to apply to Allies and associates the standard meted out for the common enemy."[55]

The Chinese Delegation proposed that the reservation could be made an annex to the Treaty of Peace, but it was again refused. Once more the Chinese Delegation proposed that its reservation be sent to the President of the Conference in the form of a declaration entirely separate from the Treaty so as to enable China to ask for reconsideration of the Shantung question after

[51] Koo, *Wunsz King Collection*, No. 19, pp. 55-57. Koo's Note to President Wilson, 5 rue Charles Lamoureux, Paris, April 24, 1919. Koo, *Reminiscences*, II. First Decade as Diplomat, C, 7-8.

[52] Koo, *Wunsz King Collection*, No. 19, pp. 59-60. Koo's Memorandum of Conversation with Colonel House, Hotel Crillon, May 22, 1919.

[53] Koo, *Wunsz King Collection*, No. 20, p. 62. Koo's Memorandum of Conversation with Lansing, Paris, May 29, 1919.

[54] Koo, *Wunsz King Collection*, No. 22, pp. 66-67. Koo's Memorandum of Conversation with James B. Scott, Paris, June 5, 1919.

[55] Koo, *Wunsz King Collection*, No. 23, pp. 68-69. Koo's Interview with Dutasta, June 24, 1919.

the signing of the Treaty; it was again rejected. Clemenceau only permitted China to send the declaration after the signing. Eventually Koo suggested a last compromise with "a further modification of the wording, so that the signing of the treaty by China might not be understood as precluding her from asking at a suitable moment for reconsideration of the Shantung question."[56] Even this was not acceptable to the Secretary General of the Conference before the formal signing of the Treaty. Since the effect of any condition or reservation after the signature of the Treaty would be void, Koo and his colleagues refused to sign.

In the meantime, the decision of the Big Three on Shantung reached China and caused the May Fourth Movement. At a routine business meeting of the Kuo-min tsa-chih she (National Monthly Society) Chang Kuo-t'ao, then a student at Peking University, moved for a general demonstration which eventually brought three thousand college students out in the streets.[57] The house of Ts'ao Ju-lin, the pro-Japanese Minister of Communications was burned, and Chang Tsung-hsiang, the pro-Japanese Minister to Tokyo, was seriously wounded.[58] The demonstration and strikes soon spread to all the major cities from the North to the South. On May 6, a special session was held by Peace Delegates in Shanghai, who were there to try to effect the peaceful unification of the two rival governments. The two chief delegates, Chu Ch'i-ch'ien, who represented the warlord government at Peking, and T'ang Shao-i, who represented the Military Government at Canton, jointly signed a cable-gram to the Chinese Delegation at Paris stating that,

> In case the Peace Conference should accede to the demand of another Power [Japan], while ignoring our claim, the four hundred million people of China, in the name of justice and righteousness, would never agree to such a decision. We request that you will not sign the treaty . . . .[59]

The populace of Shantung was so indignant that a resolution by 30,000 people was passed on May 6 at the Conference for Commemoration of National Humiliation, and a telegram was sent to the Chinese delegates in Paris saying that "If you sign any treaty which includes a clause that Japan has any rights in Shantung, we shall subject you to the same treatment as

[56] Wunsz King, *Ts'ung Pa-li ho-hui tao Kuo-lien*, p. 25.

[57] Chang Kuo-t'ao, "Wo-te hui-i" (Memoir of Chang Kuo-t'ao), *Ming-pao yüeh-k'an* (Ming-pao Monthly), I, No. 4, 88-91. Chang Kuo-t'ao was one of the founders of the Chinese Communist Party. In the 1920s he headed the China Trade Union Secretariat. He defected to the National Government in 1938.

[58] Ts'ao Ju-lin, *I-sheng chih hui-i*, pp. 195-203.

[59] American Consul-General (Thomas Sammons) to the Secretary of State, June 14, 1919, Shanghai, *Internal Affairs of China, 1910-1929*, 893.00/3119, Reel 21.

has been meted out to Chang and Ts'ao when you return . . . ."[60]

After the May Fourth Incident, the pro-Japanese ministers, Ts'ao, Chang, and Lu Tsung-yü, Director General of the Bureau of the Monetary System were "allowed to resign."[61] However, when the Central Government received the final telegram from the Chinese Delegation in Paris for a final confirmation by the cabinet to sign, President Hsü Shih-ch'ang tried to resign, but the Parliament refused on June 10. On June 13, Premier Ch'ien Neng-hsün was replaced by Kung Hsin-chan. Ten days later the new cabinet, still under the influence of the An-fu Clique of Tuan, instructed the Chinese Delegation to sign. Nevertheless, in the glaring Hall of Mirrors of the Palace of Versailles on June 28, 1919, when all the other delegations were there to sign the Treaty, the Chinese delegates were absent. Instead, Koo and his Chinese colleagues issued a release stating that:

> . . . the Peace Conference having denied China justice in the settlement of the Shantung question and having today in effect prevented them from signing the treaty without sacrificing their sense of right, justice, and patriotic duty, the Chinese delegates submit their case to the impartial judgment of the world.[62]

DISCUSSION

Although he failed to realize all the goals of China at the Paris Peace Conference, Dr. Koo had demonstrated an astuteness in Anglo-American diplomacy, which earned him the admiration of Western diplomats and the envy of Japanese rivals. He and his Chinese delegates by abstaining from the ceremony for the signing of the Treaty of Versailles saved China from disgrace and paved the way for further negotiations on the Shantung problem at the Conference on the Limitation of Armaments in Washington between 1921 and 1922. Koo had also established the reputation of modern Chinese diplomacy in the international arena to the point that his principle of geographical representation was accepted by the League of Nations. China for the first time in recent history was recognized as an acceptable member of the community of nations when she was allowed to occupy the seat of a non-permanent member of the League Council.[63] Koo himself, as the premier Chinese diplomat, so recognized by the international community, became president

[60] American Consul (George F. Dickford) to American Minister in Peking (Paul S. Reinsch). Tsinanfu, May 8, 1919. *Internal Affairs of China, 1910-1929*, 893.00/3165.

[61] Lo Kuang, *Lu Cheng-hsiang chuan*, pp. 113-14.

[62] Wunsz King, *China at the Paris Peace Conference in 1919*, p. 30. Koo, *Reminiscences*, II. First Decade as Diplomat, C, 9-11.

[63] Baker, *Woodrow Wilson and World Settlement*, pp. 233-34.

of the Council for the fourteenth session.

Dedicated and capable as they were, Dr. Koo and his Chinese colleagues were less experienced than their Japanese counterparts, Baron Makino and Viscount Chinda. Because of the scarcity in China of men educated in the West, the Chinese Government, with full awareness, had found it necessary to recruit young and somewhat inexperienced graduates, such as Dr. Koo, for highly responsible diplomatic positions.[64] It is little wonder that when Baker brought the President's decision, Dr. Koo and his colleagues were shocked.

Faction-ridden and confused though they were, there now developed a consensus among the warlords, as well as all the diplomats, concerning the restoration of China's lost rights; their dedication to Chinese nationalism was firm. Within China there was no cooperation between the Peking Government and the Canton Government even with regard to the question of selecting representatives to the Paris Peace Conference. Within the Peking Government, the wide split between the President and the Parliament on one side and the Premier and the Committee of Foreign Affairs on the other had contributed to the ephemeral restoration of the Ch'ing dynasty.[65] At Paris the cool relations between the Peking-appointed southern delegate Chengting T. Wang, Koo, and the other members of the Chinese Delegation were understandable. The lack of enthusiasm and cooperation on the part of Sao-Ke Alfred Sze as a result of the problem of seniority within the Delegation so damaged China that Great Britain could practically guarantee the victory of Japan and cancel whatever Dr. Koo might have accomplished with President Wilson and members of the American Delegation. Lou Tseng-tsiang, the French-speaking Foreign Minister, might have influenced the course of the French Government to a certain degree if he had not been so pessimistic concerning China's weakness.[66] It is perhaps indicative of Lou's lack of diplomatic vigor that he actually became inactive after the Paris Peace Conference and "exiled" himself to Switzerland a few years later.[67]

The preparations of the Peking Government for the Paris Peace Conference were not sufficient. Furthermore, government instructions to Koo and his colleagues were not consistent, and these orders were not always carried

[64] President Yüan Shih-k'ai was aware of Koo's inexperience when Ts'ao Ju-lin, Vice-Minister of Foreign Affairs, recommended Dr. Koo as the Minister to Washington. Ts'ao Ju-lin, *I-sheng chih hui-i*, pp. 147-48.

[65] Ts'ao Ju-lin, *I-sheng chih hui-i*, pp. 201-2.

[66] *Ibid.*, p. 189. Ts'ao Ju-lin commented on Lou Tseng-tsiang as "his will has ever been weak and unsteady."

[67] Lou Tseng-tsiang's request to be appointed as the Chinese Minister to Switzerland was mainly because of his bankruptcy as a result of the fall of the French war bonds while in Europe, not political interest. Lo Kuang, *Lu Cheng-hsiang chuan*, pp. 117-19, 132, 135-37.

through by Koo and his colleagues. Because of Japan's Nishihara Loans and Japan's help in establishing the War Participation Army, Premier Tuan was so indebted to the Japanese that the Sino-Japanese Military Alliance was signed on May 16, 1918, near the end of the war, and the Chinese Delegation to the Paris Peace Conference was not instructed to discuss the problem of the restitution of Shantung.[68] When Japan brought the demand of Shantung to the Council of Ten, Koo and his colleague were caught unprepared.

Nevertheless, Koo and his colleagues went their own way, and the problem of Shantung became the major theme of the Chinese Delegation. Against the clearly designated order of the Peking Government, the Chinese representatives refused to sign the Treaty of Versailles. This undutiful conduct of the Chinese Delegation was legalized afterward by a new instruction from Peking that the Delegation should refrain from signing.[69] This attitude of the Peking Government toward its representatives abroad further encouraged independent actions by the Chinese delegates in future international conferences and also enhanced the stability of the Anglo-American group and their foreign policy throughout the numerous changes of the cabinet and the civil wars among the warlords.

Also significant was the fact that Chinese public opinion, emotional and unpractical as it was, discharged an impressive duty by channeling the voice of the people of China and the feelings of the warlords from various provinces to the Delegation at Paris. For the first time in modern Chinese history newspapers and organized demonstrations exerted such a pressure that the decision-making in foreign policy of the Chinese Central Government was shared to a certain extent. With the beginning of a nationwide awareness of the citizen's role in the destiny of China, and with the respect and cooperation which Koo and his delegates exhibited toward the desires of the people, the conduct of foreign affairs was put under the supervision of the people with the blessing and tacit understanding of the various warlords in the provinces. Rather than to the Central Government in Peking entirely, the Chinese delegates in Paris were partially responsible to the Chinese people, or at least toward the educated and organized factions of Chinese society. As a matter of fact, it was due to the pressure of public opinion that the delegates were absent from the Hall of Mirrors against the government's instruction. Nevertheless, public opinion was so removed from Paris that many suggestions became not only impractical but also obsolete as a result of poor communication between the Chinese delegates and news media on one side and the underdeveloped civil

[68] Ts'ao Ju-lin, *I-sheng chih hui-i*, p. 188.

[69] Lo Kuang, *Lu Cheng-hsiang chuan*, pp. 113-15. Instruction for signing the Treaty of Versailles, June 23, 1919, and instruction for not signing the Treaty of Versailles, July 10, 1919.

communication system in China on the other.[70]

The most profound effect of the work of Koo and the rest of the members of the Anglo-American group at Paris was that after the Paris Peace Conference, Chinese foreign policy shifted fundamentally from the pro-Japanese policies instituted by the returned students from Japan to a pro-Anglo-American course by the English-speaking and American-trained diplomats under the Peking Government. The Nationalist Government after the split with the Chinese Communist Party in 1927 inherited this general policy, as well as these diplomats, including Dr. Koo. As Japanese aggression gravitated from Manchuria to North China and eventually South China, the Nationalist Government relied more and more upon the Anglo-American group in the international arena from the League of Nations after the Paris Peace Conference to the United Nations during World War II. On May 5, the Japanese delegate, Baron Makino, stated that Japan would return the entire Shantung Peninsula and its sovereign power to China, except some economic rights and a settlement in Tsingtao. The same statement was given by the Japanese Foreign Minister on May 17. But, fear and suspicion enhanced the growth of Chinese nationalism, and the options represented by these statements were not well exploited. To a remarkable extent, the representatives in Washington actually made the foreign policies of Nanking. It is little wonder that when the Chinese Communists triumphed in mainland China, the Nationalist Government felt that it had been "betrayed" by her American ally, and many American "China-hands" also regretted that "we lost China."

[70] A dispatch from the veteran statesman, T'ang Shao-i, to the Chinese Delegation at Paris on whether or not the Chinese delegates should formally take up the issue of the independence of Korea at the European Conference. American Consul-General (Thomas Sammons) at Shanghai to the American Minister (Paul S. Reinsch) at Peking, December 24, 1918. *Internal Affairs of China, 1910-1929.*

CHAPTER III

Koo at the Washington Disarmament Conference, 1921-1922

THE BEGINNING AND PRINCIPLES OF THE MEETING

The Paris Peace Conference at Versailles left many problems unsolved. The war had shifted the balance of rivalry among Great Britain, Germany, and Russia to a new competition among Britain, the United States, and Japan. Britain had faced the dilemma of whether or not to renew the Anglo-Japanese Alliance, a hard choice between their American cousin and their Japanese sweetheart; the U. S. shifted its traditional Monroe Doctrine and, as an international capitalist power, competed in trade and military development; and Japan, which had profited from the war and matured into a strong power, adopted its own form of Monroe Doctrine and applied it to East Asia.

Armament competition in particular made the problems of war-stricken economies even more serious.[1] In August of 1921, U. S. President Warren Harding sent invitations to the governments of Great Britain, France, Italy, Japan and others, to participate in a Conference on the Limitation of Armament.

The Chinese Government accepted the invitation to the Conference promptly. Dr. Sao-Ke Alfred Sze, the new Chinese Ambassador to Washington, was instructed to notify American Secretary of State Charles Evans Hughes that such a conference met with the hearty concurrence of the Republic of China.[2] Nationalist officials began to make immediate preparations for the Chinese participation in the Washington Conference. In August, they established a Division for the Preparation of the Conference on the Limitation of Armament within the Foreign Ministry, and thereafter issued a set of regulations for its operation.[3] Various governmental ministries provided personnel

[1] Chia Shih-i, *Hua-hui chien-wen lu* (Reminiscence Pertaining to the Washington Disarmament Conference), pp. 1-3.

[2] *Cheng-fu kung-pao*, Nos. 1966, 1971, and 1978; August 14, 19, and 26, 1921.

[3] *Ibid.*, No. 2010, September 28, 1921. The Committee of Specialists consisted of members from the various Ministries of the Peking Government, such as: Ministry of Internal Affairs, Ministry of Finance, Ministry of War, Ministry of Navy, Ministry of Justice, Ministry of Education, Ministry of Agriculture and Commerce, Ministry of

for a Committee of Specialists as well as a Secretariat for the Conference. The sum of 1,105,251 silver dollars was raised to finance the Delegation, chiefly from the contributions of various warlords.[4] Additionally, the Chinese leased a large private house in Washington, D. C., on Massachusetts Avenue to accommodate the Delegation. Ambassador Sze was named Chief of the Delegation, and, more significantly, included in the Delegation were the Chief Justice of the Supreme Court of China, Chung-Hui Wang (Wang Ch'ung-hui), and V. K. Wellington Koo.[5] Wu Ch'ao-shu, Deputy Foreign Minister of Canton Government, was also appointed as a delegate, but refused to attend the Conference. In late October, Dr. Koo and his wife sailed for America aboard the *Olympic*, accompanied by a valet, an English maid, and a tiny sable-colored Pekinese dog.[6]

The tentative agenda for the Conference, which had been drawn up by the American hosts and circulated to the various invited powers beforehand, had been accepted without any difficulty. Subsequently, the powers received an agenda for a Conference for the Discussion of Pacific and Far Eastern Questions.[7] This document included the topics: Territorial and Administrative Integrity; the Open Door, Equality of Commercial and Industrial Opportunity; Concessions, Monopolies, or Preferential Economic Privileges; Development of Railways; and Preferential Railroad Rates.

On November 12, 1921, in Memorial Continental Hall in Washington, the first plenary session of the Conference on the Limitation of Armament, in connection with which Pacific and Far Eastern questions would also be discussed, was held. The Secretary of State of the United States, Charles Evans Hughes, presided. The U. S. was also represented by Senator Henry Cabot Lodge, Majority Leader of the Senate and Chairman of the Foreign Relations Committee, Senator Oscar W. Underwood, the Senate Minority Leader and expert on taxation, and former Secretary of State Elihu W. Root. Root's appointment to the U. S. Delegation caused Dr. Koo some apprehension because Root tended to lean toward the Japanese position in Manchuria for pragmatic reasons.[8] Great Britain was represented by Arthur James Balfour,

Communications, and the Bureau of Tariff Affairs. "Regulations of the Committee of Specialists of the Chinese Delegation for the Conference on the Limitation of Armament." Kung Te-po, *Kung Te-po hui-i lu* (Memoir of Kung Te-po), I:65-79.

[4] *Wai-chiao kung-pao*, No. 11, May 1922.

[5] V. K. Wellington Koo, *Reminiscences*, II, D, 1 and 2.

[6] Koo Hui-lan, *Autobiography*, pp. 142-43. American Minister (Schurman) to Chinese Foreign Minister (Yen), September 12, 1921, *Wai-chiao kung-pao*, No. 4, Treaties, pp. 9-12.

[7] American Minister (Schurman) to Chinese Foreign Minister (Yen), September 12, 1921, *Wai-chiao kung-pao*, No. 4, Treaties, pp. 9-12.

[8] Wunsz King, *Ts'ung Pa-li ho-hui tao Kuo-lien*, p. 28.

Lord President of the Privy Council, Baron Lee of Fareham, First Lord of the Admiralty, and Sir Auckland Campbell Geddes, Ambassador to the U. S.[9] Japan was represented by Admiral Baron Tomosaburō Katō, Minister of the Navy, Baron Kijūrō Shidehara, Ambassador to the U. S., Prince Iyesato Tokugawa, President of the House of Peers, and Masanao Hanihara, Vice Minister for Foreign Affairs.[10]

At Hughes' suggestion, the session members created a Committee on Program and Procedure with respect to disarmament composed of chief delegates of the principal and allied powers of Britain, France, Italy, Japan, and the U. S. Similarly, an identical committee respecting the Pacific and Far Eastern questions was formed by representatives of China, Belgium, the Netherlands, and Portugal. The Committee on Limitation of Armament dealt mainly with a U. S. proposal to limit naval warship tonnage, arriving finally at the famous 5-5-3 ratio for Britain, the U. S., and Japan, respectively.[11] The Committee on the Pacific and Far Eastern Questions devoted its attention to Chinese questions such as foreign post offices in China, Chinese revenue, extraterritoriality, and the Chinese Eastern Railway. The three Chinese delegates distributed these tasks among themselves, Dr. Koo being responsible for the Subcommittee on Chinese Revenue and the Subcommittee on Drafting and Classification.[12]

A dispute developed within the Chinese Delegation over the strategy of which issue should be presented first to the Conference: whether first to present fundamental principles such as territorial and administrative integrity, or special cases such as Shantung or the Twenty-one Demands.[13] Eventually Koo and his colleagues decided that fundamental principles, once accepted, would serve as a basis for discussing any special issues and would enhance the possibilities of success. The U. S. informed the Chinese Delegation at midnight on November 15 that it would be unable to present Far Eastern questions to the Committee, and Koo and his colleagues worked overnight with the assistance of their American legal consultant, Westel W. Willoughby, to draft the Ten Points, which were read to the Far Eastern Committee the following day by Ambassador Sze. The issues included: (1) Respect for the territorial integrity of China by all powers, with the assurance by the Chinese Government not to

[9] *Conference on the Limitation of Armament, Washington, November 12, 1921-February 6, 1922*, pp. 12, 18, 34.

[10] Shidehara Heiwa Sidan (Shidehara Peace Foundation), ed., *Shidehara Kijūrō*.

[11] *Conference on the Limitation of Armament, Washington, November 12, 1921-February 6, 1922*, pp. 66, 1575-1604.

[12] Chia Shih-i, *Hua-hui chien-wen lu*, pp. 30-31.

[13] Lo Chia-lun, "Wo tui-yü Chung-kuo tsai Hua-sheng-tun hui-i chih kuan-ch'a" (My Observations on China at the Washington Conference), *Tung-fang tsa-chih*, XIX:2 (January 1922), pp. 12-25.

lease or alienate any further part of its territory; (2) Application of and respect for the open-door policy in China by all powers; (3) Treaties between powers respecting China and its area not to be undertaken without notification and opportunity to participate given to China; (4) Examination and revision of all foreign rights, privileges, immunities, and commitments in China, to be accomplished at the Conference; (5) Removal of limitations upon China's political, jurisdictional and administrative freedom; (6) Establishment of reasonable terms of duration for China's commitments; (7) Interpretation of agreements according to the principle of strict construance, and in favor of China; (8) Respect for China's neutrality; (9) Settlement of international disputes in the Far East by peaceful means; and (10) Provision for future conferences to be held.[14] Later, China's Ten Points served as the basis for the Root Resolution which was adopted by the Conference on December 10, 1921. The resolution included four points: (1) Respect for the territorial and administrative integrity of China; (2) Development of an opportunity to achieve a stable government in China; (3) Use of the Conference's influence to establish the principle of equal opportunity for all nations to practice commerce and industry in China; and (4) Non-exploitation by all powers of any situation in order to gain privileges for themselves at the expense of friendly states and likely to jeopardize the security of their subjects.[15] A realistic politician, Root confided to Koo that the Japanese position in Manchuria was inalterable except by force, and had therefore addressed his fourth point to the Japanese, trading recognition of Japan's special interests there for the acquired interests of the other powers.[16]

Root also believed it was desirable to distinguish between China proper and areas over which it exercised suzerainty, adding to the confusion, and inherent question, of "What is China?" To this Koo replied:

> The Chinese Delegation could not discuss any question which might give the impression of attempting to modify the territorial boundaries of China. . . . As regards the point of administrative integrity . . . the administration of China proper formed one unit and that of the other parts of the Republic formed other units. But this was an internal arrangement within the Republic and, so far as the outside world was concerned, it would appear clear that the principle of administrative integrity should be confirmed for the Chinese Republic as one unit.[17]

Koo obtained a confirmation of the one-China principle by resolution and, with an appeal to the American sense of fair play from representatives of

[14] *Conference on the Limitation of Armament, Washington, November 12, 1921-February 6, 1922*, pp. 866-68.

[15] Chia Shih-i, *Hua-hui chien-wen lu*, pp. 127-28.

[16] Wunsz King, *Ts'ung Pa-li ho hui tao Kuo-lien*, p. 39.

[17] *Ibid.*, pp. 882-84.

Manchurian Provincial Legislatures, Chambers of Commerce, Industry and Agriculture, and Educational Associations who asserted that "Manchuria is an integral part of China," the issue of "What is China?" was nearly silenced throughout the conference.[18]

While it may seem obscure to the non-Chinese, Koo's assignment to the Subcommittee on Chinese Revenue was of crucial importance to his government, for tariff autonomy, concerning the rates to be charged and their apportionment among different classes of articles, was ever the major concern of the Chinese Government in general and the bankrupt Peking Government in particular. Originally, Ambassador Sze was to be responsible for tariff negotiations. However because he was fully occupied by the meetings and preparations for the Nine Powers Treaty Relating to Principles and Policies Concerning China, Dr. Koo was asked to cover this matter.[19] On September 12, 1921, Jacob Gould Schurman, American Ambassador to Peking, forwarded the tentative agenda of the American Government for the Conference in connection with Pacific and Far Eastern Questions, and the Peking Government immediately instructed Ambassador Sze in Washington to deliver to Secretary Hughes the Chinese agenda which included the problem of tariffs. Hughes promised that the matter could be brought up under the topic of "administrative integrity" without amending the existing agenda.[20]

TARIFF AUTONOMY

Thus on November 23, Dr. Koo first broached the question of tariff autonomy at the Far Eastern Committee's fifth meeting. It was an historically significant statement from the viewpoint of sovereign rights, reciprocity, differentiation, revenue, and tariff revision, and it suggested that the existing arrangement of tariffs in China imposed from without constituted an infringement upon the sovereign rights which all nations enjoyed. Furthermore, the agreements deprived China of its power to make reciprocal arrangements with other powers and ran counter to the principles of equality and mutuality; a uniform rate for all kinds of commodities, without latitude to differentiate rates between luxuries and necessities has obvious disadvantage to China. Koo argued that the existing tariff system caused a serious loss of revenue to the Chinese treasury while it was exceedingly difficult to revise tariffs, even by

[18] *The North China Herald*, January 7, 1922, p. 10.

[19] Wunsz King, *Ts'ung Pa-li ho-hui tao Kuo-lien*, p. 40.

[20] Memorandum by the Secretary of State of a Conversation with the Chinese Minister (Sze), November 5, 1921. *Foreign Relations of the United States, 1921*, I:82.

modest amounts.[21] Based on these arguments, Koo concluded with the following proposals: (1) tariff autonomy should be restored to China at the end of a certain period to be agreed upon by the powers; (2) the Chinese import tariff duty should be immediately increased to 12½ per cent effective January 1, 1922, a rate mentioned in the Chinese treaties with Great Britain, the U. S., and Japan; (3) as soon as practicable, a new tariff arrangement should be agreed upon between China and the powers, whereby China should be free to levy any rate of duty it might choose on any article imported, up to a certain maximum rate to be agreed upon, thus permitting differentiation in the duties imposed.[22]

The Subcommittee on Chinese Revenue held six meetings between November 29, 1921 and January 4, 1922, under the gavel of Senator Underwood, and including members from all the nine powers participating in the Conference. Within the Subcommittee there were two sets of interests, competitive, but not at all irreconcilable: the Chinese need for tariff revision and the foreign powers' desire to have the *likin*, a local transit tax, abolished. One could be exchanged for the other. At the first meeting, Dr. Koo presented the Subcommittee with a list of six concrete proposals: (1) raise the Chinese import duty from 5 to 12½ per cent; (2) abolish the *likin* effective January 1, 1924 and simultaneously the powers permit to levy an additional surtax on all luxury goods entering China; (3) negotiate a new customs regime within five years of the agreement on the basis of a maximum rate of 25 per cent *ad valorem* on all imported goods; (4) abolish the existing reduction on goods imported overland; (5) limit the agreement to ten years (1932); (6) China voluntarily pledged not to alter the customs system in any fundamental way, and assured the Powers that the devotion of customs revenue to the payment of loans would continue.[23] There does not seem to have been serious argument over the Chinese proposal; it was accepted outright at least in principle, and there only remained haggling over details of how the transition to Chinese tariff autonomy should be achieved, and the details, naturally, varied according to the pecuniary self-interest of the individual countries involved.

At the second meeting of the Subcommittee on Chinese Revenue on November 30, Sir Robert Borden of Great Britain proposed that the revision should begin at once; however, it should be accomplished in increments instead of all at once. He proposed an immediate 5 per cent increase in Chinese tariffs, future revisions were to be at seven-year intervals beginning in four years, to

[21] *Conference on the Limitation of Armament, Washington, November 21, 1921-February 6, 1922*, pp. 920-22.

[22] *Ibid.*, pp. 924-28.

[23] *Conference on the Limitation of Armament, Subcommittees, Washington, November 12, 1921-February 6, 1922*, pp. 544-46.

7½ per cent to collect duties on certain luxury goods such as alcohol and tobacco, and that upon the abolition of the *likin*, China could raise duties to its desired 12½ per cent.

Japan claimed, through Masunosuke Odagiri, Director of the Yokohama Specie Bank, that since trade with China represented 30 per cent of its foreign trade, such an increase would present a hardship, forcing higher prices and affecting trade adversely for both China and Japan. Dr. Koo pointed out to Mr. Odagiri that an increase of 7½ per cent represented only 6,000,000 silver dollars distributed among the entire lot of Japanese business; the 30 per cent surtax proposed by the Japanese represented an increase equivalent to only 4.7 per cent, and he refused to consider an increase to 5 per cent as a concession, as the treaties already provided for that amount. Finally, Dr. Koo reminded the Japanese that upon that country's recovery of tariff autonomy in 1899, it had raised its tariffs from less than 5 per cent to 19 per cent by 1911![24]

A month later, after reconciling some differences between China and Japan at the third meeting of the Subcommittee on December 27, with Dr. Koo's concurrence, Sir Borden presented his draft Agreement on Chinese Tariff for discussion.[25] The ten articles, which included all of his original points, proposed: a Special Conference of China and others to prepare the way for the abolition of the *likin* as the precondition for the raising of tariffs to 12½ per cent; the variation of the rate from 5 per cent should be accomplished by a Revision Committee, and the revised tariff was to become effective two months after publication without ratification; this Special Conference was to be empowered to authorize a surtax at a rate not to exceed 2½ per cent *ad valorem* except for luxury goods; a further revision of the tariff every seven years; and the reduction of tariffs then applied to articles transported over land into China was to be abolished.

The discussions at the subsequent meetings of the Subcommittee concentrated on the issues of raising the import duty of 12½ per cent, the maximum surtax for luxury goods, and the allocation of the increased revenues. Odagiri still insisted that as to the agreement on the first issue to be decided at the Special Conference, the rate should be raised only to a point agreeable to all the treaty powers, to which Koo agreed.[26] Koo also inquired as to the time and method for the calling of the new Special Conference, pursuing Sir Borden's suggestion that it be convened with a view to its completion four months after the ratification of the Conference's Treaty Relating to the Chinese Tariff. Cattier, the French delegate, raised an unexpected obstacle in

[24] *Ibid.*, pp. 558-64.
[25] *Ibid.*, pp. 570-76.
[26] *Ibid.*, pp. 580-82, 594-96.

the form of the so-called "case of the golden Francs": since the major export of France to China was luxury goods, he raised the question of the maximum duty rate for such goods. After lengthy arguments, Borden and Koo agreed that the total surtax should not exceed 5 per cent. Odagiri suggested that the increased revenues be used to service China's unsecured foreign loans. Also, because of Japan's large trade with China, certain adjustments in the operation and makeup of the Chinese Maritime Customs, long exclusively controlled by the British, be made, implying that the Japanese be given greater influence therein. Koo replied that while China intended to meet its obligations, and reserved a certain amount for this purpose, he rejected any attempt to dictate any such formula; moreover he criticized the makeup of the Maritime Customs, especially the small number of Chinese nationals among its forty-four Directors, and reminded the Subcommittee of China's sole right to determine the number of foreign nationals employed on the customs staff.[27]

Koo's proposed clause on the abolition of reduced duties for goods coming into China via land routes was opposed by the French, whose colony of Indochina and China shared a long frontier. Koo defended his proposal, explaining that the 1886 special arrangements no longer existed, e.g., that China-Russia trade, once carried by caravans, had been replaced by railway transportation, second, that the existing system cost China 2,000,000 silver dollars a year, and finally, that such an arrangement was contrary to the Open Door. Senator Underwood added American weight to Koo's arguments, stating that he did not believe the U. S. would support any treaty detrimental to its most-favored-nation status. After lengthy debate, the delegates reached a compromise formula whereby discriminatory duties then existing could not be increased, however thereafter uniform custom taxes would be levied on goods coming into China whether by land or sea.[28] Thus, the Subcommittee completed its work, and the draft treaty, together with Koo's Declaration of Intention not to Disturb the Present Administration of the China Maritime Customs, were submitted to the Committee on Pacific and Far Eastern Questions for action.

At the seventeenth meeting of the Committee on Pacific and Far Eastern Questions, Senator Underwood, Chairman of the Subcommittee on Chinese Revenue, reported the completion of his Subcommittee's work. He outlined to the Far Eastern Committee the two phases of tariff readjustment for China. Immediate revision called for a Committee of Revision to meet at Shanghai to change the existing tariff to a basis of 5 per cent effective. This revision would become effective two months after publication of this agreement

[27] *Ibid.*, pp. 594-96.
[28] *Ibid.*, pp. 596-98, 608-20, 622-24.

without awaiting ratification. It would provide additional revenue amounting to about $17,000,000 silver. Long-range revision would involve a Special Conference representing China and the powers charged with the duty of preparing the way for the speedy abolition of *likin*. It would likewise put into effect a surtax of 2½ per cent, which would secure additional revenue amounting to approximately $27,000,000 silver, and a special surtax on luxuries, not exceeding 5 per cent, which would provide additional revenue amounting to $2,167,000 silver. The total additional revenue would amount to $46,167,000 silver. The tariff had produced $64,000,000 silver revenue for 1920. If this were added to the additional revenue provided by the Agreement, the total yield from customs duties would be $110,167,000 silver. These measures, he hoped, would secure sufficient revenue to the Chinese Central Government to maintain a stable government and thus improve trading conditions in China.[29] Underwood also focused the attention of the Committee on problems such as equal opportunity of trade, years for revision, and the maintenance in China of large military forces as a serious drain on the finances of China.

Following Senator Underwood's statement, Dr. Koo spoke on the re-establishment of tariff autonomy, a matter to which the Chinese people attached extreme importance. He regretted that the Agreement presented by the Senator did not include the restoration of tariff autonomy to China. Based on political, financial, economic, and social reasons, he reiterated his points presented previously to the Committee on November 23. The existing treaty provision on China's tariff constituted not only an infringement on its sovereign rights but also a detriment to its well-being. The maintenance of the existing tariff meant a continued loss of revenue to the Chinese Government, the customs import duty of 3½ per cent being less than the average rate of 15 to 60 per cent levied by other powers. The present uniform low duty encouraged a disproportionate increase in the importation of luxuries such as wine and tobacco which in turn had a deleterious effect on social and moral habits of the Chinese people. It was also an impediment to China's economic development because under the existing tariff agreement China enjoyed no reciprocity from any of the powers, and China's produce, on entering any of these countries, was subject to maximum tariff rates. Finally, the regulation of China's tariff by treaty inevitably must work unjustly, Koo said, since the powers, in order to avoid the burden of the increased rate, would hardly give their unanimous consent to any proposal by China for revision. The Chinese Delegation, Dr. Koo concluded, felt duty bound to declare that it was their desire to bring the question of tariff autonomy up again for consideration on all appropriate occasions in the future.[30] With the powers' assent, the report

[29] *Ibid.*, pp. 1162-64.
[30] *Ibid.*, pp. 1532-36.

of the Subcommittee on China's revenue was referred to the Subcommittee on Drafting to put it in final form. At the eighteenth meeting of the Far Eastern Committee, held on January 16, 1922, the Drafting Committee presented the report of the Subcommittee on Chinese Revenue in two classes of provisions. One set was a draft Agreement on the Revision of the Chinese Tariff for the revision of the customs schedule under the proposed treaties making the rates equivalent to 5 per cent effective in accordance with the existing treaties. The other was a draft resolution regarding revision of Chinese Customs Duties, which as a formal treaty, modified the existing treaties. Both instruments were unanimously adopted formally by the Far Eastern Committee.

Lord Balfour brought up the question of nonsignatory powers at the Committee meeting. The tariff reform would not go into effect until every nation in the world which had a treaty with China providing for a tariff on imports and exports not exceeding 5 per cent had decided to sign. One signatory power alone, by refusing to agree, could prevent for an indefinite period the application of the existing agreement because the signatory powers were liable for a uniform rate *ad valorem* at all land and maritime frontiers of China, according to the proposed draft treaty, as well as the most-favored-nation treatment.[31]

Senator Underwood agreed with Lord Balfour and declared that should any nonsignatory powers refuse to become parties to the convention and attempt to enter into agreements with China under the old treaty rate of 5 per cent, China would have the right to renounce the old treaties if it thought proper. When conditions changed and the old trading agreements worked a great disadvantage to one or another of the contracting parties in the past, it had been recognized that such trade conventions might be eliminated. Since China had to have a stable financial base if it were to function as a government, the Powers agreed with China on a plan to raise taxes. If one nation in the world stood out alone on the basis of some previous treaty or agreement against the sentiment and the consensus of the Powers sitting at the table, and tried to prevent China from getting this additional money, the Chinese Government would be entirely justified in denouncing that treaty or agreement.[32] The Committee eventually approved the proposed change of Article IX, which then read "The provisions of the present Treaty shall override all stipulations of treaties between China and the respective Contracting Powers which are inconsistent therewith, other than stipulations according most favored nation treatment." In later years, Spain, Denmark, Sweden, and Norway also joined the treaty.

[31]*Ibid.*
[32]*Ibid.*, pp. 1536-40.

An unexpected controversy was raised at the last moment by Lord Balfour when he asked the Committee to embody China's intention not to affect any change in or to disturb the existing administration of the Chinese Maritime Customs in the form of a preamble, an annex, or a solemn declaration at the Plenary Meeting. Dr. Koo stated that it had been a voluntary declaration of policy of the Chinese Government without suggestion from any power. There was no international treaty or convention in which this policy had been stipulated. He felt certain that his colleagues of the Committee would not wish to make it a treaty obligation of the Chinese Government. He preferred the presentation of it in a form of declaration as originally suggested by him. China had voluntarily offered it, and the offer should be accepted in good faith, as it had been tendered, Koo said.[33] Senator Underwood agreed that the powers ought not to be in a position to force China, as a sovereign state, to put foreign nationals in the administration of its custom service. He also objected to putting the Chinese declaration into the Treaty because he might have difficulty defending it with the American people, who might feel that their government had coerced China into an obligation concerning China's local affairs.[34] However, at the insistence of Lord Balfour, Dr. Koo promised a solemn and formal declaration invested with the character of permanency.

RESTORATION OF SHANTUNG MEETING INITIALS

Another outstanding international question facing the Conference, which China sought to settle, was the issue of the restoration of rights in Shantung Peninsula to China from Japan. To at least one contemporary, Wellington Koo was the principal figure in the controversy.[35]

China had previously refused to sign the Treaty of Versailles in 1919, in which the Allies had granted Japan jurisdiction over the former German colony in Shantung. Both Great Britain and the U. S. had at the time urged Japan to return the rights in the province to China, however the latter had insisted upon direct bilateral negotiations between itself and China. China, fearing it might become the victim of Japanese expansionism, preferred that the question be settled through mediation at an international conference. China had considered bringing the case to the League of Nations, through Koo, their representative in that body, but had decided against such a move because the U. S., China's steadfast sympathizer, would not be present, and support was

[33] *Ibid.*, p. 1198.
[34] *Ibid.*, p. 1548.
[35] *New York Times*, November 20, 1921, p. 1.

not to be found elsewhere.[36]

To the Japanese Government, its policy supported by the Japanese public, the Shantung question was one of "sole concern to certain particular Powers or such matters that may be regarded accomplished facts [and] should be scrupulously avoided," and it had remained suspicious toward the Conference's planned discussion of the issue until it had been precisely informed as to the nature and scope of the problems to be discussed.[37] Although no formal understanding among Britain, Japan, and the U. S. had been reached concerning the agenda of the Conference, the Department of State informed Ambassador Sze that "the right of any sovereign nation to exercise its discretion about discussing any particular question would no doubt apply to this matter."[38]

Before the commencement of the Conference, Japan, fearing it would be "tried" on the issue by the participating powers, attempted to dispose of the troublesome matter beforehand. In July 1921, Japanese Ambassador to Washington Baron Shidehara asked Secretary Hughes to suggest to China the possibility of undertaking bilateral negotiations and promised to "take the matter up with the most generous dispositions and make terms which would be entirely satisfactory to China."[39] Hughes feared that the tangential matter of Shantung at the Conference could interrupt progress on the essential task of disarmament and had therefore endorsed the Shidehara initiation, emphasizing that since France, Britain, and Italy were signatories to the Versailles Treaty, they would have difficulty dealing with the issue at the Conference, Ambassador Sze responded to Secretary Hughes by asking the U. S. to act as an intermediary and guarantee a satisfactory solution.[40] Following a second conversation between Shidehara and Hughes in August, the Japanese offered an outline of Proposed Terms of Settlement Respective of the Shantung Question: (1) to abandon the former German leasehold of Kiaochow; (2) to abandon plans for settlement in Kiaochow provided the Chinese open it as a port of trade; (3) to operate the Kiaochow-Tsinanfu Railway jointly with

[36]The Minister in China (Schurman) to the Secretary of State, Peking, November 5, 1921. *Foreign Relations of the United States, 1921*, I:629-30.

[37]The Chargé d'Affaires in Japan (Bell) to the Secretary of State, Tokyo, July 13 and 26, 1921. *Foreign Relations of the United States, 1921*, I:31, 45.

[38]Memorandum by the Chief of the Division of Far Eastern Affairs, Department of State (MacMurray), Washington, August 13, 1921. *Foreign Relations of the United States, 1921*, I:58.

[39]Memorandum by the Secretary of State of a Conversation with the Japanese Ambassador (Shidehara), July 21, 1921. *Foreign Relations of the United States, 1921*, I:613-14.

[40]Memorandum by the Secretary of State of a Conversation with the Chinese Minister (Sze), August 11, 1921. *Foreign Relations of the United States, 1921*, I:615-16.

China; (4) to renounce preferential rights involved in the former Sino-German Treaty of 1898; (5) to grant rights relating to the further development of railroads in the province to the International Financial Consortium in China; (6) to make the Tsingtao Customs House an integral part of China's customs; (7) to transfer the operation of the public works to China provided their operation was arranged previously; and (8) to establish a special police force to safeguard the railway and to withdraw Japanese troops upon its organization.[41]

After a careful study of the outline, Secretary Hughes informed Ambassador Baron Shidehara that, in the first place, Japan's suggestion to "restore" the Shantung Railroad to China and yet retain a half-interest in it, was a contradiction and, furthermore, since China intended to eventually establish a unified rail system, it certainly would want to control the enterprise exclusively. However, Hughes again advised Ambassador Sze that Japan would gain a strong position if its terms, which appeared reasonable to the average person, were ignored or rejected, and reiterated his desire that China and Japan seek accord before the Conference.[42]

China responded to the Japanese proposals in October 1921.[43] The Ministry of Foreign Affairs of the Peking Government outlined the reasons for its decision not to negotiate directly with Japan, claiming the unacceptability of the Japanese proposals. It considered and responded to the Shidehara outline point by point, announcing its agreement with the Japanese suggestions to open Kiaochow Wan as a port, to consult with the International Financial Consortium in developmental matters, to establish Chinese control of Shantung customs, and to forming a Chinese police to secure the railroads. Most importantly, however, it insisted that the Sino-German Treaty of 1898 had expired immediately upon China's declaration of war against Germany and any subsequent occupation of the territory could only be considered temporary pending its restoration to China. Peking rejected any joint operation of the railways with Japan and any similar arrangement in mining; moreover, it called for the immediate withdrawal of Japanese troops from the province, disdaining to meet Japanese preconditions.

The Japanese delivered a second note to the Chinese which was also rejected

[41]The Japanese Ambassador (Shidehara) to the Secretary of State (Hughes), Outline of the Proposed Terms of Settlement Respective of the Shantung Question, Washington, September 8, 1921. *Foreign Relations of the United States, 1921*, I:617-18.

[42]The Secretary of State to the Minister in China (Schurman), Washington, September 19, 1921. *Foreign Relations of the United States, 1921*, I:619-20.

[43]The Chinese Minister (Sze) to the Secretary of State, Telegram from the Wai-chiao Pu (Ministry of Foreign Affairs), dated October 5, 1921, on China's reply to the Japanese Proposals for the Readjustment of the Shantung Questions. Delivered to the Japanese Minister at Peking on the same day. Received by the Chinese Legation in Washington on October 6, 1921. *Foreign Relations of the United States, 1921*, I:622-24.

as being "too far from the hopes and expectations of the Chinese Government and people."[44] The Chinese Government was at this time under heavy pressure to act in different ways on the issue and feared to act at all. As a consequence officials took no direct preliminary action on the Shantung problem, leaving the matter postponed until it was later taken up in Washington where it became the responsibility of Wellington Koo.

Earlier, when plans for an international conference to include the discussion of the Shantung problem were announced, Chinese public opinion had been initially favorable and hopeful that all the rights Japan had seized and all the unequal treaties Japan had forced on China during the European War would be settled. Numerous societies had been formed in the country to support the Conference and to study the Shantung question. These groups had coalesced into two prominent ones by the opening of the Conference in November of 1921, the Association for Chinese People's Diplomacy and the National Association of Teachers and Merchants.[45]

The most important aspect of these groups was their opposition to direct negotiations of any kind between China and Japan on the question of Shantung. Direct negotiations, regardless of place, they believed, would be to China's disadvantage; the "good offices" of third parties was an unacceptable alternative to full mediation because good intentions were insufficient to guarantee a positive result. Direct negotiations would be tantamount to recognition of the Twenty-One Demands, which China had signed only under protest, and the Treaty of Versailles which it had refused to be party to. They believed their Government's decision to reject the Shidehara proposals had been correct, and any change in this posture would compromise Chinese diplomatic integrity in the world. Further, members of these groups were convinced that even if the Shantung matter were taken before the Conference, as they and the Government wished, the Japanese would, through diplomatic stalling, or outright treachery after an amicable agreement, gain sovereignty over the province.[46]

On October 12, the National Association of Teachers and Merchants dispatched Yü Jih-chang and Chiang Meng-lin to Washington to confer with and assess the Chinese Delegation as well as to influence the situation there by other means, disseminating their views in public.

[44]The Chinese Minister for Foreign Affairs (W. W. Yen) to the Japanese Minister in China (Obata), Peking, September 3, 1921. *Foreign Relations of the United States, 1921*, I:632-35.

[45]Ts'en Hsüeh-lü, *San-shui Liang Yen-sun hsien-sheng nien-p'u*, II:171-72.

[46]Ho Szu-yüan, "Hua-sheng-tun hui-i chung Shan-tung wen-t'i chih ching-kuo" (The Story of the Shantung Question at the Washington Conference), *Tung-fang tsa-chih*, XIX:2 (January 1922), p. 58.

The Conference, now underway and into its third week, was making progress on other issues. Reluctant to allow the problem of Shantung to affect Japan's attitude of participation in the Conference, both Secretary Hughes and Lord Balfour suggested separately to Admiral Baron Katō of the Japanese Delegation and to Ambassador Sze that "it would be most desirable if the representatives of China and Japan were to resume in Washington the discussion of the Shantung question," and both offered their good offices in any way acceptable to the two parties. In the meantime, the U. S. State Department and the British Foreign Office instructed their ambassadors in Peking to "impress upon Foreign Minister Yen with the utmost earnestness the necessity to take this only practicable way."[47] In order to save the self-respect and dignıty of China and Japan, a formula was suggested wherein talks separate from but parallel to the Conference were to be held, that Hughes and Balfour would introduce the negotiators, offer their good offices, and then withdraw. The meeting would also be attended by two American observers, J.V.A. MacMurray and Edward Bell, and two British observers, Sir John Jordan and Miles Lampson, all of whom would take no part in the proceedings unless so requested.[48] Under increasing public pressure from so-called "representatives of the Chinese people" in Washington and diplomatic pressure from Hughes and Balfour, the Chinese Delegation moved toward a decision on the Shantung matter and opted for bilateral discussions with the Japanese, with the good offices of the Americans and British.[49] Consequently, Secretary Hughes announced in an executive session of the Committee on Far Eastern Questions that both China and Japan had agreed to suggestions for the initiation of conversations between their representative delegates in Washington.[50]

The existence of the various pressure groups in Washington, and the anti-Peking groups in China, e.g., the Canton Government, with their negative and contradictory activities, exacerbated the already difficult diplomatic position of the Chinese at the Conference. The qualifications of Dr. Koo and his Chinese colleagues to speak for China were often questioned. Koo and the Chinese Delegation were constantly depicted by the Canton Government as "unrepresentative of the country at large . . . subject to the influence of Japan, and of the military party in North China." After hearing of the

[47]The Secretary of State to the Minister in China (Schurman), Washington, November 25, 1921. *Foreign Relations of the United States, 1922*, I:934-35.

[48]The Secretary of State to the Ambassador in Japan (Warren), Washington, November 30, 1921. *Foreign Relations of the United States, 1922*, I:937.

[49]Ho Szu-yüan, "Hua-sheng-tun hui-i chung Shan-tung wen-t'i chih ching-kuo," *Tung-fang tsa-chih*, XIX:2 (January 1922), p. 56.

[50]*New York Times*, December 1, 1921.

bilateral negotiations on the Shantung issue, Yü Jih-chang and Chiang Meng-lin of the National Association of Teachers and Merchants met with and questioned the Chinese Delegation on November 29 and 30, but without gaining any satisfactory accord of views.[51]

On December 1, ninety minutes before the opening ceremony of the Sino-Japanese meeting, many Chinese students and journalists marched to the Headquarters of the Chinese Delegation under the banner of "Oppose the Direct Negotiations!" and "Return Us Shantung!" In response to the demonstrators on one side and to the assembled diplomats on the other, Dr. Koo explained that the negotiations were neither direct negotiations nor taking the issue to the Conference, neither exclusively the use of good offices nor full mediation, rather something in between all of these and, moreover, that holding the meetings at the U. S. State Department with four Anglo-American observers would provide effective attention to Chinese interests.[52] Dr. Wang Chung-Hui added that refusal to accept the Anglo-American good offices would damage their sympathy toward China and that while good feeling alone might not help China, bad feeling would certainly do harm.[53] At 3:00 p.m. all the representatives were at the meeting place except the Chinese. When Secretary Hughes telephoned and offered help in calling the police to disperse the crowd, Dr. Koo declined the offer. Dr. Koo has since related that the Delegation was adamant in its determination not to consent to anything and that China could not afford to be delinquent from the meeting while representatives of other countries were waiting.[54] The demonstrators eventually allowed Dr. Koo and Dr. Wang to proceed to the meeting after a delay of forty-five minutes.

This small crisis averted, the first meeting of the Sino-Japanese negotiations opened in the afternoon of December 1. Secretary Hughes' short speech expressing his confidence in a fair and mutually satisfactory settlement was followed by Lord Balfour's formal offer of his friendly intervention if it should be needed. Baron Katō of the Japanese Delegation pointed out that:

> . . . the term of the Shantung Question is itself a misnomer. The question is not one which affects the whole Province of Shantung. The important points now awaiting adjustment relate only to the manner of restoration to China of an area of territory less than one-half of one per cent of the Shantung Province, and also to the disposition of a railway 290 miles long and its appurtenant mines, formally under the exclusive management of the Germans. There is absolutely no question

---

[51] Ho Szu-yüan, "Hua-sheng-tun hui-i chung Shan-tung wen-t'i chih ching-kuo," *Tung-fang tsa-chih*, XIX:2 (January 1922), pp. 54-64.

[52] *Ibid.*, pp. 62-64.

[53] *New York Times*, December 2, 1921.

[54] Interview with Dr. Koo, November 19, 1966, New York.

> of full territorial sovereignty being exercised by China throughout the length and breadth of the Province.[55]

After Dr. Sze pointed out that the Shantung question stood out as one of the most vital and important to China, Dr. Koo made two significant suggestions. First, all the communications exchanged between Japan and China relating to the Shantung question should be made the basis of future discussions. Second, it would be best for the purpose of facilitating the progress of the conversations to foretell the chance of any treaties between China and Japan, as well as treaties between other governments being drawn up, and discussions should be based upon the actual facts rather than on academic points of view. Baron Katō expressed his approval, and these two points became the guiding principles throughout the negotiations.[56]

KIAOCHOW-TSINANFU RAILWAY

If the heart of China's concern at the Conference was the Shantung question, the heart of the Shantung question was, no doubt, the Tsingtao-Tsinanfu Railway. It occupied most of the minutes of the thirty-six meetings of the Sino-Japanese negotiators, consumed more time than all the other items combined, and ground to a halt at least three times within the short span of two months. The Sino-Japanese arguments were centered on whether the railway should be a joint enterprise or a Chinese Government line, valuation of the railway, and the mode and period of payment.

At the first business meeting, Dr. Koo brought the railway question before the assembled diplomats:

> [He] felt that . . . the question of the Shantung Railway was one to which the Government and people of China attached the greatest importance. Japan had proposed that the Shantung Railway should be made into a joint Sino-Japanese enterprise . . . but, the Chinese Government could not see their way to accept the principle of joint enterprise. . . . If this railway were to be handed back to China and were to be administered as a Chinese Government railway, it was understood that the restitution would, of course, be effected subject to the condition proposed by the Chinese Government in their note of November 4; namely, the Chinese

---

[55] *Conversations between the Chinese and Japanese Representatives in Regard to the Shantung Question, Treaty for Settlement of Outstanding Questions Relative to Shantung, Agreed Terms of Understanding Recorded in the Minutes of the Japanese and Chinese Delegations Concerning the Conclusion of the Treaty for the Settlement of Outstanding Questions Relative to Shantung; Minutes Prepared by the Japanese Delegation*, pp. 1-2. (Hereinafter referred to as *Conversations.*)

[56] *Ibid.*, pp. 4-6.

> Government would be prepared to redeem or purchase half of the total amount of the valuation of the railway and its appurtenances.[57]

Dr. Koo's statement met with strong opposition from the Japanese Delegation. Masanao Hanihara, Vice Minister for Foreign Affairs, stated first that, China had in two previous treaties with the Germans already agreed to a joint Sino-Japanese operation of the railroads in the event the Germans gave up possession of the railway, and second, because Japan had acquired the railway at considerable sacrifice of lives and treasure, it was offering the very reasonable prospect of a joint venture in the same kind of arrangement by which many other railroads operated in China.[58] Dr. Koo quickly reminded his Japanese colleague of the understanding by which the discussions were to be based on actual facts instead of academic points of view. Therefore the Sino-German treaties of 1915 and 1918 referred to by Mr. Hanihara should be put aside—these had been a source of suspicion and misapprehension on the part of the Chinese people.[59] Furthermore, Dr. Sze also remarked that it would be most advantageous to the commerce of all powers that China develop a unified system for management and operation of the Chinese railways. Dr. Koo added:

> It was difficult for him to understand how a power could rightfully acquire a property belonging to another power which was situated in the land of a friendly country without the consent of that friendly country. He also wished to add that a joint enterprise was a thing which would not work satisfactorily unless the two parties to it were coming together in a spirit of willingness and accord. It was something like the matrimonial contract which would not be a success if the contracting parties were forced into it.[60]

A deadlock thus resulted at the first business session, and both parties agreed to discuss other matters at the next meeting. These first exchanges had been just what Dr. Koo had advised against—academic positions—and it seemed that their initial vocalization was a necessary and unavoidable statement of principles. While the Japanese never relinquished their right to retain interests in the railway based on the principle of treaties and the law of war, nor the Chinese their principle of exclusive ownership based on sovereignty, nevertheless the two sides thereafter followed Koo's advice and took a more practical, businesslike, dollars-and-cents approach.

One week later at the ninth meeting on December 10, Dr. Koo offered, according to the Chinese note of November 4, to reimburse the Japanese for half the assessed value of the railroad in order to take it over completely.[61]

[57] *Ibid.*, pp. 8-9.
[58] *Ibid.*, pp. 9-10.
[59] *Ibid.*, pp. 10-11.
[60] *Ibid.*, p. 12.
[61] *Ibid.*, pp. 66-67.

Baron Shidehara argued quite convincingly against the Chinese proposal, stating that since the railroad had been valued at some 53,406,141 gold marks or 30,000,000 yen by the reparation commission of the Paris Peace Conference and since Japan was to credit that amount toward Germany's reparation debt if the Chinese paid them only half that amount, Japan would lose 15,000,000 yen. If China wished to take over the whole property, he said, then it should pay the full price. Unaware of such an arrangement between the Japanese and the Germans, China conceded this argument and proposed to pay Japan the full value of the railroad.

Hanihara, pressing further, inquired of the Chinese if they proposed only to pay the price Japan was allowing the Germans, or would they also compensate the Japanese for their additional improvements made to the line during their occupation. Dr. Koo replied that the permanent improvements the Japanese had made could be included, provided the revenue of the line be used for this purpose, less a certain amount for depreciation.[62]

The value of the Kiaochow-Tsinanfu railroad having now been agreed upon, there remained consideration of the mode of payment. Baron Shidehara advanced a concrete proposal to finance the Chinese purchase of the railroad with a long-term loan between the Chinese Government and Japanese capitalists and suggested that the new railroad retain the services of a Japanese Chief Engineer, Traffic Manager, and Chief Accountant, subject to a Chinese Manager, repeating that this arrangement was similar to others in China.[63]

Surprisingly, the Chinese Delegation did not favor a loan of any kind, but preferred a cash payment for the railroad. The Japanese were suspicious of this bold Chinese posture, and Baron Shidehara inquired of Dr. Koo the reason why the Chinese preferred a cash payment to a loan contract. He understood that a great sum of debt remained unpaid by China, on a large part of which even the interest was in arrears. Why was China in such a hurry to make payment in cash for the Shantung Railway while various other debts remained unpaid?[64]

The Chinese Delegation had difficulty in allaying Shidehara's suspicions. Dr. Koo and his Chinese colleagues agreed privately that their readiness to pay for the railway in cash arose primarily out of their desire to effect Japanese removal from the railway and Shantung Province. Publicly, Dr. Koo, speaking for the Chinese Delegation, said that the Japanese Delegation was doubtless aware that the whole Shantung question had exercised the minds of the two peoples to such an extent that it was thought desirable to remove, once and for all, this cause of prolonged misunderstanding. Far from entertaining

[62] *Ibid.*, pp. 67-105.
[63] *Ibid.*, p. 136.
[64] *Ibid.*, p. 134.

discriminatory treatment of the Japanese, the Chinese Delegation had in view the larger interests of both Japan and China.[65] Furthermore, since the Shantung Railway was very profitable, the Chinese bankers would naturally desire to participate in the profits, and it was difficult for the Chinese Government to refuse these legitimate demands of its nationals.[66] Besides, the very fact that there were a number of loans on which the payments of interest were in arrears served as further explanation as to why the Chinese people desired to contract no further foreign loans.[67]

The Chinese idea for cash payment had been for a single payment or a series of payments to a foreign bank in China on a certain date or dates after the New Year when interest rates would be lower, and China would not forfeit the interest on its own funds by withdrawing them from banks all at once. The Chinese delegates preferred the cash payment which was to be effected at the end of nine months from the date of the agreement when the transfer of the railway was to be completed. Baron Shidehara suggested that, if China preferred cash payment rather than a loan contract, immediately or before the commencement of the transfer of the railway, China should deposit the total amount of the payment with a bank of a third power in China, after which it was to be handed over to Japan when the transfer was complete.[68] In six months, then, the transfer of the properties would be accomplished.

The mode of payment discussions went back and forth, around and around, between the delegates; the Chinese continued their insistence upon a cash payment, but proposed times and dates favorable to their interests. Japan continued to press for a commercial loan in order to retain some manner of control over the railroad, at the same time specifying terms for a cash payment that would guarantee delivery of the money in exchange for the property. Dr. Sze proposed a division of the payment into three periods: at the end of three months from the date of the agreement, two-fifths of the whole amount should be deposited; one-fifth at the end of six months; and the remaining two-fifths at the end of nine months. This plan would meet the Japanese purpose without any serious effects upon the money market.[69] To Hanihara's question of a guarantee on the Chinese cash payment, Dr. Koo added that the proposed undertaking ought to be made bilaterally on the basis of mutual confidence. Speaking of a guarantee, China might ask with equal pertinence what assurance there would be that after making deposit of the money the transfer would be made to its satisfaction. In as much as the

[65] *Ibid.*, p. 116.
[66] *Ibid.*, p. 117.
[67] *Ibid.*, p. 119.
[68] *Ibid.*, pp. 160-61.
[69] *Ibid.*, p. 163.

Chinese proposal was to proceed with the deposit of money in conjunction with the progress of the transfer of the railroad properties, i.e., that the deposit and the transfer should be made *pari passu*, it seemed to him that the Japanese proposal to have the whole amount deposited at once was rather exacting.[70] No agreement was reached at this time.

Nevertheless, on December 16 at the fourteenth meeting, Dr. Koo conceded that in order to accommodate the wishes of the Japanese delegates to retain Japanese interests in the railway, China would not pay for the railway in cash but in installments, extending for three years, at intervals of six months each. Only at the end of three years from the transfer would the railway be entirely redeemed. The first installment would be paid in cash. For the remaining five installments, the Chinese Government would deliver to Japan the amount in treasury notes secured on the revenue of the Kiaochow-Tsinanfu Railway. Pending the maturity of the notes, China proposed that interest at a reasonable rate should be paid every six months.[71] Dr. Koo urged his Japanese colleagues to help him out of the embarrassing position of being pressed to accept a loan which was opposed by the Chinese people.[72]

Baron Shidehara considered the payment period of three years to be too short and not advantageous for the Japanese bankers.[73] He referred to railway loans that had been concluded since 1913; most had maturity dates ranging from forty to fifty years, the average time being forty-five years. If they were to deduct twenty-two years therefrom, which represented the number of years since the railway concession had been established, there would remain twenty-three years, and he thought this to be a reasonable period.[74]

Dr. Koo remarked that all of China's railway loans mentioned by Baron Shidehara had been made for lines merely projected, not for those already constructed. Therefore, the status of the Kiaochow-Tsinanfu Railway was different from others.[75] Moreover, according to Baron Shidehara's calculation, China ought to have purchased the railway a few years previously. Koo cited specifically the Nanking-Hangchow Railway matter, observing that the term fixed had been forty-five years, but according to the contract, right of purchase had been possible after fifteen years. In the Kiaochow case, the contract had been made in 1899; if three years were added to the elapsed time, loans would have been outstanding for twenty-five years.[76] Furthermore,

[70] *Ibid.*, p. 164.
[71] *Ibid.*, p. 119.
[72] *Ibid.*, p. 118.
[73] *Ibid.*, p. 137.
[74] *Ibid.*, p. 129.
[75] *Ibid.*, pp. 125, 128.
[76] *Ibid.*, p. 129.

Koo reminded Shidehara that in most of the railway contracts there had been provisions for the repurchase or redemption after a short period from the date of the contract.[77]

Dr. Koo now proposed to lengthen the payment period from the original three years to ten, and finally to twelve years, with the understanding that after three years all the unpaid portion of the sum could be paid upon suitable notice.[78] Koo said that his Delegation had made many concessions on the period of payment issue and, therefore, he hoped that in regard to the question of expert assistance those concessions would be considered.[79]

Immediately, Baron Shidehara complained that the period of payment was not of much importance to China; what was important was the period after which it could exercise the option to redeem the whole liability. The Chinese Delegation had not yielded at all on that material point.[80] Responding to Shidehara, Dr. Koo agreed that the Chinese Delegation would issue a statement that six months' notice would be given to Japan before China paid the outstanding balance at the expiration of three years after the agreement. In that form, the period of redemption would be three and a half years.[81] Baron Shidehara asked whether the Chinese would give him satisfaction on the question of experts to fill the three management and operations posts. If so, the Japanese Delegation would be ready to accept the Chinese plan with some modifications.[82]

Thus, negotiations now focused on the employment of Japanese experts as chief officials of the Kiaochow-Tsinanfu Railway. As in the opening ceremonies of the discussions, the diplomats vented harsh invective, perhaps for outside consumption, before setting into the less dramatic but necessary business at hand. Baron Shidehara attacked the inefficiency and corruption of the Chinese railway system and used these arguments to demand the use of Japanese personnel on the Kiaochow-Tsinanfu line. Dr. Koo responded with praise for the Chinese railway system and reminded his Japanese colleague that the Chinese desire was for the immediate reversion of the line to China, hence there was no need for any Japanese experts. The Chinese railways were probably not nearly as corrupt as Shidehara claimed they were nor as sterling in their operation as Koo attested; however, these diatribes serve to underscore the importance the issue of foreign experts had in the discussions and to indicate that the issue was one to be solved by deliberate negotiation, which

[77] *Ibid.*, p. 130.
[78] *Ibid.*
[79] *Ibid.*, p. 157.
[80] *Ibid.*, p. 157.
[81] *Ibid.*
[82] *Ibid.*, p. 147.

was the nature and task of these two diplomats.

Dr. Koo explained that the practice of employing foreign experts had developed from the fact that in building railways China had borrowed foreign capital. In the process of negotiating railway-loan contracts, foreign bankers had used the opportunity to ask for these positions. In the case of the Shantung matter, however, the railway was already in operation, and quite evidently was in a different class.[83] Moreover, on the big trunk lines nearest to the Shantung Railway, there was no foreign traffic manager, though there was a foreign engineer. After the connection of the two lines had been effected, it would be awkward to have a Japanese traffic manager on the system. If the Chinese Delegation consented to the presence of a Japanese traffic manager on the Shantung line they would find it difficult to give an explanation, either to their Government or to their people.[84] Furthermore, the work of a traffic manager was of such a nature that he was bound to have frequent contact with the shippers. The Shantung line ran through the part of the Shantung Province which was most densely populated. In the nature of things, the traffic manager would have much more to do with the Chinese people than with Japanese.[85] Therefore, Dr. Koo concluded that in the interest of friendly relations and cooperation between Japan and China, it would be more advisable to give the post of engineer instead of traffic manager to a Japanese national to insure similar treatment on both the Kiaochow-Tsinanfu line and the Tientsin-P'uk'ou line because the function of the Chief Engineer was of a technical nature and had less contact with the Chinese shippers. Koo did not forget to remind Shidehara of the Chinese desire to acquire the line by cash payment and thereby control it fully; it was hardly necessary to add that the three positions in question would amount to effective control of the operation.[86]

Dr. Sze commented that in his personal opinion, none of the three experts was necessary for the Shantung Railway, but by way of compromise, he suggested that a Japanese engineer might be employed to supervise the maintenance of the line in the Shantung district.[87]

Baron Shidehara insisted that since the Shantung Railway was already completed, an engineer might not be necessary. However, since a manager for the traffic department would always be required, a special person for that post would be needed.[88] Finally, after lengthy argument, Baron Shidehara

[83] *Ibid.*, p. 122.
[84] *Ibid.*, p. 154.
[85] *Ibid.*
[86] *Ibid.*, p. 138.
[87] *Ibid.*, pp. 150-51.
[88] *Ibid.*, p. 152.

asked the Chinese delegates whether it would be possible for them to agree to an arrangement wherein China would appoint its own traffic manager as well as a Japanese expert to act as associate traffic manager. After the consolidation, both would serve under the general control of the Chinese traffic manager for the whole system, which would consist of the Tientsin-P'uk'ou and Shantung Railways. In the same way a Japanese associate accountant could be appointed to cooperate with the Chinese accountant, a significant compromise which the Japanese Government later refused to sanction.[89]

Since the traffic manager and accountant positions would involve *de facto* control of the railway, both Japan and China declared that this arrangement went beyond the limit of their instructions from the home governments. The Japanese delegates found it necessary to consult with Tokyo when the talks reached this impasse.

The delegates' respective positions at this point in the negotiations can be summarized as follows: the Japanese proposed a commercial loan to China to finance the acquisition of the Kiaochow-Tsinanfu Railway, the period of the loan to be fifteen years with an option of redemption after five years and appointment of a Japanese traffic manager and an accountant, with further details to be worked out in Peking.[90] The Chinese proposed two alternative plans. The first provided for Japan to transfer the railway and its appurtenances to China within nine months after the agreement. China would pay Japan the sum of 53,406,141 gold marks plus compensation for Japanese improvements in the line, two-fifths of the sum in three months, one-fifth after six months, and then the remaining two-fifths nine months after such date. China could not promise to employ Japanese nationals, but the delegates suggested a joint commission to arrange details and oversee the agreement. The second plan was identical to the first, except that payments would be deferred over twelve years with an option of redemption after three years, upon giving six months' notice to the Japanese. China would make the first payment on the day of transfer and subsequent installments would be secured by the revenues from the properties. Additionally, China reserved the right to select and employ the Japanese engineer. The Japanese Delegation agreed to recommend the first plan to its Government on condition that the cash payment be deposited in a third-power bank prior to the transfer of properties; furthermore, they would support the seond plan if a Japanese associate traffic manager and associate accountant under the authority of a Chinese general manager were added to the personnel.[91]

At this critical juncture, January 1, 1922, when the Washington diplomats deadlocked on substantive matters, several serious crises developed in China

[89] *Ibid.*, p. 160.
[90] *New York Times*, December 21 and 22, 1921.
[91] *Conversations*, p. 183.

which threatened to abort the talks altogether. There was a political crisis in Peking arising out of budget problems that was serious enough to cause the resignation of Premier Chin Yün-p'eng and the designation of Foreign Minister W. W. Yen as Acting Premier, until Liang Shih-i was appointed to the post, enabling Dr. Yen to return to his work as Foreign Minister.

Japanese Ambassador, Torikichi Obata, visited the two men and, quite understandably, the subject of Shantung arose. Obata threatened the Foreign Minister that Japan would have to discontinue the Washington talks if China insisted on cash payment and immediate recovery of the Kiaochow-Tsinanfu Railway. He also pressed Yen on the matter of the Japanese plan-loan agreement by insisting that Japanese personnel serve as traffic manager, chief accountant, and chief engineer. When Minister Yen mentioned the possibility of hiring Japanese experts as "associates" in these positions as suggested by Baron Shidehara, Obata objected immediately saying that this was the idea of the delegates and not of the Government.[92] In a noncommittal manner, Yen told Obata that the matter would be considered at a cabinet meeting that evening.

When Obata visited Premier Liang two days later, Liang informed him that "a loan would be sought by China and the railway operated under Chinese management, and that all details would be arranged in Washington."[93] The Premier neither promised to get the loan from Japanese sources nor excluded the possibility of their use. After the two Chinese plans arrived in Peking on January 2 from the Chinese plenipotentiaries in Washington,[94] the Foreign Ministry sent instructions to them on January 5 saying that the second Chinese plan, deferred payment by means of government treasury notes, seemed more practicable and that in the selection of the Japanese experts as associate traffic manager and associate accountant, the Chinese Government should have full freedom of choice.[95]

The causative spark which ignited another crisis came on January 5 when Baron Shidehara told Secretary Hughes that Premier Liang had made a proposal to Obata which was very similar to the one the Japanese Delegation

[92] Record of Conversation between Foreign Minister (Yen) and the Japanese Minister (Obata) to Peking, December 27, 1921, Peking, *Wunsz King Collection.*

[93] Ministry of Foreign Affairs (Yen) to Plenipotentiaries Sze, Koo, and Wang at Washington, December 31, 1921, Peking. Archives of the Ministry of Foreign Affairs at the Institute of Modern History, Academia Sinica, Taipei.

[94] Plenipotentiaries Sze, Koo, and Wang to Ministry of Foreign Affairs, December 30, 1921, Washington. Archives of the Ministry of Foreign Affairs at the Institute of Modern History, Academia Sinica, Taipei.

[95] Ministry of Foreign Affairs (Yen) to Plenipotentiaries Sze, Koo, and Wang at Washington, January 5, 1922, Peking. Archives of the Ministry of Foreign Affairs at the Institute of Modern History, Academia Sinica, Taipei.

had presented at Washington, namely, a long-term Japanese loan. At the same time, Ma Soo, personal representative of Dr. Sun Yat-sen of the Canton Government, informed the press in Washington that Premier Liang of the Peking Government had accepted the conditions of Obata concerning the Japanese loan and, furthermore, the Chinese plenipotentiaries in Washington were about to receive instructions from Peking not to press the Japanese representatives further on the rights of railway and mines along the railway because the Peking Government badly needed new capital from Japan. The Chinese delegates in Washington sent their telegram back to Peking for verification.[96]

The exposure of this news, although not well-founded, produced reverberations in both China and Washington. In Washington, the representatives of the Chinese students and the "Chinese people" took to "berating the delegates in Washington for their supposedly weak-kneed policy toward Japan."[97] On the other hand, the Chihli Clique, which had been one of the sponsors of the Liang Government, now demanded the immediate removal of the Premier from office, or the six provinces under their rule, Shantung, Honan, Shensi, Kiangsu, Hupei, and Kiangsi, would secede from the central government. Under the command of warlord Wu P'ei-fu,[98] largc bodies of troops began to move northwards from Hupei. Public opinion in Shanghai and elsewhere approved Wu's actions immediately.[99] Premier Liang dispatched telegrams to the Washington delegates on January 12 denying that he had reached any understanding with the Japanese Ambassador concerning a loan and instructing them to shift the negotiations to Peking. He also sent telegrams and statements to various provinces denying that he had ever sent any instructions to the delegates at Washington pledging his full support to them.[100]

All explanations were in vain. There were more emergency meetings by the various trade circles and groups interested in the Washington talks, more demonstrations in the cities, and more telegrams dispatched to Dr. Koo and the Chinese Delegation urging them not to obey the order of Liang Shih-i.[101] Premier Liang was forced out of office on January 25, after having been in office only a month. Dr. W. W. Yen, became Acting Premier once again. The removal of the Fengtien Clique-supported premier served as the direct cause of

[96]Plenipotentiaries Sze, Koo, and Wang to the Ministry of Foreign Affairs (Yen), January 4 and 10, 1922, Washington. Archives of the Ministry of Foreign Affairs at the Institute of Modern History, Academia Sinica, Taipei.

[97]Koo Hui-lan, *Autobiography*, p. 146.

[98]*The North China Herald*, January 14, 1922.

[99]*Ibid.*, January 7, 1922, pp. 9, 22.

[100]Liang Shih-i to Wu P'ei-fu, January 7 and 12; Ts'en Hsüeh-lü, *San-shui Liang Yen-sun hsien-sheng nien-p'u*, II:180-84, 188-90, 210-25.

[101]*The North China Herald*, January 14, 1922, p. 113.

the Fengtien-Chihli War three months later in April 1922 between Marshal Chang Tso-lin's Manchurian Army and Marshal Wu P'ei-fu's Chihli Army, which resulted in the total defeat of the Fengtien Clique and its retirement from the metropolitan province back to Manchuria. The Peking Government thereafter fell under the complete domination of the Chihli Clique.[102]

Public opinion in Washington and in China, led by Marshal Wu, endorsed the actions of the Chinese Delegation. Premier Liang's statements in speeches in the various provinces and to the press in China provided valuable support for the diplomats, while the guidance of veteran Foreign Minister Yen strengthened their position in the Washington discussions. Since the Washington diplomats were under the scrutiny of an aroused Chinese public at home, determined Chinese students in Washington, and various provincial warlords, in addition to the uninterrupted support of Foreign Minister Yen in Peking, they felt confident of their ability to reject any unreasonable demands made by Japan.

When the Sino-Japanese negotiations were resumed after the New Year through the efforts of Hughes and Balfour, the Japanese Delegation's attitude became less conciliatory. On January 4, Baron Shidehara first reported to the eighteenth meeting that the Japanese Government only approved of the plan involving the loan agreement and emphasized that that was the limit of their concessions.[103] Nevertheless, at the next meeting on January 5, Dr. Koo presented the revised Chinese plan for cash payment. In order to satisfy Japanese desires, the Chinese delegates were ready to accept the plan of a single deposit on a specific date, instead of three deposits to be spread over nine months, leaving to Japan the decision of whether it should be made before or at the time of the beginning of transfer of the railway.[104]

In the meantime, Dr. Koo explained the various reasons for maintaining China's position. The Chinese Delegation would not be able to justify a Japanese loan to the Chinese people when Chinese bankers had offered to raise the capital. The Shantung railway question differed from others involving loans because previously such loans had been contracted for the construction of new lines instead of existing ones. The Delegation's diplomatic instructions were clear in telling them not to go beyond the two Chinese alternative plans. The Japanese loan plan was not wise because it would give rise to misgivings among the Chinese people and, on the other hand, the outright reversion of the railroad to China by Japan would foster good relations between the two countries.[105]

The negotiations were again at a standstill. Thus, Dr. Koo suggested at the

[102] *Wu P'ei-fu chuan*, pp. 61-65.
[103] *Conversations*, p. 176.
[104] *Ibid.*, p. 189.
[105] *Ibid.*, pp. 189-90.

nineteenth meeting that it was appropriate to seek the good offices Hughes and Balfour had offered.[106] The Japanese objected, however, and the two gentlemen could not, of course, participate without the express invitation of Japan. Baron Shidehara remarked that the Japanese delegates were "not in a position" to request such good offices, and Hanihara even questioned the productivity of such a move, other than embarrassment, as neither side was prepared to go further.[107] Nevertheless, Sir John Jordan suggested that he and MacMurray should report to their respective chiefs and let them decide for themselves as to their attitude.[108] Thus, the British and Americans intervened again in an attempt to penetrate the impasse.

As instructed by Balfour and Hughes, Jordan and MacMurray visited the Chinese and Japanese Delegations separately on January 7 and 8, during which they presented four alternative plans involving adjustments of phraseology, such as considering the Kiaochow-Tsinanfu Railway to have been built with funds "borrowed from Japanese capitalists by the Chinese Government"; combinations of period and mode of payment, such as twelve years to pay the actual value in treasury notes with option to redeem after five years; and ideas for the expert staffing of the line, such as dual positions of Japanese and Chinese engineers, traffic managers, and accountants.[109] All these efforts were found to be unacceptable to both the Chinese and Japanese, although the fourth alternative plan, providing for a twelve-year loan and dual sets of experts, became the kernel of the eventual agreement. Finally, on January 18, Lord Balfour received and considered the Japanese Delegation's last formula:

> Deferred payment by Chinese treasury notes running for fifteen years, but redeemable at any time after five years; appointment of a Japanese chief accountant, and of a Chinese chief accountant, of coequal powers, both of them subject to the control of the Chinese director-general of the railway; and appointment of a Japanese traffic manager subject to the control of the Chinese director-general with the understanding that, in anticipation of the probable redemption of the road by China at the end of two and one-half years a Chinese assistant traffic manager. . . .[110]

On January 19 and 22, Secretary Hughes received the Chinese Delegation at his residence and advised Dr. Koo and his colleagues to accept this last formula. The Secretary stated that Japan had made a great concession by giving up her original plan of making the Kiaochow-Tsinanfu Railway a joint Sino-Japanese enterprise. At the time, the Shantung Railway was under

[106] *New York Times*, January 7, 1922.

[107] *Conversations*, pp. 199-203.

[108] *Ibid.*

[109] Chia Shih-i, *Hua-hui chien-wen lu*, pp. 149-50.

[110] The Secretary of State to the Minister in China (Schurman), Washington, January 22, 1922. *Foreign Relations of the United States, 1922*, I:942.

Japan's actual control. Short of a war to force it out, there was no better settlement than the present one.[111] Lord Balfour also advised the Chinese Delegation that thoughtful consideration should be given to this formula considering the fact that in only five years China would have full possession of the line. The Sino-Japanese negotiations resumed on January 23.[112] On January 25, Secretary Hughes escorted Ambassador Sze to see President Harding, who told Dr. Sze that "he [Harding] considered it would be a colossal blunder in statecraft if China were not to take advantage of the opportunity now offered her for the settlement of the Shantung question as the alternative might involve a risk of losing the province."[113]

Shortly after the conversations with the Chinese delegates on January 22, Secretary Hughes dispatched a long telegram to American Ambassador Schurman in Peking with instructions that he was to impress upon Foreign Minister Yen the view that this arrangement represented the limit to which Japan was prepared to go, which in fact China must be prepared to accept as the only available means of realizing the goal of reestablishing itself in Shantung within the forseeable future or else see its hopes indefinitely and hopelessly postponed. If necessary, the Minister was authorized to tell Yen:

> [He had] the President's authority for stating this to be the attitude of our Government. Various American expressions of sympathy with an academic position may have misled the Chinese. Before deciding against such a settlement the Chinese should realize that if they choose to break off negotiations on the relatively unimportant issues outstanding and thus bring upon themselves the disaster which may be expected, they cannot count on any support either from public sentiment in the United States or from this Government.[114]

The same pressure was exerted later by British Ambassador Alston in Peking.

In the meantime, Premier Liang had been granted "sick leave" by President Hsü as a result of another cabinet crisis caused by Marshal Wu. Foreign Minister Yen again became Acting Premier and, favoring the latest solution being discussed in Washington, Yen brought the case to the Cabinet meeting on January 26, where both President Hsü and the Cabinet approved it. Thus, Yen cabled formal authorization that same night to the Chinese delegates at Washington to sign the treaty with the Japanese[115]

[111] Wunsz King, *Ts'ung Pa-li ho-hui tao Kuo-lien*, p. 34.

[112] *New York Times*, January 23, 1922.

[113] The Secretary of State to the Minister in China (Schurman), Washington, January 25, 1922. *Foreign Relations of the United States, 1922*, I:945.

[114] *Ibid.*, January 22, 1922, I:942-43.

[115] The Minister in China (Schurman) to the Secretary of State, Peking, January 26, 1922. *Foreign Relations of the United States, 1922*, I:945-46.

OTHER SETTLEMENTS ON SHANTUNG DISCUSSION

The issues of tariff autonomy and Shantung were the most important and dramatic of the Conference. There were many other parallel matters which were considered at the same time as these, but with less attention, spectacle, and rancor. These should not be overlooked, for herein too, just as with the resolution of the major issues, can be marked the conciliatory and expeditionary efforts of Wellington Koo.

Restitution of leased territory was accomplished by requiring Japan to turn over the former German territory of Kiaochow and the fifty kilometer zone around Kiaochow Wan, together with the German archives and documents necessary for the transfer to Chinese administration. The delegates, quite predictably, varied the period of transfer according to their interests. Dr. Sze demanded one month; Baron Shidehara objected, hoping for a prolonged period. Dr. Koo suggested at the twenty-seventh meeting that the one-month limit be allowed to stand tentatively, thereby stimulating progress until, at the thirty-fifth meeting, Baron Shidehara suggested a six-month period. The final agreement provided for both Japan and China to appoint commissions with powers to make and carry out detailed arrangements relating to the transfer. The exchange was to be completed as soon as possible, but not later than six months from the effective date of the agreement.[116]

The Asian powers agreed that Japan would undertake to transfer to China all public properties in the leased territory of Kiaochow, whether formally possessed by the German authorities or purchased or constructed by the Japanese administration, except such public properties as were required for the Japanese consulate to be established in Tsingtao and those required more especially for the benefit of the Japanese community, including public schools, shrines, and cemetaries. Originally, Hanihara had demanded compensation not only for Japan's investments in the province but for Germany's as well, against which Koo had argued that such properties constituted a natural fixture of the land and, moreover, that the annual contribution of 20 per cent of the total customs revenues from Tsingtao made to the Japanese provided compensation.[117] Dr. Sze observed that the Japanese budget for Shantung administration in 1919 showed a surplus of 6,888,000 yen, a considerable revenue from the public works in Tsingtao for compensation.[118] China agreed to refund a fair and equitable proportion of the expenses actually incurred by Japan for such properties purchased or constructed by the Japanese authorities or such improvements and additions to those formally possessed by the

[116] *Conversations*, pp. 263-377.
[117] *Ibid.*, p. 34.
[118] *Ibid.*, p. 35.

German authorities, having regard to the principle of depreciation and continuing value.[119]

On January 11, at the twenty-first meeting, Dr. Sze introduced the question of the withdrawal of the 2700 Japanese troops from the province, and Baron Shidehara responded with an assurance that the troops along the Tsingtao-Tsinanfu Railway would be withdrawn as soon as the Chinese were ready to assume such duties within a prearranged schedule, possible nine months.[120] Dr. Koo felt that the mutual presence of Chinese and Japanese troops during the transfer might precipitate untoward incidents and, therefore, proposed the idea of withdrawal in stages. Concerning the Japanese garrison forces at Tsingtao, Baron Shidehara suggested withdrawal within thirty days from the date the transfer of the Tsingtao administration was completed; Dr. Koo concurred with the proposal that the garrison be withdrawn no later than that date, lest their continued presence create an impression among the Chinese people that the Japanese intended to delay their departure from the province.[121] Again, as with the question of transfer of leased territory and many other matters during the Conference, the diplomats found accommodation in the phraseology of their work:

> The Japanese garrison at Tsingtao should be completely withdrawn, if possible, simultaneously with the transfer of the administration of the leased territory of Kiaochow, and in any case not later than thirty days from the date of such transfer.[122]

Apart from the Tsingtao garrison, the Japanese troops remaining in the province, stationed along the railroad and its branches, were to be withdrawn in prearranged stages as Chinese troops replaced them, and the complete withdrawal was to be accomplished if possible within three months, and not later than six months from the date of the agreement.[123]

China and Japan agreed that upon the effective date of the agreement, the custom-house at Tsingtao would be made an integral part of the Chinese maritime customs and that the provisional agreement of August 6, 1915[124] between Japan and China relative to the issue would be terminated.

119 *Ibid.*, p. 377.
120 *Ibid.*, p. 210.
121 *Ibid.*, pp. 218-19, 226.
122 *Ibid.*, p. 227.
123 *Ibid.*, p. 378.
124 Agreement about the reopening of the Office of the Chinese Maritime Customs at Tsingtao, and its Functioning in the Territory Leased to Germany and Now in Consequency of the Germany-Japanese War, under the Military Government of Japan, August 6, 1915, signed by R. Hioki, Japanese Minister to China, and F. A. Aglen, Inspector General of Customs of China. MacMurray, *Treaties and Agreements with and Concerning China, 1894-1919*, vol. II, no. 1915/12.

Relating to the further extension of the Tsingtao-Tsinanfu Railway, namely, the Tsinan-Shunteh and the Kaomi-Hsuchow lines, the delegates decided after some discussion that the concessions would be thrown open for the common activity of an international group on terms to be arranged between the Chinese Government and the group.[125]

Agreements were also reached concerning opening Kiaochow as a trading port and the cable and wireless service. The entire area of the former German leased territory of Kiaochow would be open to foreign trade, and foreigners would be permitted freely to reside and to carry on commerce, industry, and other lawful pursuits within that area. The Chinese local authorities would consult with the foreign residents of Kiaochow as to such municipal matters as might directly affect the latter's welfare and interests.[126] All the rights, titles, and privileges concerning former German submarine cables between Tsingtao and Chefoo and between Tsingtao and Shanghai were vested in China, with the exception of those portions of the two cables which had been utilized by the Japanese Government for the laying of a cable between Tsingtao and Sasebo.[127] The Japanese wireless stations at Tsingtao and Tsinanfu would be transferred to China upon the withdrawal of the Japanese troops at those two places with fair compensation for the value of the stations.[128]

The Japanese had originally proposed joint operation of the mines appurtenant to the railroads, just as they had for the railroads and, as might be expected, the Chinese had expressed their desire to take control of the mines, allowing foreigners, including Japanese, to invest 50 per cent of the total capital. There were three mining districts in question: the coal mining districts of Tsechuan (Tzu-ch'uan) and Fangtse (Fang-tzu), and the iron mining district of Chinlingchen (Chin-ling-chen).[129] According to the temporary Chinese Government mining regulations of November 1915, which Koo had presented, iron extraction had been placed under the general supervision and control of the Chinese Government. Private investors could own such mines only by special permission of the Ministry of Agriculture and Commerce, foreign capital was not permitted, unauthorized export of ore was forbidden, and the Chinese Government retained rights of priority in buying out the mining interests.[130] Shidehara had expressed his dissatisfaction with the intent of the Chinese Government to form a "Chinese Corporation" in conformity with "Chinese Law." He believed that the status of the Chinese company was

[125] *Conversations*, p. 379.
[126] *Ibid.*, pp. 56, 238, 251, 380-81.
[127] *Ibid.*, pp. 54, 297, 380-81.
[128] *The North China Herald*, January 28, 1922.
[129] *Conversations*, p. 378, 379, 277, 278, 281.
[130] *Ibid.*, pp. 281-82.

difficult to define either as a juridical entity or as a limited or unlimited liability. According to Shidehara, Chinese laws governing mines had been the subject of discussion in Peking, but at that point, none of the governments of the treaty powers had yet recognized the Chinese mining regulations, and although mining rights had been formerly granted to German interests, Japan had at that time actual possession.[131] Therefore, he demanded that the mines of Tsechuan, Fangtse, and Chinlingchen should be handed over to a Sino-Japanese combination in which Chinese and Japanese capital should stand on an entirely equal footing. The mode and terms of such joint enterprise should be arranged between the Japanese and Chinese commissions which were to be appointed for that purpose and which should meet immediately upon the effective date of the agreement.[132]

After lengthy bargaining, Dr. Koo had accepted the Japanese version with the provision that the three mining districts, for which the mining rights had been granted by China to Germany, should be handed over to a company to be formed by special charter of the Chinese Government. Japanese capital might not exceed the amount of Chinese capital.[133]

The issue of the Shantung salt mines was solved amicably, but not without some vigorous argument and discussion. The controversy surrounding this industry derived from its economic importance and profitability to the region under Japanese occupation and, potentially, to China after reversion of the area. The prosperity of salt mining, which had increased almost 350 per cent under the Japanese occupation, provided them with a valuable product and considerable revenue. Additionally, the gabelle levied against production had served for many years as security for international loans to the Chinese Government.[134]

The Chinese were understandably interested in incorporating the salt industry into its government production monopoly and removing it from its sheltered status under the Japanese which had created unfair competition with the industry in other parts of China.[135] Dr. Koo had assured his Japanese counterparts that fair compensation would be paid and that provisions would be made for export of salt to Japan to continue.

The Japanese were equally concerned about compensation for this valuable industry and had inquired after details of payment, i.e., compensation for actual investments, whether the Chinese would pay for the liquidation of Japanese businesses and the prospective losses therefrom.[136] After receiving

[131] *Ibid.*, p. 282.
[132] *Ibid.*, pp. 282, 294.
[133] *The North China Herald*, January 21, 1922.
[134] *Conversations*, p. 59.
[135] *Ibid.*, pp. 60-61.
[136] *Ibid.*, pp. 73-75.

instructions from Tokyo, Hanihara presented his proposal: (1) Japanese nationals in Kiaochow involved in salt production were to be allowed to continue their activities, subject to China's right to purchase their businesses according to terms decided by the Chinese and Japanese Commissions; (2) provision to be made for the exportation of salt, the details of which were to be decided by the Commissions; (3) the question of the duty or royalty to be imposed upon the salt industry carried on by the Japanese nationals should be made the subject of a separate arrangement.[137]

After lengthy argument, Dr. Koo introduced his revised proposal stating that whereas the salt industry was a government monopoly in China, it was agreed that the establishments of Japanese nationals along the coast of Kiaochow Wan which had been actually engaged in the industry were to be purchased by the Chinese Government on payment of their appraised value and that exportation to Japan of a quantity of salt produced by such establishments was to be permitted on fair terms. Arrangements for these purchases, including the transfer of the establishments to the Chinese Government, would be completed by the Chinese and Japanese Commissions within a certain month from the date of the agreement. In case the two Commissions could not agree on any point, it would be referred to arbitration.[138] Koo's revised proposal, after minor adjustments including the deletion of the clause on arbitration at the insistence of Baron Shidehara, was adopted by the Japanese delegates.[139] The final agreement on the Shantung salt mines had specified transfer of the properties in question to be arranged by the two Commissions as soon as possible, and in any case not longer than six months from the date of the agreement.[140]

DISCUSSION

One by-product of the Washington Conference was the relative national unity it created in China. However short-lived, however illusory, and however regional, China's participation in the Conference symbolized a national endeavor to recover lost rights and, for the first time in modern Chinese history, all provincial warlords, except a few provinces under the control of the Canton Government, voluntarily contributed their share toward the expenditures of the huge Chinese Delegation. The contributions ranged from $100,000 silver of Marshal Chang Tso-lin of Manchuria to $5,000 silver from Military Governor Ma of Suiyuan Province in Inner Mongolia. Moreover,

[137] *Ibid.*, p. 305.
[138] *Ibid.*, pp. 308-9.
[139] *Ibid.*, pp. 310-13.
[140] *Ibid.*, p. 312.

when the Chinese Delegation was engaged in negotiating the Japanese loan for the Kiaochow-Tsinanfu Railway, nationalistic fervor increased in intensity. Warlords, many civic organizations, and numerous private citizens, including Dr. Koo himself, contributed funds for purchasing the railway with Chinese capital rather than accept the Japanese loan plan. This mass support was significant even though in the end much of the necessary cash behind the impressive commitments did not materialize. All the accounts of the Conference were well recorded and publicized, and despite geographical distinctions and warlordism, China had been united in championing its cause of recovering its national rights from foreign powers.

Regarding tariff revision, the concrete achievements of Dr. Koo and the Chinese Delegation were modest. Unity and strength were more apparent than real. China was not in a position to make its demand heard by the powers even with capable representatives like Koo and Sze. Acquiring an effective duty rate of 5 per cent *ad valorem*, in accordance with existing treaties concluded between China and the powers without the delay required for ratification, as provided in Article I of the Treaty, was perhaps the most concrete result Dr. Koo achieved at the Conference as far as the tariff problem was concerned.[141] His major proposal to raise the import duty from 5 per cent to 12½ per cent effective as written into the draft agreement of Sir Robert Borden was considered "out of the question" by Odagiri of Japan. The Japanese recommendation that "since the problem of raising the rate to 12½ per cent needs more complete study by all the treaty Powers, it is advisable to refer this matter to a special conference" became Article III of the Treaty, and the Special Conference mentioned was only empowered to authorize the levying of a surtax rate of 2½ per cent *ad valorem* except on certain articles of luxury.[142] In his opening speech on the question of the administration of the Chinese customs during the fifth meeting of the Committee on Pacific and Far Eastern Questions as well as in his concluding speech during the seventeenth meeting of that body, Dr. Koo asked only that the powers agree to the restoration to China of its tariff autonomy.[143] He did not list tariff autonomy as one of his seven concrete proposals for the Subcommittee on Chinese Revenue to consider nor did he propose a specific time limit for the complete restoration of China's tariff autonomy.[144] Nevertheless, he laid a foundation for convening the Special Conference on Chinese Tariff

[141] *Conference on the Limitation of Armament, Washington, November 12, 1921-Februry 6, 1922*, pp. 1633-34.

[142] *Conference on the Limitation of Armament, Subcommittee, Washington, November 12, 1921-February 6, 1922*, pp. 560, 572, 580.

[143] *Ibid.*, pp. 922, 1174-76.

[144] *Ibid.*, p. 546.

which eventually met in October of 1925 in Peking, at which the thirteen powers present agreed on the final restoration of China's tariff autonomy to begin in 1929.[145]

The settlement on the Kiaochow-Tsinanfu Railway might not have recovered everything immediately and completely for China, but it produced a much better bargain than Foreign Minister Yen had thought possible and a better settlement than the Chinese Government had originally demanded.[146] It was perhaps the only alternative for China because Japan was in actual possession, and China had no means of evicting Japan forcibly. The settlement eliminated two thousand Japanese employees at the price of retaining only two of them under restricted conditions. According to one understanding as recorded in the minutes, the Chinese Managing Director of the railway would appoint the entire subordinate staff of the Japanese Traffic Manager and Japanese Chief Accountant, and Japan disavowed any intention of claiming that China was under any obligation to appoint Japanese nationals as members of the subordinate staff of those positions.[147] Another understanding was that upon taking over the Shantung Railways, the Chinese authorities were to have full power and discretion to continue or to remove employees of Japanese nationality in the service of the railway. The two remaining Japanese managerial personnel would be under the direction, control, and supervision of the Chinese Managing Director, who would enjoy the power to remove them. With a vigorous and effectual Managing Director, then, the Japanese would be well controlled.

It proved an economic boon to China to accept the settlement on Shantung, and at the same time it provided a means to restore the province in the quickest way possible. The Japanese budget for the Shantung administration in 1919 showed a surplus of 6,888,000 yen.[148] The total assets of the Kiaochow-Tsinanfu Railway were estimated at 53,406,141 gold marks by the reparation commission of the Paris Peace Conference. With Japanese improvements and additions, minus depreciation, the total figure still stood at 40,000,000 yen. Dr. Chengting T. Wang, Director of the Sino-Japanese Joint Commission on Shantung, estimated that the railway would pay for itself in fifteen years. The surplus of the first three years would be sufficient to pay the interest, and the surplus of the remaining twelve years would pay the capital, or in other words, its annual surplus would be around 3,330,000 yen. The yearly production of the Tsingtao salt field would produce 1,200,000 tons with a potential capacity five times greater than this amount. The annual

[145] Wunsz King, *Ts'ung Pa-li ho-hui tao Kuo-lien*, p. 50.

[146] Westel W. Willoughby, *China at the Conference*, p. 332.

[147] *Ibid.*, p. 324.

[148] *Conversations*, p. 35.

revenue of the Tsingtao salt operation was at least 5,000,000 yen with an expectation of yielding more than 25,000,000 yen.[149] The total annual revenue of the Shantung administration, the Kiaochow-Tsinanfu Railway, and Tsingtao salt mines would yield more than 15,000,000 yen, and these figures did not include the taxes and profits of the mines, the gabelle, the Maritime Customs, cables, and many other indirect revenues. No government could afford to ignore such figures, least of all the hard-pressed Peking Government and its Chihli Clique, the prospective recipient of the profits.

The great burden of the Chinese Delegation at the Washington Conference was that of negotiating the recovery of control over things and circumstances then preventing China from attaining viable nationhood and a posture of dignity and integrity with some of the very powers who recognized and respected China's integrity and sovereignty least. The problem of representing China was compounded by the various upheavals, monetary crises, and changes in government at home in China; while other problems included the frequent challenges made to the Peking Government's authority to negotiate on behalf of the nation and attacks upon its integrity, strategy, e.g., the order of the agenda, such as Shantung versus tariff revision and accomplishments. Some of these strategic arguments originated within the Chinese Delegation itself. All this was contradictory and embarrassing and served to lend validity to the worst Japanese accusations concerning the Chinese constitution.

The Canton Government, as previously mentioned, alleged the Peking Delegation in Washington to be "unrepresentative of the country at large, subject to the influence of Japan, and of the military party in North China"[150] and went so far as to communicate its own program for the Conference, via its own Ministry of Foreign Affairs, to Secretary of State Hughes. The first condition for the permanent settlement of the Chinese question, Canton specified, was "the withdrawal of recognition from the administration of Hsu Shih-chang (Hsü Shih-ch'ang), which was illegal in origin and impotent and disintegrating in operation."[151] There was the obvious problem of the empty seat left by the absence of Wu Ch'ao-shu, representative of the Canton Government. Even the Chinese delegates themselves were not certain of their status. When the Peking Government instructed the Chinese Delegation to accept the Japanese loan plan for the Kiaochow-Tsinanfu Railway, Wang Chung-Hui told Chiang Meng-lin and other representatives of the Chinese people that "in fact we have come here not representing the Chinese people,

[149] *Ibid.*, p. 49.

[150] The American Minister (Schurman) to Secretary of State, Peking, April 12, 1922. *Internal Affairs of China, 1910-1929.* Reel No. 29, 893.00/4264.

[151] *Ibid.*, No. 28, 893.00/4171. The Republic of China (Canton Government) to 644 Munsey Building, Washington, D. C., December 1921.

but the Peking Government. Now we even cannot represent the Peking Government anymore."[152]

The problem of Chinese credentials at the Conference was ameliorated partly by compromises, such as the Powers' propitious acceptance of Dr. Koo's suggestion that designated China, instead of Peking, as the sponsor for the future Special Conference regarding the Chinese Custom Tariff in order to avoid the difficulty of choosing between the Peking Government and the Canton Government.[153] China's position was buoyed, too, by the fact that it had an ally in the United States, especially in the person of Senator Underwood, who was sympathetic to China and usually ready to endorse a Chinese idea or intervene to break an impasse.

If the Chinese delegates were under extraordinary pressure from their own people, the Japanese delegates were perhaps equally pressured from their own country and its influential circles.[154] An authoritarian ruling elite with popular support was leading Japan to assumed grandeur. Consequently, the Japanese representatives in Washington might have experienced as much difficulty as did Dr. Koo and his Chinese colleagues, who represented a weak and divided China. It was not unusual for Baron Shidehara to emphasize in negotiating that the Japanese delegates went beyond their instructions. Foreign Minister Uchida abruptly told American Ambassador Warren in Tokyo that "the Japanese delegates to the Washington Conference had exceeded their powers in proposing forms in payment."[155] Further substantiation came when Chinese Foreign Minister Yen mentioned the fact that when Japanese representatives had proposed to employ Japanese experts as Associate Engineer and Associate Accountant in charge of the Kiaochow-Tsinanfu Railway after its amalgamation with the Tientsin-P'uk'ou Railway, Obata, Japanese Ambassador to Peking, had replied that "the Japanese Government would never give its consent."[156] The attacks from influential politicians, such as Kotaro Mochizuki, a leader of the Kenseikai Party, were even more shocking.[157] Nevertheless, Baron Shidehara's diplomacy of disarmament, international cooperation with the great powers of the West, and noninterference in China

[152] T'ung Chih-jen, "Tsai-chi Hua-sheng-tun hui-i chung Shan-tung wen-ti chih ching-kuo," *Tung-fang tsa-chih*, XIX:9 (May 1922), pp. 81-87.

[153] Wunsz King, *Ts'ung Pa-li ho-hui tao Kuo-lien*, pp. 43-44.

[154] The Minister in China (Schurman) to the Secretary of State, Peking, January 18, 1922. *Foreign Relations of the United States, 1922*, I:940.

[155] The Ambassador in Japan (Warren) to the Secretary of State, Tokyo, December 26, 1921. *Foreign Relations of the United States, 1922*, I:938.

[156] Record of Interview between Foreign Minister (Yen) and Japanese Minister in Peking (Obata), Peking, December 27, 1921. Archives of the Ministry of Foreign Affairs at the Institute of Modern History, Academia Sinica, Taipei.

[157] *The North China Herald*, January 28, 1922.

might have provided Dr. Koo and China with the only opportunity to settle the problem of Shantung and other issues with a reasonable person on reasonable terms.[158]

The strategy of Koo and the Chinese Delegation on the priority of principles first and special claims second was basically correct, although it caused great criticism, particularly among the educated overseas Chinese and the "representatives of the Chinese people," including Chiang Meng-lin, representative of the Chinese in Shanghai, Liang Lung, representative of the overseas Chinese in England, and Ho Szu-yüan, of the Shantungese in America.[159] Their unanimous view was that the problems such as Shantung should be of the first priority rather than touched upon in the so-called "Ten Points" of the Chinese Delegation, which they believed were vague, uncertain, and inappropriate. Nevertheless, the Chinese Delegation was able to bring the various special questions as planned to the Conference in the following order: tariff autonomy; abolition of extraterritoriality; abolition of spheres of influence; restoration of leased territories; withdrawal of foreign troops, railway guards, foreign police stations, post offices, foreign telegraphic and radio stations; abolition of the Twenty-one Demands; and the Shantung issue.[160] All of these caused considerable debate if not concrete results. Westel W. Willoughby, legal consultant of the Chinese Delegation, made the observation upon the strategy contained in the Ten Points:

> On November 16, the Chinese Delegation presented what have since been known as China's Ten Points. This maneuver upon the part of the Chinese Delegation was undoubtedly a wise one, since the result was that, from that time forward the work of the Committee assumed almost exclusively the character of an examination of the Pacific and Far Eastern situation from the point of view of China.[161]

Contrary to certain opinions represented at the Conference by Chinese students, people's delegates in Washington, and even some members of the Chinese Delegation itself, including Dr. Wang Chung-Hui and General Huang Fu, the policy of Dr. Koo and the Chinese Government was basically sound, if not quite independent, in regard to negotiating with the Japanese on the restoration of Shantung and accepting the settlement on the Kiaochow-Tsinanfu

[158] Sidney DeVere Brown, "Shidehara Kijūrō: The Diplomacy of the Yen," in *Diplomats in Crisis: United States-Chinese-Japanese Relations, 1919-1941*, edited by R. D. Burns and E. M. Bennett (Santa Barbara, Calif.: ABC-Clio Press, 1974).

[159] Lo Chia-lun, "Wo tui-yü Chung-kuo tsai Hua-sheng-tun hui-i chih kuan-ch'a," *Tung-fang tsa-chih*, XIX:2 (January 1922), p. 32.

[160] Ho Szu-yüan, "Hua-sheng-tun hui-i chung Shan-tung wen-t'i chih ching-kuo," *Tung-fang tsa-chih*, XIX:2 (January 1922), p. 56

[161] Westel W. Willoughby, *China at the Conference*, p. 32.

Railway. China might have pursued an irresponsible policy, refused any direct negotiation with the Japanese, and declined to accept the settlement on the Shantung Railways, but as a consequence, the Sino-Japanese negotiations would never have begun or would certainly have broken off. China might have submitted the issue to the plenary meeting of the Conference, where it probably would have found little sympathy from the leading powers because the British and French were committed to their Versailles agreements, the United States was estranged, and Japan would have been insulted. The issue might have offered an excuse for Japan to boycott the Conference entirely. Although the Shantung question had been one of the key issues for the failure of President Wilson's Democratic Party, it was not vital to President Harding. The U. S. Senate would not oppose the Administration's efforts, for unlike the situation at Versailles, influential senators were members of the American Delegation at Washington. American public opinion and the opposition party would not offer immediate and practical help. The Shantung question would have remained unsettled with no occasion for discussion at any significant international forum until, perhaps, after World War II. Within two decades, Shantung and the Kiaochow-Tsinanfu Railway would have been submerged under Japanese exploitation and Japanization. Consequently, China would have had to face the difficult problems presented by a Japanized generation such as the Nationalists experienced with the Taiwanese. When the case of the "Manchurian Incident" is considered, it seems apparent that China's appeal to the League of Nations would not have produced any concrete results either.[162]

It was perhaps the most practical alternative for China to pay Japan with national treasury notes maturing after fifteen years, but redeemable at the option of China at the end of five years. The author of Liang Shih-i's biography may be right when he said that it made no real difference between the payment in national treasury notes in the Shantung settlement and loans as in other railway settlements. He condemned the makers of the Shantung agreements as cheats who not only cheated others, but also themselves.[163] The voluntary contributions of the Chinese people to redeem the railway, while nobly inspired, proved a failure. In December 1921, the Ministry of Communication sent an assortment of telegrams to various provinces to ask people to contribute their share for the line. Lecturing groups and a lantern parade were organized as an advertisement of the fund-raising campaign.[164] Within three days the National Salvation and Fund-Raising for Redeeming the Kiaochow-Tsinanfu Railway Association was established.[165] Premier Liang Shih-i himself

[162] Liang Ching-tun, *Chiu-i-pa shih-pien shih-shu* (The Manchurian Affair), pp. 382-93.
[163] Ts'en Hsüeh-lü, *San-shui Liang Yen-sun hsien-sheng nien-p'u*, II:205.
[164] *Ibid.*, pp. 191-92.
[165] *The North China Herald*, February 18, 1922.

promised three million silver dollars,[166] and the military governors of various provinces made impressive commitments.[167] Dr. Koo contributed one thousand silver *yüan*. In the end, however, the fund never materialized, and in later years, the Government's call for shareholders did not create any significant response either. By the time of the Lukouchiao (Marco Polo Bridge) Incident on July 7, 1937, when the eight-year Sino-Japanese War had started on a national scale, only the annual interest of the national treasury notes on the railway had been paid.[168]

It is debatable whether a resident minister should be appointed as a regular member of a delegation to the host state. The friendship established between the Koos and Hughes, Balfour, and other members of the American and British Delegations afforded tremendous influence and convenience the Japanese delegates did not enjoy;[169] yet the same friendships could become obstacles in case of conflicts of policies and national interests. Maintenance of the status of *persona grata* for a resident minister to a host government and cultivation of friendships with local officials could tie the hands of an envoy. It would certainly demand more personal sacrifice and effort when there was no alternative for the leading diplomats of the Peking Government, including Dr. Koo. These Chinese diplomats minimized the sacrifices in posts at London or Washington, where they were trained, closely attached in spiritual and physical life with their Western counterparts, and where they all retired. It is no wonder that some said Dr. Koo had no choice but to listen to Balfour, and Dr. Sze had to listen to Hughes. There might be a grain of truth in what was alleged by some public opinion in various countries, that "the Chinese delegates were working for the State Department of the United States and Hughes was the great-grand plenipotentiary of the Chinese

[166] Ts'en Hsüeh-lü, *San-shui Liang Yen-sun hsien-sheng nien-p'u*, p. 190.

[167] *The North China Herald*, February 1, 1922. The Ministry of Communications received the following offers for the redemption of the railway:

a. Tuchün of Shantung, General T'ien Chung-yü	$3,000,000
b. Tuchün of Hupei, General Hsiao Yao-nan	$3,000,000
c. Tuchün of Shensi, General Feng Yü-hsiang	$1,000,000
d. Tuchün of Honan, General Chao T'i	$1,000,000
e. Tuchün of Kiangsi, General Ch'en Kuang-yüan	$1,000,000
f. Inspector-General of Manchuria, Marshal Chang Tso-lin	$3,000,000
g. Inspector-General of Chihli-Shantung-Honan, Marshal Ts'ao K'un	$3,000,000
h. Similar commitments were made by Tuchün of Kansu and Anhwei provinces.	

[168] Wunsz King, *Ts'ung Pa-li ho-hui tao Kuo-lien*, p. 36.

[169] Koo Hui-lan, *Autobiography*, pp. 125, 147.

plenipotentiaries."[170] In this respect, Japanese teamwork seem more successful. Hanihara, who was sent directly from the Foreign Ministry in Tokyo, functioned as the alter ego of Baron Shidehara while Dr. Wang, who was directly appointed in Peking, did not involved himself as much as did Hanihara. The course of the Conference might have been changed if Chengting T. Wang had been appointed as an outspoken member of the Chinese Delegation, or if Wu Ch'ao-shu of the Canton Government had not boycotted the meetings.

Dr. Koo and his Chinese colleagues may not have possessed all the qualities of statesmanship or great national leadership as demanded by Lo Chia-lun, a representative from Shanghai, or the experience as required by T'ung Chih-jen.[171] They did, however, have outstanding intelligence, adequate training, and patriotic devotion. Perhaps no other case reveals more of Dr. Koo's diplomatic talent, which was productive, imaginative, and exacting, than the negotiations on the Kiaochow-Tsinanfu Railway. His resourcefulness and forcefulness was unmatched by either his Japanese counterparts or his Chinese colleagues throughout these marathon negotiations and their myriad confusing plans coming from both the Japanese and the Chinese delegates. He took unusual pains to make his objections and criticisms clear but not insulting, and only under special circumstances did he condemn the Japanese with deliberate calculation. He was shrewd enough to detect any meaningful implication concealed in the diplomatic expressions of the Japanese delegates. He never forgot to flatter his American or British colleagues or enemies whenever an opportunity arose. Nor did his admirable memory apparently ever fail to remind him in time of a particular document or wording vital for the case under discussion. Occasionally, Dr. Koo maneuvered his commitments to the powers into the concealed minutes of the proceedings rather than into part of the treaty or agreement for publication. For example, in the case of the Shantung telephone enterprise wherein Koo assured Hanihara that due consideration would be given to the extensions and improvements to be required by the residents, China committed itself to employ Japanese-speaking personnel as operators and staff of the telephone service for the convenience of the Japanese residents; this was not to be incorporated into the final agreement, rather only recorded in the minutes of the negotiations.[172]

A word must be inserted here concerning the role of W. W. Yen, Foreign Minister of the Peking Government for the period of the Washington Con-

[170] Lo Chia-lun, "Wo tui-yü Chung-kuo tsai Hua-sheng-tun hui-i chih kuan-ch'a," *Tung-fang tsa-chih*, XIX:2 (January 1922), pp. 12, 43, 47.

[171] *Ibid.*, XIX:2 (January 1922), p. 46.

[172] T'ung Chih-jen, "Tsai-chi Hua-sheng-tun hui-i chung Shan-tung wen-ti chih ching-kuo," *Tung-fang tsa-chih*, XIX:9 (May 1922), p. 87.

ference. While the focus of events was concentrated on the Chinese delegates at Washington, the role of Yen, the very center of stability and continuity of Peking Government policy and his close cooperation with Doctors Koo and Sze in Washington, was greatly neglected. A senior member of the influential Anglo-American Group in Peking, he became Foreign Minister of Chin Yün-p'eng's cabinet of the Peking Government on August 11, 1920, long before the idea of a Washington Conference was conceived. During the cabinet crisis when Chin resigned on December 18, 1921, Foreign Minister Yen acted as the Premier until the new Premier Liang Shih-i was sworn in on December 25. Yen acted as Foreign Minister of Liang's cabinet until its fall shortly thereafter, when he again acted concurrently as Premier. It was during this period that the Treaties of the Washington Conference were signed. He remained in his cabinet post as Acting Premier until April 8, 1922 when Chou Tzu-ch'i formed a new cabinet. Yen continued in his ministerial post through the change in presidency until the end of July 1922, when Dr. Koo came home to replace him. Fortunately for Dr. Koo and China, as his Chinese colleagues and he were struggling for China on the diplomatic front in Washington, Yen coordinated policy with their efforts and shielded them throughout all the dangerous cabinet changes, warlord politics, and civil war.

Rodney Gilbert, the popular contemporary reporter of the *North China Herald*, did not conceal his feelings when the decision on the Kiaochow-Tsinanfu Railway was announced:

> China has an opportunity to acquire what is hers by abstract right. By abstract right the writer means what China as a nation is entitled to in keeping with our Occidental conceptions of national sovereignty and independence, as opposed to what she deserved or earned.
>
> At the end of the Peace Conference, China acquired or recovered many abstract rights which, concretely she had not earned, either through deserving efforts toward reform at home or through diplomatic conquests abroad. These rights were not given or restored to her through charity, but through the application to the East on the part of the other delegations of our Occidental theories of national right.
>
> The foreign trained Chinese in whose keeping is China's diplomatic objective is face rather than concrete advantages, know how to play upon the Occidental regard to abstract right and to lead all discussion away from the concrete question of China's preparedness, fitness, or deserts.[173]

Yet, despite the rather chauvinistic, condescending, and cynical tone of Gilbert's remarks, one cannot fail to notice that, nevertheless, they are paying a form of tribute to Wellington Koo's abilities. Moreover, Senator Underwood, who was generally sympathetic to China's cause, but not unreservedly, directing himself to Dr. Koo's urging for Chinese tariff autonomy before the

[173] *The North China Herald*, February 18, 1922.

Committee for Pacific and Far Eastern Questions, stated that:

> [He] did not think there was any doubt in the minds of the men on the Subcommittee as to the question that if China at present had the unlimited control of levying taxes at the customs house, in view of the unsettled conditions now existing in China, it would work, in the end, to China's detriment and to the injury of the world; . . . if [he] was a judge of the situation, a judge of the temper of conditions in the balance of the world, [he] felt sure that when China herself established a parliamentary Government of all the provinces of China and dispensed with the military control that now existed in many of the provinces of China, so that outside Powers might feel that they were dealing with a Government that had entire and absolute and free control of the situation, China could expect to realize the great ideals of sovereignty that she asked for at this table.[174]

Again, the message of an oblique if disguised tribute to Wellington Koo emerges, for Koo was the individual in the forefront of China's attempt at the Washington Conference to restore its dignity, ensure its viability, and "realize the great ideals of sovereignty that she asked for at this table."

[174] *Conference on the Limitation of Armament, Washington, November 12, 1921-February 6, 1922*, p. 1182.

CHAPTER IV

The Linch'eng Kidnapping and International Control of Chinese Railways, 1923

THE LINCH'ENG KIDNAPPING OF RAILWAY PASSENGERS

The north-bound express train from P'u-k'ou to Tientsin was ambushed by more than a thousand bandits between Linch'eng Station and Shakou Station, Shantung, at 2:00 a.m., May 5, 1923.[1] One British subject, Bothman, was killed, and two Chinese passengers were badly wounded. Six Western passengers escaped. Nineteen foreigners, including sixteen Americans and James B. Powell, editor of the *China Weekly Review*, Shanghai, and more than two hundred Chinese passengers were taken as hostages to the bandits' den, Pao-tu-ku, on the crest of a nearby mountain.[2]

The bandit chief, Sun Mei-yao, was a native of Kiangsu. He was a former lieutenant of General Chang Ching-yao.[3] For many years he had been active as a bandit in Kiangsu and Shantung provinces. Sun's followers numbered several chiefs and about ten bands with a total strength of over six thousand men under the banner "The National Reconstruction and Autonomy Army, 5th Route." They had some affiliation with the An-fu Clique and had been used by the Feng-chün (Manchurian Army) to harass the rear echelons of the Chihli Army during the Feng-Chih War in 1922.[4] The bandits' den was located on a mountain with a perimeter of 50 *li*, east of the Tientsin-P'uk'ou Line. Historically the area was a strategic battlefield; remnants of the Nien rebels had resisted the government troops here for years during the Kuang-hsü period.[5]

In the beginning the Chihli Clique in power suspected that the Linch'eng incident had been caused by the retaliatory activities of the Chiao-t'ung

[1] *Tung-fang tsa-chih*, XX:8 (April 1923), p. 2; The Minister in China (Schurman) to the Secretary of State, Tsinanfu, May 6, 1923. *Foreign Relations of the United States, 1923*, I:631.

[2] Pao-tu-ku, or Paotzeku as it appears in the *Foreign Relations of the United States*, or Pao-tze-kang, as usually given in the local Chinese papers.

[3] Chang Ching-yao served as Commander of the 7th Division of President Yüan Shih-k'ai's Peiyang Army in 1916 and as Premier Tuan Ch'i-jui's Military Governor of Hunan in 1918. Refer to *Liu Ju-ming hui-i lu* (Memoir of Liu Ju-ming), pp. 6, 30.

[4] *Tung-fang tsa-chih*, XX:8 (April 1923), pp. 2-4.

[5] *Li* is a measure of length reckoned at 360 paces, or about 1,890 feet English measure.

(Communications) Clique under Liang Shih-i, who as Premier had been ousted the previous year by Marshal Wu P'ei-fu of the Chihli Clique.[6] Marshal Ts'ao K'un, head of the Chihli Clique, demanded that the Peking Government send a formal diplomatic note to the British Minister in Peking insisting that Liang Shih-i, Yeh Kung-ch'o, and other leaders of the Chiao-t'ung Clique be expelled from Hong Kong.[7]

Then it was alleged that Japan was behind the bandits. The Reverend Hugh W. White of the American Southern Presbyterian Mission wrote to the American Government that Japanese complicity was evident in the aggressive tone of the Japanese press, which was trying to turn American opinion against China. Furthermore, White stated, no Japanese had been captured, yet three Japanese advisers were present at the bandit camp, and the bandits demanded that pro-Japanese General Chang Ching-yao be made military governor of Shantung.[8]

At the same time the bandits were also thought to be connected with disbanded Anhwei troops because a report from the Anhwei Director of Military Affairs to the Minister of Foreign Affairs stated that "the newly recruited troops have just been disbanded and brigandage is rife. I request that you temporarily cease to issue permits to foreigners for travel in the Northern Anhwei District."[9]

During the two weeks from May 5 to May 20, shortly after the incident, the diplomatic corps held conferences, and sent more than eight notes from the diplomatic body in Peking to Prime Minister Chang Shao-tseng, Acting Foreign Minister, V. K. Wellington Koo, and the Minister of Communications, Wu Yü-lin.[10] The Powers insisted that all possible steps should be taken immediately to secure the release of the foreign captives and that the Chinese Government should pay the necessary ransom afterwards. Moreover, the

[6] *Wu P'ei-fu chuan* (Biography of Wu P'ei-fu), pp. 61-65.

[7] Ts'en Hsüeh-lü, *San-shui Liang Yen-sun hsien-sheng nien-p'u*, II:254-56.

[8] Dispatch from the Reverend Hugh W. White of the American Southern Presbyterian Mission, Yencheng, Kiangsi Province. Consular Report to the Secretary of State from J. C. Huston, American Consul in Charge, American Consulate General, Tientsin, July 5, 1923. *National Archives Microfilm Publications Microfilm No. 329, Records of the Department of State Relating to Internal Affairs of China, 1910-1929*. National Archives and Records Service, Washington, 1960. Reel No. 34, 893.00/5121-22. (Hereinafter referred to as *Internal Affairs of China, 1910-1929.*)

[9] A Formal Note from Chang Shao-tseng, Special Commissioner of Foreign Affairs, May 3, 1923. Report of Samuel Sokobin, American Consul, American Consulate, to J. G. Schurman, American Minister in Peking, Kalgan, May 9, 1923. *Internal Affairs of China, 1910-1929*, 893.00/5023.

[10] *Chung-kuo wai-chiao chi-kuan li-jen shou-chang hsien-ming nien-piao* (Table of the Names and Titles of the Successive Heads of the Organ of Foreign Affairs of China), pp. 54-55.

diplomats believed strong military action should be taken to suppress brigandage in Shantung; and while pressing for an official inquiry of the entire affair, the diplomatic corps reserved the right to demand a progressive indemnity for every foreigner who remained captive after May 12. The British Minister proposed at a meeting of the diplomatic corps on the afternoon of May 8 that after the matter was settled:

> A demand should be made on the Chinese Government for adequate police protection of the Tientsin-P'uk'ou line to be supplied by the railway itself and paid for out of its earnings and that to this end there should be appointed a foreign traffic manager, chief accountant, and police officers.[11]

He further suggested that the officers might be appointed from the countries of the bondholders.[12] A suggestion to use the Linch'eng occurrence as a protest for reforming China generally and to establish an international regency was seriously discussed.[13] The diplomatic body also applied pressure on Marshal Ts'ao K'un, Inspector-General of Chihli, Shantung, and Honan, General T'ien Chung-yü, Military Governor of Shantung and former Chief of Staff of Ts'ao K'un, and other military commanders in charge of operations against the bandits.[14]

After the Washington Conference, Dr. Koo had left New York for his post in London. Inasmuch as he had been away from China for seven years, he was eager to report personally on the Washington Disarmament Conference. Moreover, "another more important reason made him decide to return to China a few weeks after their arrival in England. The political situation in Peking was unsettled and Wellington Koo was anxious to get the feel of the country."[15] On March 30, 1922, Dr. Koo, accompanied by Madame Koo and their three children, boarded the vessel *Khyber* and arrived in Shanghai on May 13. In Shanghai Dr. Koo made a number of speeches. To the reporters of the *North China Daily News* he argued that the South and the North should set aside their differences and come to an understanding. He also promoted the cause of establishing the redemption fund of the Shantung Railway before the Chinese General Chamber of Commerce and the Association for the Redemption of the Shantung Railway.[16]

[11]The Counselor of Legation at Peking (Bell) to the Secretary of State, Peking, May 8, 1923. *Foreign Relations of the United States, 1923*, I:632.

[12]The Minister in China (Schurman) to the Secretary of State, Peking, June 6, 1923. *Foreign Relations of the United States, 1923*, I:653.

[13]*Ibid.*, May 26, 1923, I:648.

[14]*Tung-fang tsa-chih*, XX:8 (April 1923), p. 5.

[15]Koo Hui-lan, *No Feast Lasts Forever*, pp. 152-54, 164. Koo Hui-lan, *Autobiography*, pp. 153-62.

[16]*The North China Herald*, May 13 and 20, 1922.

On May 23, Dr. Koo arrived in Peking amidst a welcoming crowd and moved into the historical palace of 200 rooms bought and renovated by his father-in-law, in the Iron-lion Lane. The palace had been built in the seventeenth century for the legendary beauty Ch'en Yüan-yüan, concubine of General Wu San-kuei, who collaborated with the Manchus and established Ch'ing in China proper. Here also, Dr. Sun Yat-sen, founding father of the Chinese Republic, died in 1925. From this prestigious residence, he became Foreign Minister in T'ang Shao-i's cabinet on August 5, 1922 and remained in that position until Wang Chung-Hui, acting for Premier T'ang, resigned on November 25 of that year. On January 1, 1923, Dr. Koo succeeded Huang Fu as Foreign Minister of Chang Shao-tseng's cabinet.[17]

The Peking Government was again in chaos and lacked the internal cohesiveness to meet a crisis effectively.[18] While the Fengtien and Chihli forces were actively preparing for an unavoidable confrontation, the Minister of Marine and Minister of Justice were directing police strikes to compel President Li Yüan-hung to resign, thus preparing the way for Marshal Ts'ao K'un to assume power. Because of pressures created by the dissatisfaction of Ts'ao Jui, a brother of Marshal Ts'ao K'un and Civil Governor of Chihli, and the failure of Chang Ying-hua, Finance Minister, to arrange a loan for Ts'ao K'un's presidential campaign, the cabinet under Chang Shao-tseng resigned *en bloc* on June 6.[19] President Li offered Dr. W. W. Yen the premiership without success, and the manager of Ts'ao K'un's presidential campaign notified Dr. Koo frankly that the Chihli Clique did not want him to accept the offer either.[20] While General Feng Yü-hsiang, Inspector-General of the Army and Tupan of Frontier Defense for the Northwest, and General Wang Huai-ch'ing, Commander-in-Chief of the Metropolitan Forces and Commander of the 13th Division, were threatening to resign, their army units and police surrounded the presidential palace and Li's private home from June 10 to June 12 until Li fled to Tientsin.[21] The pro-Ts'ao Jui members of the cabinet, Kao Ling-wei, Wu Yü-lin, and others, then informed the press that their cabinet was exercising the powers of the president.[22]

[17]Koo, *Reminiscences*, III. Services In China, E and F.

[18]The Minister in China (Schurman) to the Secretary of State, Peking, April 10, 27, May 4, June 7 and 9, 1923. *Foreign Relations of the United States, 1923*, I:505-11.

[19]*The North China Herald*, June 9, 1923.

[20]*Ibid.*, June 16, 1923.

[21]*Wu P'ei-fu chuan*, pp. 84-87.

[22]Telegrams of President Li Yüan-hung to the Public, June 9 and 12, 1923. *Cheng-fu kung-pao* (Government Gazette), Nos. 2602 and 2605. Telegrams of the State Council (Cabinet), June 16 and 17, 1923, *Cheng-fu kung-pao*, Nos. 2609 and 2610.

THE NEGOTIATIONS BETWEEN THE GOVERNMENT AND THE BANDITS

While the diplomatic body in Peking was meeting to consider proposals from consular and military officers for such measures as a naval demonstration and possible international control of Chinese railways, the provincial governments of Shantung and Kiangsu were fully occupied with the task of obtaining the prisoners' release. Military Governor T'ien Chung-yü commissioned General Cheng Shih-ch'i, Commander of the 5th Division of the Chihli Army,[23] as the Commander-in-Chief of the Bandits Pacification and Extermination Command in coordination with other·generals for the operation. Ch'i Hsieh-yüan, Military Governor of Kiangsu and Inspector-General of Kiangsu, Anhwei, and Kiangsi, also dispatched Ch'en T'iao-yüan, Defense Commissioner of Hsuchow, and Wen Shih-chen, Commissioner of Foreign Affairs of Nanking, to Tsao-chuang. The government established a provisional headquarters at Tsao-chuang near the bandits' den, and the Chung-hsing Coal Mine Company served as the temporary location for the subsequent conferences.[24] Some earlier meetings which had been arranged between Yang I-te, Commissioner of Police of Tientsin, and the bandits had broken off, and before the dawn of June 21, Government troops once again surrounded Pao-tu-ku.[25]

Both Governor T'ien and Minister Wu Yü-lin went to Peking and persuaded the President, the State Council, Marshal Ts'ao K'un, as well as the diplomatic body, to adopt a firm policy against the bandits. The diplomatic body eventually realized that Western dissension and unreasonable demands only weakened the Chinese Government's ability to deal with the bandits.[26] On May 18 Minister Schurman found out that his French and British colleagues were in accord with him that a naval demonstration was unnecessary and would only exaggerate the importance of the captives and encourage the bandits to demand higher terms.[27] Japan also declared her objection to the proposal.[28] In order to facilitate the military and rescue operations, troops were dispatched from neighboring provinces, including Chihli, Shantung, Honan, and Kiangsu and placed under the unified command of General Cheng Shih-ch'i. A Provisional Association of National Public Bodies at Tsao-chuang was established on May 28 by Feng Shao-shan, representative of commercial circles from Shanghai, and Chiang Ching-yüan, representative of commercial

[23] *Wu P'ei-fu chuan*, p. 96.
[24] *Tung-fang tsa-chih*, XX:8 (April 1923), p. 5.
[25] *Ibid.*, XX:9 (May 1923), p. 2.
[26] *Ibid.*, XX:2 (January 1923), pp. 3-4.
[27] *Foreign Relations of the United States, 1923*, I:642-43.
[28] *The North China Herald*, July 7, 1923, p. 11.

circles from Peking to coordinate various relief measures, including sending food packages to the captives.[29] This consolidated front so weakened the position of the bandits that they finally released James B. Powell on May 26 with two bandit secretaries to reopen negotiations with General Cheng Shih-ch'i, General Ch'en T'iao-yüan, and Roy S. Anderson,[30] an American citizen and advisor to the President of the Peking Government who was to emerge as the negotiator in whom the bandits placed their trust.

On June 1, initial agreement on terms was reached, and General Ch'en T'iao-yüan, Commissioner Wen Shih-chen, and several secretaries went to the bandits' den in order to establish rosters for integrating the bandits into the national army. Military Governor T'ien Chung-yü dispatched personnel to Tientsin for two thousand military uniforms and 50,000 silver dollars for distribution after the integration was completed.[31]

In order to confirm Anderson's status as the representative of the Government and to approve the terms that he had made with the bandits,[32] Marshal Ts'ao K'un, President-apparent, sent him an urgent and confidential telegram from Pao-ting on June 8, which reached Tsao-chuang the next day:

> . . . as the case has now been discussed and a solution has been found, please do not hesitate to give the several guarantees demanded by the bandits, in order that both Chinese and foreign captives may be relieved from danger at an early date. I greatly hope that the case will now be settled in this manner. I, therefore, send you this telegram trusting that you will note the same. Ts'ao K'un.[33]

On June 12, Anderson and Commissioner Wen Shih-chen signed a pledge with the bandits which was witnessed by Chiang Ching-yüan, representative of Commercial Guild of Peking, Sun Fu-chi, representative of Commercial Guild of Shanghai, and nine members of the local gentry:

> To the Most Honorable Chief Sung (Sun Kuei-chih) and all other Chiefs. I, Roy S. Anderson, am an American citizen and a friend of China, in life and death. As the brethren in the mountains are having hard times, as all Tan Chai [Chiefs] have shown genuine sincerity in their actions and words in all the conferences, and as they are willing to submit, I am willing to guarantee that my brethren will be organized into an army and made officers and privates. There shall be no more than three thousand people and the number of unarmed men shall not exceed five hundred. The Government will undertake to support two thousand and seven

29 *Tung-fang tsa-chih*, XX:9 (May 1923), p. 5.

30 Roy S. Anderson's biography see "Memorial Tombstone of Mr. Roy S. Anderson"; composed by Cheng Hung-nien in 1925 and translated by Chu Pao-chin in 1968. *Roy S. Anderson Papers on Modern Chinese History*, San Diego. (Hereinafter referred to as *Anderson Papers*.)

31 *Tung-fang tsa-chih*, XX:9 (May 1923), p. 4.

32 *Foreign Relations of the United States, 1923*, I:651-52.

33 *Anderson Papers.*

> hundred people while all Tan Chai [Chiefs] shall make arrangements to pay the remaining three hundred men, themselves. I am also willing to guarantee that after the brethren are "called and pacified," all their former crimes will be pardoned by the Government. After they are organized, their pay as agreed upon will be given to them according to their ranks, every month, by the Government. This guarantee shall be effective three years from the day of signing . . . .[34]

Sung Kwei-chi (Sun Kuei-chih), who represented the bandits, also made a pledge to Anderson which was witnessed by the same parties:

> I, Sung Kwei-chi (Sun Kuei-chih) representing all brethren here, beg to say that we are willing to be "called and pacified" and organized into a national army. From this time on, we will be permanently loyal to the country and commit nothing that will disturb the order of the army or hurt the reputation of soldiers. On behalf of all brethren, I beg to make this important declaration that we have full confidence in Mr. Anderson and to the person of Mr. Anderson we pledge that we will permanently observe the above things.[35]

As soon as the agreements were concluded, Anderson and Wen came down from the bandits' den with all of the foreign captives and four Chinese hostages.[36] By June 24, the first reorganized regiment under the general command of Sun Mei-yao, marched out of the mountains. The reorganization of the second regiment was delayed, but eventually it also moved out of the mountains. However, shortly after their reorganization, Sun Mei-yao, the newly appointed brigadier general was shot, and his followers were marched into an ambush and were disarmed and disbanded.[37] All the negotiations were conducted with the tacit approval of the diplomatic corps and without the active participation of Foreign Minister Koo and the Chinese Ministry of Foreign Affairs.[38]

THE DEMANDS OF SIXTEEN NATIONS

In order to ascertain whether or not there was collusion between the train crew and the brigands, to determine the degree of responsibility of the civil

[34] *Ibid.*

[35] *Ibid.*

[36] *Tung-fang tsa-chih*, XX:11 (June 1923), p. 6.

[37] *Ibid.*, XXI:3 (February 1924), pp. 8-9; XX:11 (June 1923), p. 7. Various reasons were offered to explain why the Government wanted to terminate these bandit regiments: (a) The Government wanted to discourage other bandits from kidnapping foreigners as hostages in order to blackmail the Government for pay and ammunition; (b) Sun's followers continued their bandit behavior due to lack of pay; (c) Sun refused to submit captured ammunition to his superiors after a successful pacification operation against other bandits.

[38] V. K. Wellington Koo to Chu Pao-chin, November 12, 1968, New York.

and military authorities, and to investigate the measures taken by the Chinese Government to protect against the recurrence of similar incidents, Schurman, Minister of the United States, proposed on May 23 the establishment of an International Military Commission at Tientsin which would consist of military commanders or substitutes named by the legations.[39] After resistance by the Chinese Government, the Ministry of War reluctantly directed Liang Shang-tung to accompany the military attachés of seven countries to Tsao-chuang.[40] On June 1, the entire party left Tientsin in special cars and arrived at Tsao-chuang the next day. After several days of on-the-spot investigation, the commission returned to Tientsin, and its senior member, Brigadier General William D. Connor of the United States Army, submitted its reports on June 6 to the dean of the diplomatic corps in Peking.[41] Its findings and recommendations became the basis for the subsequent discussion and demands of the diplomatic corps.

Both the American and British governments and their legations in China were under pressure from their residents for strong action. In early June, the American Association of China and the American Chambers of Commerce in Shanghai and Peking transmitted to the United States a statement which was approved in its entirety by both the British and China Association and the British Chamber of Commerce in Shanghai:

> An intolerable condition has been created in China by the Washington decision and failure to act aggressively in the present crisis. American lives and liberty throughout China are in danger. Prestige and business are being destroyed by lack of action.... We demand (1) Suspension of all benefits to China under the Washington Conference; (2) Disarmament of troops and return to their homes and placing of Chinese finances under foreign control; (3) Foreign guards be placed upon lines of communication, both land and water; (4) Foreign guards be placed at strategic points throughout China; (5) Suspension of return of Boxer Indemnity; (6) Co-operation with Great Britain in providing remedies for present conditions.[42]

At the annual meeting of the China Association held in London on July 27, 1923 at the offices of the P. and O. Steam Navigation Company under the

[39] The Minister in China (Schurman) to the Secretary of State, Peking, May 23, 1923. *Foreign Relations of the United States, 1923*, I:646.

[40] *Tung-fang tsa-chih*, XX:9 (May 1923), p. 4.

[41] Senior Member of the International Military Commission (William D. Connor of the United States Army) to Dean of the Diplomatic Corps in Peking, Headquarters of American Forces in China, Tientsin, China, June 6, 1923. Dean's Circular No. 143 on the Report of the International Military Commission, Peking, June 7, 1923. *Internal Affairs of China, 1910-1929*, 893.00/5107.

[42] *The North China Herald*, June 13 and July 21, 1923; The American Consul General (Edwin S. Cunningham) to the Secretary of State, Shanghai, June 25, 1923. *Internal Affairs of China, 1910-1929*, 893.00/5094.

leadership of Sir James Jordan, the organization issued a statement that the Chinese Central Government had practically ceased to exist and that the presence of foreign troops in the treaty ports was needed.[43]

In the meantime, Chinese public opinion, particularly that of merchants and students, reacted strongly to these recommendations of foreign merchants, and they declared that "these recommendations will lead to international complications . . . the remedy proposed will prove to be worse than the disease."[44]

President Warren G. Harding and Secretary of State Charles E. Hughes were also convinced that any general military or financial control would be useless and would involve foreign interests in a crisis with dangers disproportionate to the degree of protection afforded. This objection was reaffirmed in a memorandum from Hughes to the British Embassy,[45] and on June 1, Minister Schurman was instructed accordingly.[46] Schurman also opposed the occupation of the railway because he thought it might increase anti-foreign sentiment and lead to acts of hostility against unprotected foreigners in Shantung and elsewhere, cause difficulties and dissension among the Powers occupying the railways, and could not free the countryside from bandits unless the Chinese themselves solved the problem.[47] He was opposed to a progressive indemnity, which was proposed at a rate of $500 for each captive for the first three days he was held and $100 for each day thereafter, for the reason that such an indemnity would not be allowed by a court of equality of justice and it would interject a new principle for the assessment of damages against the Government of China. Nevertheless, he concurred with the French proposal that the Chinese railway police should be put under supreme control from Peking by either a foreign officer or a Chinese officer with a foreign inspector associated with him.[48] While not formally opposing the British Government's program of international control over Chinese railways,[49] the Japanese Government was inclined toward the French proposal of leaving railway police under

[43]*Ibid.*, Reel No. 34, 893.00/5137.

[44]*Ibid.*, Reel No. 33, 893.00/5096.

[45]The Department of State to the Minister in China (Schurman), Washington, June 1, 1923. *Foreign Relations of the United States, 1923*, I:681-82.

[46]The Secretary of State to the Minister in China (Schurman), Washington, June 1, 1923. *Foreign Relations of the United States, 1923*, I:650-51.

[47]The Minister in China (Schurman) to the Secretary of State, Peking, June 6, 1923. *Foreign Relations of the United States, 1923*, I:653.

[48]The Secretary of State to the Minister in China (Schurman), Washington, June 21, 1923. *Foreign Relations of the United States, 1923*, I:663-64; The British Charge (Chilton) to the Secretary of State, Memorandum, Washington, June 30, 1923. *Foreign Relations of the United States, 1923*, I:673.

[49]*The North China Herald*, July 1 and 7, 1923.

Chinese control but subject to foreign inspection and report.[50]

On June 14, shortly after the release of the captives under the Anderson-Sung Agreements, the diplomatic corps appointed a committee for recommendations regarding demands under three headings: (1) compensation, (2) guarantees for the future, and (3) sanctions. This committee consisted of the ministers of Belgium, France, Great Britain, Italy, Netherlands, the United States and the chargé d'affaires of Japan.[51]

On June 20, the committee demanded the punishment of Military Governor T'ien and three other military officers as being the officials responsible for the incident. Two days later the committee adopted plans for three payments of indemnity for (A) direct losses, (B) progressive indemnities, and also (C) the reimbursement of relief expenses.[52]

In regard to an agreement between the Powers on the establishment of an international railway police force and foreign control over the railway revenues and traffic management, the committee was not able to formulate a precise wording concerning guarantees for the future in the draft note and could only assert that "the diplomatic body reserved the right, after a more thorough study of the question, to present their scheme when elaborated to the Chinese Government."[53]

Finally on August 20, the committee meeting of the diplomatic corps adopted the British proposals concerning the railway defense question:

1. A railway defense administrative bureau shall be established by the Ministry of Communications with a foreign officer as its chief, and police authority over all national railways throughout the country should be accorded to the new bureau.
2. Railway defense officers shall be established for all Chinese railways and the officers shall be managed by foreign officers.
3. Railway standing guards belonging to the Railway Defense Administrative Bureau shall be organized, and these guards shall be stationed on all Chinese railways.

[50] The Minister in China (Schurman) to the Secretary of State, Peking, June 15 and July 16, 1923. *Foreign Relations of the United States, 1923*, I:660, 679.

[51] "International Control of Railways and Railway Police," *Tung-fang tsa-chih*, XX:16 (August 1923), p. 5.

[52] The Minister in China (Schurman) to the Secretary of State, Peking, June 20 and 22, 1923. *Foreign Relations of the United States, 1923*, I:662-63, 664-65; The Minister in China (Schurman) to the Secretary of State, Peking, June 20, 1923. *Internal Affairs of China, 1910-1929*, 893.00/5054.

[53] The British Chargé (Chilton) to the Secretary of State, Memorandum. *Foreign Relations of the United States, 1923*, I:671-72. The principles of the formation of a Chinese police force controlled by foreign officers were agreed to by the Powers on August 6. *The North China Herald*, August 11, 1923.

4. In order to guarantee the expenses of the railway standing guards, foreign accountants and superintendants of railway affairs shall be appointed.[54]

Great Britain was strongly insistent upon these demands, France blindly acquiescent, Japan neutral, and the United States disappointed.[55] In Japan the *Jiji Shimpō* newspaper alone supported the proposals declaring that "some such steps are necessary to ensure proper protection of foreign residents in China." Other papers declared that "the proposal is the thin end of the wedge of international control which is held inconsistent with the true peace policy and spirit of the Nine Power Treaty." The *Yomiuri Shimbun* expressed the opinion that "the proposal is a manifestation of British ambition toward China . . . it may do good if it awakens China to realization of the need for unification and restoration of internal order."[56] The Chinese press regarded it as a conspiracy among all the Powers to invade China's sovereign rights and to impose foreign control upon China.[57]

As regards measures for enforcement, the British Minister in the committee meeting of July 15 suggested the use of force, i.e., a naval demonstration, and advocated united action by the Powers, especially by the United States, Japan, and Great Britain in the event that the demands were resisted by the Chinese Government.[58] This position won the support of the British cabinet and the British Government advised the Secretary of State of the United States to take united action.[59] The use of force for the purpose of achieving the desired ends brought strong objections, and Secretary of State Hughes frankly informed the British chargé d'affaires to Washington, Chilton, on July 9 of his doubt about the efficacy of a naval demonstration; the familiarity of the Chinese with the presence of foreign vessels of war in their ports, coupled with the necessary limitations, and the vagueness of action involved in such a course, appeared likely to render such a demonstration ineffective.[60] The Japanese chargé d'affaires had been unresponsive to the proposal of a naval demonstration in the meeting of June 15 in Peking, and on July 9, the Japanese Counselor informed the Chief of the Division of Far Eastern Affairs of the State Department that since a naval demonstration might require the

[54] *The North China Herald*, August 25, 1923.

[55] *Yi-shih Pao*, August 21, 1923.

[56] *The North China Herald*, August 25, 1923.

[57] *Ibid.*, September 1, 1923.

[58] The Minister in China (Schurman) to the Secretary of State, Peking, June 15, 1923. *Foreign Relations of the United States, 1923*, I:660.

[59] The British Chargé (Chilton) to the Secretary of State, Memorandum, Washington, June 30, 1923. *Foreign Relations of the United States, 1923*, I:673.

[60] The Secretary of State to the British Chargé (Chilton), Washington, July 9, 1923. *Foreign Relations of the United States, 1923*, I:676.

landing of forces and lead to further complications, his government did not favor such action.[61]

Instead, Hughes forwarded to London the suggestion of Minister Schurman to turn the present political crisis to advantage[62] with such measures as the withdrawal of recognition of the present Chinese Government or the withholding of recognition from any new government that might seek to assume power in the present political crisis, such nonrecognition to involve a suspension of release of customs and salt surpluses.[63] The withdrawal of recognition from the Peking Government would not involve the withdrawal of legations from Peking; they would continue to function for the maintenance of *de facto* relations with the Chinese authorities.[64]

On August 10, 1923, the diplomatic corps in Peking delivered a "Note of Sixteen Countries"[65] to Dr. Koo, who had taken office as Chinese Minister for Foreign Affairs on July 23. Eliminated from the Note were the original proposals of the Committee on the settlement of four outstanding problems: (1) the improvement of the Shanghai harbor, (2) the extension of the International Settlement of Shanghai, (3) the Maintenance of the Whangpoo (Huang-p'u) Conservancy Board agreement, and (4) the reorganization of the Mixed Court. The State Department was in accord with the British Foreign Office in reasoning that these demands appeared irrelevant to the essential purpose of the Linch'eng affair, and their inclusion would expose the Powers to the charge of attempting to exploit the occasion for the purpose of obtaining ulterior advantages.[66]

KOO'S ANSWER OF SEPTEMBER 24

Immediately after the "Note of Sixteen Countries" had been received, Koo held a special conference of the State Council, and an Ad Hoc Committee

[61] The Minister in China (Schurman) to the Secretary of State, Peking, June 16, 1923. *Foreign Relations of the United States, 1923*, I:660; *The North China Herald*, July 7, 1923.

[62] *Ibid.*, June 15, 1923. *Foreign Relations of the United States, 1923*, I:660.

[63] The Secretary of State to the British Chargé (Chilton), Washington, July 9, 1923. *Foreign Relations of the United States, 1923*, I:676.

[64] The Secretary of State to the Minister in China (Schurman), Washington, July 24, 1923. *Foreign Relations of the United States, 1923*, I:680.

[65] For both English and French texts see Report from the Minister in China (Schurman) to the Secretary of State, Peking, August 14, 1923. *Internal Affairs of China, 1910-1929*, Reel No. 35, 893.00/5329.

[66] The Secretary of State to the Minister in China (Schurman), Washington, June 21, 1923. *Foreign Relations of the United States, 1923*, I:663-64; The British Chargé (Chilton) to the Secretary of State, Memorandum, Washington, June 30, 1923. *Foreign Relations of the United States, 1923*, I:672.

consisting of two members from each of the related ministries, including the Ministries of Foreign Affairs, Interior Affairs, Finance, Army, and Communications, was appointed to draft the answer. The group completed their task by the thirteenth, but the response was not sent to the diplomatic corps in Peking until September 24, one and a half months later. On the one hand, domestic opposition from warlords of various provinces, particularly Shantung where Military Governor T'ien still retained a powerful voice in military circles,[67] had gained strength, and Marshal Wu P'ei-fu and Marshal Ch'i Hsieh-yüan had sent telegrams to the Peking Government protesting foreign intervention in China's internal affairs.[68] On the other hand, any immediate rejection of foreign demands would have invited harsher reprisals because the British proposal concerning international control of China's railways was under debate by the diplomatic corps, and a delay would offer an opportunity for diplomatic maneuvering.[69]

By the end of August, the various diplomatic missions of China received instructions from Dr. Koo that all efforts should be made to soften the terms of the demands. At the same time, he provided three principles to guide the revision of the Committee's work: (1) to apply the term relieving grants for "indemnity"; (2) as soon as Military Governor T'ien quit office on his own, the Government would state that the governor had been punished; and (3) international control of Chinese railways was unnecessary because the Chinese Government had already taken proper measures with the establishment of the Division of Railway Police under the Ministry of Communications and the issuance of orders concerning nationwide operations to exterminate the bandits and to protect foreigners.[70] The draft answer was revised upon these principles, and after discussion by the Cabinet on August 28, it was taken to Loyang by a councilor of the Ministry of Foreign Affairs and submitted to Marshal Wu, who eventually gave his consent.

The originally-designated date of delivery, September 10, had to be postponed because of the absence of the dean of the diplomatic corps, who was vacationing at Pei-tai-ho, a resort on the seashore, and Military Governor T'ien's reluctance to tender his resignation. Fearing that further delay would bring more complications, Dr. Koo, on September 24, invited the Portuguese Minister, de Freitas, to the Ministry after the latter had returned to Peking

[67] Koo's Answer to the Note on Linch'eng of the Sixteen Nations, *Tung-fang tsa-chih*, XX:18 (September 1923), p. 2.

[68] *Wu P'ei-fu chuan*, p. 89. Also, *Wu P'ei-fu hsien-sheng nien-p'u* (Chronological Biography of Mr. Wu P'ei-fu), no place, no publisher, no date, p. 26. (Copy kept by East Asiatic Library of the University of California, Berkeley, California.)

[69] *Tung-fang tsa-chih*, XX:18 (September 1923), p. 2.

[70] *Ibid.*, XX:18 (September 1923), p. 3.

and presented the Note from the Chinese Government personally.[71]

In the Note, Dr. Koo first denied the responsibility of the Chinese Government for the Linch'eng case; nevertheless, he accepted the three categories of damages, (A), (B), and (C), as the basis for "relieving grants by reason of the sympathy of the Chinese Government," not compensation toward the foreign victims as claimed by the diplomatic body. Also rejected were the supplementary indemnities for individual cases:

> It is, however, reassuring to observe that the incident under consideration, deplorable as it was, was not a case of anti-foreign demonstration nor did it betray any symptom of special animosity against foreigners as such. It arose simply from an act of lawlessness committed by Brigands .... Careful consideration of the case leads to the conclusion that no liability for damages can be predicated on the Chinese Government. In view, however, of the circumstances of their capture as well as the suffering and indignities sustained by them in consequence ... the Chinese Government desires of their own accord, to do, in the fullest measure possible, what is equitable in the way of reparation for the foreign victims .... For this purpose they are ready to accept as the basis of classification and assessment the three categories of damages A., B., and C. outlined in your Excellency's Note under reply. The reason for the progressive increase in the amount of compensation from week to week for captives during the period of captivity, however, does not seem clear, since the delay in their release was due to the adoption of negotiation with the bandits as the safest means of effecting their release, a course which was followed in harmony with the express wishes of the Diplomatic Body .... As regards ... "supplementary indemnities" for individual cases, they appear to be in the nature of indirect remote or consequential damages and the Chinese Government does not feel themselves in the position to include them in the basis of assessment for the compensation ....[72]

Secondly, in regard to guarantees for the future, Dr. Koo rejected the demand of the diplomatic corps for international control of Chinese railways and reiterated China's determination to rely upon her own measures and plans for railway reforms in order to prevent foreign Powers from further infringing upon China's domestic affairs:

> ... the territory covered by the Peking-Hankow, Lung-Hai, Peking-Mukden, and Tientsin-P'uk'ou railways is now divided into four principal districts, in each of which troops are stationed at strategic points along the railway .... In addition, the Ministry of Communications has undertaken to reorganize the special

[71]Koo, *Reminiscences*, III. Service in China, G. Questions Arising in My Terms of Office as Foreign Minister, 1922-1928, 5.

[72]Note of V. K. Wellington Koo to the Portuguese Minister J. B. de Freitas (dean) on the Rejection of Their Note on Measures Concerning Damages, Guarantees, and Sanction on Linch'eng Case, September 24, 1923. *Wai-chiao kung-pao*, No. 29, November 1923, Political Affairs, pp. 1-2. The Responding Note on Linch'eng Case Issued by the Cabinet Acting for the President. *Hua-kuo yüeh-k'an* (Hua-kuo Monthly), September 1923, No. 3, pp. 11-14.

railway police which has heretofore been established for each Government railway to maintain order on the train, as well as at the stations; and in order to avail itself of the experience of other countries in this field of railway management it has decided to engage such foreign expert assistance as, in their opinion, may be necessary or desirable . . . .

. . . the Chinese Government looks upon the whole matter of railway policing and protection as an urgent problem of China's internal administration. The Chinese Government, however, appreciates the interest which the Diplomatic Body takes in this problem and its readiness to collaborate; and while they do not feel free, in loyalty to their duty, to commit themselves to any scheme which the Diplomatic Body may desire to present . . . .[73]

Thirdly, in regard to sanctions against officials responsible for the case, Dr. Koo was in a strong position to safeguard China's judicial integrity as a result of the Government's farsightedness with the action it had already taken against the officials responsible for the Linch'eng Case:

The gravity of the incident undoubtedly calls for the most condign punishment upon all those responsible for it. If the Chinese Government does not see their way to accede to the request of the Diplomatic Body, it is only because they feel bound by the existing treaties under which the matter of the punishment of Chinese officials, as well as of Chinese citizens in general, are to be dealt with by China in accordance with Chinese law.

. . . in fact, sincerely desirous of setting a deterring example to the future and stimulating greater vigilance henceforth on the part of all provincial authorities, they have promptly punished or are already considering for punishment those to whom responsibility could be justly attributed for the incident. By a Presidential Mandate of May 9th, 1923, three days after the attack by the bandits, the Ministry of the Interior and the Ministry of War were ordered to consider the punishment for the Military Governor of Shantung, T'ien Chung-yü; while the other civil and military officials were forthwith removed from office, pending investigation and further punishment. By a Mandate of June 26th, 1923, Ho Feng-yü, Defense Commissioner at Yen-chou-fu and Commander of the 6th Mixed Brigade of Shantung, were dismissed from duties and ordered to await further investigation and punishment. General Chang Wen-t'ung, Commander of the Tientsin-P'uk'ou railway police, and Chao Te-chao, the officer in command of the guard on the train which was attacked on May 6th, were summarily dismissed from their duties by the Ministry of Communications.[74]

KOO'S ACCEPTANCE OF THE DEMANDS

At the September 29 meeting among the British, French, Japanese, and American Ministers in Peking to consider a reply to the Chinese note of

[73] *Hua-kuo yüeh-k'an*, September 1923, No. 3, pp. 12-13.
[74] *Ibid.*, pp. 13-14.

September 24, Minister Schurman suggested that in view of the unwarranted nature of the acts, the reply should be sent within a few days, and that in its reply the diplomatic corps should merely state that it found in the note of September 24 no reason for changing the demands presented in the diplomatic corps' note of August 10. The French Minister revised the reply. Not only did he renew the earlier demands, but he added a few words to refute Koo's contention that the outrage at Linch'eng was not aimed at foreigners and to point out Koo's evasion of the fact that this affair was merely an incident. The diplomatic body accepted the revised document at the second meeting on October 1.[75]

As soon as Koo learned of these stiff terms he instructed Dr. Alfred Sze, Minister of China to Washington, to request a meeting on October 2 with Secretary of State Hughes and ask him to approve the Chinese Government's reply. The next day, Minister Sze gave the Department of State a copy of a telegram from Koo, dated October 3, which stated that "sheer insistence on original demands without given reason would create the impression that the Diplomatic Corps wish to impose its will on China as law in a matter which is clearly subject to negotiation."[76] However, Portuguese Minister de Freitas personally delivered the answer of the diplomatic body to Dr. Koo at the Ministry of Foreign Affairs on October 4 before the American Minister received any response from Washington.[77]

The unified position of the diplomatic corps addressed several issues. In the first place, the message of October 4 reasserted the existence of a situation, not a movement, resulting from the development of brigandage in China and threatening the life, liberty, rights, and property of foreigners residing in China. The diplomats observed that the Linch'eng example had been copied recently by the Hupei brigands who had murdered their hostage, Father Melotto, and Honan bandits who had carried off two foreign women missionaries. The diplomatic body deemed Chinese measures against bandits, outlined in Koo's note of September 24, ineffective because the local authorities, who employed their best forces in the civil wars, did not manifest any zeal in the repression of brigandage. In conclusion, the Note candidly informed Koo that the diplomatic representatives found "themselves compelled to maintain in their entirety the consideration and conclusion of their

[75]The Minister in China (Schurman) to the Secretary of State, Peking, October 2, 3, and 5, 1923. *Foreign Relations of the United States, 1923*, I:701-5.

[76]The Secretary of State to the Minister in China (Schurman), Washington, October 4, 1923, 1:00 p.m., and October 4, 1923, 2:00 p.m. *Foreign Relations of the United States, 1923*, I:702-3.

[77]*Tung-fang tsa-chih*, XX:21 (November 1923), p. 2.

collective Note of August 10."[78]

As soon as Koo received the second Note from the diplomatic body, he delivered it to the State Council. Assuming that the Congress would elect Marshal Ts'ao President the next day, the Council decided that the case should be postponed until Marshal Ts'ao was sworn in; nevertheless, the group recommended that Marshal Ts'ao remove Military Governor T'ien from office in order to placate the diplomatic body.[79]

On October 4, 1923, the Peking Government issued a mandate to extend the terms of members of Parliament as one condition for their cooperation,[80] and the next day Ts'ao K'un was elected President by 480 votes which had been purchased at the rate of 5,000 silver dollars per vote.[81] The diplomatic corps intimated by unanimous agreement that they would not attend Ts'ao K'un's inauguration, an act which implied nonrecognition of the new President by the Powers. Furthermore, both Sun Yat-sen and Marshal Chang Tso-lin, the Manchurian warlord, telegraphed de Freitas that the nation opposed Ts'ao K'un because he was illiterate, had looted Peking in 1912, and bore responsibility for the illegal and corrupt election. They requested the foreign Powers and their representatives in Peking "to avoid any act which could be construed by new Peking usurper as an intimation or assurance of international recognition and support."[82]

Minister Schurman's plan to use the presidential crisis to secure compliance with the Linch'eng demands was so successful that the Tientsin-Paoting faction of the Chihli Clique sent emissaries to the dean and to the heads of missions to learn on what conditions the Linch'eng affair could be settled. After several conferences with de Freitas lasting from October 12 to 14, Dr. Koo was finally apprised of the terms which the diplomatic corps desired as the price for attending the diplomatic reception.[83]

Because Chinese public opinion believed Koo had yielded to the foreigners' Linch'eng demands as a mere "social courtesy," Dr. Koo refused to state in writing that the Chinese Government would receive and consider the diplomatic body's railway police scheme. After the dean threatened to terminate negotiations, a tacit agreement was reached: Koo would inform the Cabinet

[78]Note of de Freitas to Foreign Minister Koo, October 4, 1923. *Wai-chiao kung-pao*, No. 29, November 1923; Political Affairs, pp. 23-24.

[79]*Tung-fang tsa-chih*, XX:21 (November 1923), p. 2.

[80]*The North China Herald*, October 6, 1923.

[81]Ts'en Hsüeh-lü, *San-shui Liang Yen-sun hsien-sheng nien-p'u*, I:265-71.

[82]The Minister to China (Schurman) to the Secretary of State, Peking, October 12, 1923. *Foreign Relations of the United States, 1923*, I:519-20; *The North China Herald*, October 13 and 20, 1923.

[83]The Minister to China (Schurman) to the Secretary of State, Peking, October 12, 1923. *Foreign Relations of the United States, 1923*, I:705-6.

and President that the dean's acceptance of the terms of Koo's note was conditional upon the understanding that the Chinese Government without pledging itself to acceptance would receive and consider such plans for railway police as the diplomatic body might present—in other words:

> The Chinese Government was given time to submit to the diplomatic body a scheme of their own which is to be framed with the diplomatic body's scheme confidently before them. (And only then the diplomatic body would examine it and the Chinese Government would put it into effect.)[84]

In order to save face for the Chinese Government and at the same time secure their ends, the British, French, and American Ministers accepted the dean's proposal.

On October 14, the draft note from the Chinese Foreign Ministry containing assurances in regard to the other demands of the Linch'eng Note from the diplomatic corps was circulated among the heads of the missions in Peking. The draft was to be dated October 15, the day of the President's diplomatic reception, and was to be placed in the hands of the dean of the diplomatic corps in the evening of October 14. The British, French, and American Ministers considered the document to be satisfactory. The note accepted the three categories of indemnities, (A), (B), and (C) and the supplementary indemnities in principle. It further stated that the Ministry of War, which had been instructed to determine the punishment to be inflicted upon Military Governor T'ien, had decided to relieve him of his post, and an order would be issued to that effect. In regard to the proposal of collaboration in the preparation of the railway police scheme, the diplomatic corps received assurances by "oral understanding between the dean and the Minister of Foreign Affairs supplementing the vaguer language of the note"[85] as described above. Nevertheless, the Ministers in Peking postponed their departure for the Presidential Palace until the Note from the Chinese Government had been handed to de Freitas.[86] The President's diplomatic reception, held at 11:00 a.m. on October 15 in the Huai-jen t'ang Hall of his palace, found the Ministers, including Japanese Minister Yoshizawa in attendance. Dr. Koo introduced them to President Ts'ao K'un.[87]

The Chinese version, however, differs from the English text:

[84] *Ibid.*, October 20, 1923, I:708-9.

[85] *Ibid.*, October 14, 1923, I:521-22.

[86] *The Far Eastern Times*, Peking, October 16, 1923; The American Consul General (Stuart J. Fuller) to the Secretary of State, American Consulate General, Tientsin, October 17, 1923. *Internal Affairs of China, 1910-1929*, Reel No. 35, 893.00/5279.

[87] *North China Star*, Tientsin, October 16, 1923, *Internal Affairs of China, 1910-1929*; *The North China Herald*, October 15, 1923.

1. As regards the supplementary indemnities, this Foreign Minister may declare that this Government will also agree in principle and consider it an additional basis for calculation. Nevertheless, the nature as well as the appropriate amount of such indemnities will be left for further discussion.
2. The Ministry of War which was instructed to determine the punishment to be inflicted upon Military Governor T'ien Chung-yü has already submitted its report to this Government. Based upon this recommendation, this Government on October 14 requested and received a Presidential Mandate approving this resignation [not deciding upon relieving him of his post].
3. This Foreign Minister specially states that his Government is in a difficult position [not "the Chinese Government cannot commit themselves," as read in the English text] to accept the various schemes designed by the Diplomatic Corps for improving railway protection, nevertheless, is profoundly grateful for their concern and assistance over the problem of railway police. This Government is firmly convinced that the vigorous plans concerning bandit-pacification and the measures for railway protection adopted recently will certainly . . . improve the situation as regards the safety of travel and residence in the interior of China.[88]

Military Governor T'ien Chung-yü was eventually removed, and his simultaneous promotion to a marshalcy was canceled when both dean de Freitas and Dr. Koo threatened to resign. These maneuvers were skillfully arranged, and they were supported by the Chinese *Government Gazette* which explained that the "sequence of two mandates had been inverted through error" and T'ien's appointment was to be taken as preceding his dismissal from the post of Military Governor so that his promotion should be considered nugatory.[89] The Chinese Government eventually paid $351,567.92 to foreigners in full payment of the Linch'eng (A) and (B) claims. No record of payment of Linch'eng (C) claims or the supplementary claims has been found. The Chinese Government submitted its own scheme based on the diplomatic body's plan for railway police for approval. In short, Dr. Koo, who represented China,

[88] *Tung-fang tsa-chih*, XX:21 (November 1923), p. 2; Koo to Chu Pao-chin, December 23, 1968. Koo recalled that "As regards the proposal of collaboration in the preparation of a scheme for an effective railway police, I remember I made it very clear to the diplomatic corps I could not accept anything as a demand for participation. It was a matter pertaining to China's domestic competence. But I told them the Government would, in its earnest desire to improve the protection of the railways, naturally be disposed to receive any suggestion from any quarter—Chinese or foreign—without any implication of a right to intervene. Actually, if I remember correctly, the final scheme was adopted and promulgated without consulting the diplomatic corps at all. It might or might not have adopted any suggestion embodied in the diplomatic corps' proposal. Even if it did, it did not imply any acceptance of foreign intervention but simply proved that the Government was sincere and earnest in wishing to improve the system of protection for the railways."

[89] *The North China Herald*, October 18, 1923.

accepted the demands of the Powers in the Linch'eng case in principle.[90] On October 27, Chinese authorities appointed General T'ang Tsai-li Director General (Tupan) of the Railway Protective Bureau.[91] Nevertheless, the noted German General Munthe declined an offer to be Co-Director General since his ambitious proposal for 22,000 railway guards with an annual budget of around 2,000,000 silver dollars was drastically reduced by the Chinese Government.[92]

DISCUSSION

When Dr. Koo accepted the office of Foreign Minister of the Peking Government under the control of the Chihli Clique, he sent a circular telegram throughout the country on July 23, 1923, that stated he was "taking office because the majority of the members of the Parliament had urged him to do so, and because he deemed it his duty to undertake upholding China's international position."[93] The *North China Daily News* interpreted this statement to mean that to the Chinese politicians:

> Dr. Koo's assumption of office is not half so significant as the pains he took, before going to the Ministry of Foreign Affairs, to disassociate himself from his colleagues, to let the world know that politics were not his and to make it plain that he was not coming in to please Ts'ao K'un or the Tientsin Clique, but because in his opinion no matter how bad conditions in China might be there ought to be someone in the Foreign Office to tell the Powers from day to day that they are not so bad as they look.[94]

Perhaps, his attitude can be better described by his own words to Chinese journalists on July 23 in Peking. "Despite the fact that there has been no actual materialization regarding international control of China's railways, [and no] cancellation of the resolution of the Washington Conference . . . the international standing of China has been [badly] effected already," said Dr. Koo, and he expressed the hope that his assumption of office "would help clear up the false impression which has been current that China is in a

[90]The Minister in China (Schurman) to the Secretary of State, Peking, February 23, 1923. *Foreign Relations of the United States, 1923*, I:709.

[91]*The North China Herald*, October 26, 1923.

[92]*Tung-fang tsa-chih*, XX:16 (August 1923), pp. 5-6.

[93]*Peking and Tientsin Times*, Tientsin, July 24, 1923; American Consul in Charge (J. C. Huston) to the Secretary of State, American Consulate General, Tientsin, July 25, 1923. *Internal Affairs of China, 1910-1929*, Reel No. 34, 893.00/5146.

[94]*North China Daily News*, Peking, July 25, 1923; American Consul General (Edwin Cunningham) to the Secretary of State, American Consulate General, Shanghai, China, August 3, 1923. *Internal Affairs of China, 1910-1929*, 893.00/5161.

state of not being governed."[95]

Dr. Koo was not discouraged by the invidious experience arising out of the Linch'eng case. His service as Foreign Minister, and later as Acting Prime Minister for President Ts'ao K'un and his Chihli Clique, continued without interruption until the "Capital Revolution" or Coup of Peking of October 23, 1924, when General Lu Chung-lin, under the command of Christian General Feng Yü-hsiang, secretly led his army back to Peking from the Jehol front and took over the capital through collaboration with General Sun Yüeh, Garrison Commander of the Capital.[96]

There was good reason to believe that Dr. Koo felt compelled to bow to pressures from presidential circles. It's possible that Dr. Koo, for all his wisdom and keenness of the traditional bureaucrat, was reluctant to give up his boyhood ambition to remain high in the bureaucratic echelon.[97] It was surely true that because of Koo, a person oriented in Western learning, connected with Anglo-American envoys in Peking, and respected by the foreign communities in China, the Linch'eng case was closed with limited damage to China, at a time when the Government lacked leadership, money, power, and unquestioned legitimacy. It was more significant that the Powers did not use the Linch'eng case as a pretext to launch allied operations in China as they had in 1900. Dr. Koo's activities may not have recovered much of the estate for the "sick man of Asia," but he had limited the losses of Chinese resources.

[95] *Peking and Tientsin Times*, Tientsin, July 24, 1923.

[96] Ch'en Hsi-chang, *Pei-yang ts'ang-sang shih-hua*, pp. 387-90, 399-410, 414-17; *Chung-kuo wai-chiao chi-kuan li-jen shou-chang hsien-ming nien-piao*, pp. 55-56.

[97] Koo Hui-lan, *Autobiography*, p. 150.

CHAPTER V

Koo, Chengting T. Wang, and the Restoration of Sino-Soviet Relations, 1923-1924

SINO-RUSSIAN RELATIONS—OUTER MONGOLIA AND CHINESE EASTERN RAILWAY

China's disastrous defeat at the hands of Japan in 1894 ended the relatively cordial relationship which had existed between China and Russia since the Treaty of Nerchinsk in 1689.[1] As China's fortunes declined in general, the problems of Outer Mongolia and the Chinese Eastern Railway assumed serious proportions in Sino-Russian relations.

Perhaps nothing could have alienated the Mongols from the Manchu Court more than its colonial policies. After news of the Chinese Revolution of October 10, 1911 reached Urga, Russian and Mongolian troops disarmed the few Chinese forces in Urga on November 19, and the Imperial Agent, San To, was escorted to Kiakhta a few days later. The living Buddha and new Emperor of the Great Mongolian Empire, Cheptsun Damba Hut'ukht'u, declared independence of China at Urga on November 18 and established his regime with the pro-Russian Prince Handa Dorji as Foreign Minister.[2] On October 21, 1912 the Mongolian Government, won over by a Russian Loan of 2,000,000 rubles, signed the Russo-Mongolian Treaty with Korostovets, former Russian minister to Peking. In exchange for Russia's pledge of support for the autonomous regime against Chinese troops, the Mongolian Government granted Russian subjects rights and privileges to engage in all enterprises at any time, at any place, without payment of any duty or tax, including the exclusive rights over mining, railway, postal and telegraphic systems.[3] The Mongolian Government secured its position further when China accepted the Russian-drafted Declaration of November 5, 1913, which included Russia's recognition of China's suzerainty over Mongolia, China's recognition of Mongolian

[1] *Chung-wai t'iao-yüeh hui-pien* (Treaties between China and Foreign States, 1687-1932), pp. 323-51.

[2] Ch'en Lu, *Chih-shih pi-chi* (Notes of Ch'en Lu), pp. 182-87.

[3] Wang Kuang-ch'i, *K'u-lun t'iao-yüeh chih shih-mo* (The Complete Story of the Russo-Mongolian Treaty at K'u-lun, 1912), pp. 18-80. Originally published in German under the title *Von Cinggis Khan zur Sowjetre-publik* (From Chinggis Khan to Soviet Republic), by Korostovets.

autonomy, and China's commitment not to keep any civil or military officials there and not to allow colonization.[4] In the Tripartite Agreement among China, Outer Mongolia and Russia, signed June 7, 1915, Outer Mongolia accepted the Sino-Russian Declaration with the understanding that the Chinese Resident General at Urga, his deputies at Uliasutai and Kobdo, and the Russian Consuls would enjoy the protection of a small number of military escorts.[5]

Taking advantage of the Russian Revolution of 1917, General Hsü Shu-cheng, Commissioner of the Northwestern Frontier, made the Outer Mongolian Government formally abolish its autonomy on November 22, 1919 and abrogate the Tripartite Agreement on Outer Mongolia of 1915. When Hsü's Frontier Defense Army was wiped out by Marshal Wu P'ei-fu during the Chihli-Anhwei War in July 1920, Outer Mongolia restored its independence on February 3, 1921 in collaboration with White Russian forces under Baron von Ungern-Sternberg.[6]

Another thorny problem between China and Russia was the Chinese Eastern Railway, the product of China's foreign policy of alliance with Russia against Japan after the Sino-Japanese War in 1894-95. When Grand Secretary Li Hung-chang was sent to St. Petersburg as Special Envoy for the Coronation of Tsar Nicholas II, Count Sergei Witte, the Tsar's Minister of Finance, impressed upon Li that in order to support the territorial integrity of the Chinese Empire, Russia needed a railway across the shortest possible route (via Chinese Manchuria) to Vladivostok.[7] Li's Sino-Russian Treaty of Alliance, signed on June 3, 1896, opened diplomatic doors for the Contract for the Construction and Operation of the Chinese Eastern Railway in September 1896 and the Sino-Russian Agreement regarding the Russo-Chinese Bank in August 1896, concluding details for the construction of the railway.[8]

The Russian Government acquired 700 shares out of the 1,000 issued by the company. The remaining 300 shares were transferred on May 18, 1896, to the Russian Government by an agreement between the Russian Government and the Russo-Chinese Bank.[9] Dissatisfied with investment alone, Russia also

[4]Pi Kuei-fang, *Wai-Meng chiao-she shih-mo chi* (The Complete Story of Negotiations on Outer Mongolia), pp. 20-22.

[5]John V. A. MacMurray, *Treaties and Agreements with and Concerning China, 1894-1919*, II:1066-67.

[6]Ch'en Ch'ung-tsu, *Wai-Meng chin-shih shih* (Modern History of Outer Mongolia), pp. 64-83.

[7]Sergei Witte, *The Memoirs of Count Witte*, translated by A. Yarmolinsky, p. 89.

[8]*Ch'ing-mo tui-wai chiao-she t'iao-yüeh chi, Kuang-hsü t'iao-yüeh* (Treaties between China and Foreign States in the Latter Part of the Ch'ing Dynasty, Kuang-hsü's Reign), II:360-68.

[9]Hsü Ching-ch'eng, *Hsü Wen-su-kung i-shu* (Papers of the Late Hsü Ching-ch'eng), II, 13a-17b.

seized judicial, police, and tax powers, mines, and other rights within the railway zone.

During World War I, the revolutionary turmoil between Horwath, the White Russian Associate Director of the railways, and Rutin, the Red leader at Harbin, offered an opportunity for the local Chinese garrison to return to the railway zone. When the workers of the line went on strike on March 11, 1920, the third anniversary of the Russian Revolution, Pao Kuei-ch'ing, Military Governor of Heilungkiang and Director of the Chinese Eastern Railway, discharged Horwath and recovered control of both the administration and the police of the line.[10]

In view of the situation in the Chinese Eastern Railway Zone, the White All-Russia Government at Omsk, and the Allied intervention in Siberia, the Soviet Government considered China to be the "most reliable rear base for world revolution."[11] Consequently, on June 25, 1919, the Soviet Government, in the name of Leo Mikhailovich Karakhan, acting People's Commissariat of Foreign Affairs of the Far Eastern Republic in Irkutsk, dispatched its First Declaration to the Chinese people and the Governments at Peking and Canton inviting the two groups to start negotiations immediately concerning abolition of all the unequal treaties and agreements between China and Russia:

> In short, all and everything, either plundered by Tsarist Government alone or in collaboration with Japan and other Allied Powers, would be returned to the Chinese people. . . . The Soviet Government is willing to return to China, without demanding any kind of compensation, the Chinese Eastern Railway. . . . The Soviet Government abandons the indemnity of Boxers Uprising in 1900. . . . In case they (Russians) commit any crimes they should be subject to the Chinese law and local jurisdiction.[12]

Following the arrival of M. L. Yurin in China as Representative of the Far Eastern Republic, the Foreign Minister of the Peking Government, W. W. Yen informed Imperial Russian minister Prince Koudachev on August 1 that the Chinese Government no longer considered him to be the legal recipient of the Russian share of the Boxer Indemnity; later, on September 23, 1920, the Chinese president issued a mandate to the effect that Minister Koudachev was no longer the recognized representative of his country.[13] Meanwhile, the Peking Government moved to control the Russian concession in Hankow and

[10] Liu Yen, *Chung-kuo wai-chiao shih* (Diplomatic History of China), supplemented by Li Fang-ch'en, p. 761.

[11] Stalin, "Do Not Forget the East," *Soviet Russia and the East, 1920-1927*, edited by Xenia Joukoff Eudin and Robert C. North, p. 156.

[12] *Chung O hui-i ts'an-k'ao wen-chien* (Documents for Reference on Sino-Russian Conference), II; *Chung O wen-t'i lai-wang wen-chien* (Documents and Notes Exchanged between China and Russia on the Sino-Russian Problems), pp. 1a-3a.

[13] *China Year Book, 1921-1922*, pp. 626-27.

nineteen Russian consulates in China proper and Urga in order to prepare the way for Sino-Soviet negotiations.[14] Furthermore, the Chinese Ministry of Communications signed the Supplementary Contract for the Management of the Chinese Eastern Railway on October 2, 1920 with the Peking and Shanghai branches of the Russo-Chinese Bank. Under this agreement, the Ministry would execute all management and operational functions and assume all privileges concerning the line on behalf of the Russian government until a settlement was reached between China and a Russian Government duly recognized by China.[15]

As White resistance in Siberia began to collapse, Karakhan dispatched to the Chinese Ministry of Foreign Affairs, on September 27, 1920 his Second Declaration of eight principles, a document which manifested a much stiffened tone. It deviated from the first in that the returned fund for Boxer Indemnity could only be used for education and the Soviet use of the Chinese Eastern Railway was taken for granted and subject only to negotiations between the Chinese Government and the Soviet Government. Both declarations ignored the problem of Outer Mongolia.[16]

Responding to the request for negotiations by Krassin, Soviet representative in London, the Ministry of Foreign Affairs telegraphed instructions to Dr. Koo, then Chinese Minister to London, to present to Krassin another set of conditions for opening any negotiations:

1. The Soviet delegates for negotiation were to be informal representatives for commercial affairs, not inheriting the title and function of the former Russian minister.

2. The Soviet delegation would refrain from making (Communist) propaganda or carrying with them propaganda papers.

3. Chinese merchants in Russia would be exempted from all forced services, and their goods would not be subject to any confiscation, and no force or limitations would be laid on Chinese workers.

4. All damages suffered by Chinese residing in Russia would be compensated by the Soviet Government according to the results of investigation jointly conducted by China and Soviet Russia.[17]

With the establishment of the Chinese Communist Party in Shanghai on July 1, 1921, as a result of the activities of Grigorii Naumovich Voitinsky,

[14] *The North China Herald*, October 2, 1920.

[15] *Chung O hui-i ts'an-k'ao wen-chien*, III; *Chung O lin-shih hsieh-ting* (Sino-Russian Provisional Agreements), pp. 3a–4b.

[16] *Chung O hui-i ts'an-k'ao wen-chien*, II; *Chung O wen-t'i lai-wang wen-chien*, pp. 4a–5b.

[17] Ministry of Foreign Affairs to Minister Koo in London (February 14, 1921), *Chung O wen-t'i lai-wang wen-chien*, p. 13a–b.

member of Yurin's mission, and the garrisoning of Soviet troops in Outer Mongolia after the defeat of Baron von Ungern-Sternberg, despite the objections of the Peking Government, the Sino-Soviet negotiations ground to a halt.[18] The brief mission of the first Soviet official representative, A. K. Paikes, in China in early 1922 did not change the situation in any apparent way.[19]

In North China the Chihli Clique forces defeated the Japanese-trained and Japanese-equipped Ting-kuo Army of the An-fu Clique and the Fengtien (Manchurian) Army on April 28 and June 18 of 1922 respectively. With the pro-Japanese An-fu Clique and the anti-Russian Fengtien Clique off the scene, the general situation became more conducive to a renewed rapprochement between the Peking Government under the domination of the Chihli Clique and the Soviet Government.[20]

The arrival of the veteran Soviet diplomat Adolf Abramovich Joffe in Peking on August 12, 1922 and the consolidation of the Russian diplomatic missions in China after the incorporation of the Far Eastern Republic into the Soviet Union only produced more exchanges of protests by both sides. Finally Joffe decided that without settlement of the key issues between China and Russia, the Chinese Government would not consider recognition of the Soviet state or begin negotiations. He left Peking for Shanghai for "medical treatment." The Peking Government did not appoint Dr. Chengting T. Wang Chinese plenipotentiary for Sino-Soviet negotiations until March 27, 1923 after the famous Sun-Joffe Declaration delineated cooperation between the Kuomintang and the Chinese Communist Party.[21]

WANG-KARAKHAN PRELIMINARY AGREEMENTS

As soon as C. T. Wang had been appointed Director General of Sino-Soviet Affairs by Premier Chang Shao-tseng on March 26, 1923[22] he began to organize his staff and to generate support for his policies among the powerful warlords in various provinces. After his *Ch'ou-pan Chung O chiao-she shih-i kung-shu chan-hsing chang-ch'eng* (Provisional Regulations on the Administration of Sino-Russian Negotiations) had been approved by the

[18] Georgii Vasilevich Chicherin, People's Commissar of Foreign Affairs to Minister of Foreign Affairs (June 14, 1921); Minister of Foreign Affairs to Minister Koo (June 30, 1921), *Chung O wen-t'i lai-wang wen-chien*, pp. 14a-16a.

[19] Soviet Representative to Ministry of Foreign Affairs (March 29, 1922); Ministry of Foreign Affairs to Soviet Representative (April 15, 1922), *Chung O wen-t'i lai-wang wen-chien*, pp. 23a-25a, 33a-34a.

[20] *Wu P'ei-fu chuan*, pp. 66-77.

[21] *Tung-fang tsa-chih*, XX:2 (January 1923), p. 10.

[22] *Cheng-fu kung-pao*, CVIII, No. 2529.

cabinet,[23] Wang declared on May 8 that his administration had started to function.[24] However, he lost no time in strengthening his support by visiting Marshal Ts'ao K'un at Paoting, Marshal Wu P'ei-fu at Loyang, General Ch'i Hsieh-yüan at Nanking, and Marshal Chang Tso-lin at Mukden under the banner of "diplomacy above political dispute."[25] The pledge of March 26 by Marshal Wu, the strong man of the Chihli Clique, greatly enhanced Wang's hand within the Chihli-controlled Peking Government.[26] Wang improved his political position further with his visit to Mukden and his extensive trips in late April to Harbin, Kirin, Hei-ho, Changchun, and Manchouli to investigate present conditions of the Chinese Eastern Railway, maltreatment of the Chinese residents in Soviet Russia, and navigation on the Sungari River, in the company of General Yang Yü-t'ing, General Chief of Staff of Marshal Chang Tso-lin.[27] Later Lu Yung-hua (Lü Jung-huan), who represented Marshal Chang, arrived in Peking on September 17 accompanied by a number of experts on Sino-Soviet relations from Manchuria to participate in the negotiations.[28]

In the company of General Uborevitch, Commander-in-Chief of the Soviet Far Eastern Forces, M. Mileff, Chief of the Railway Department of the Chita Administration, and M. Matowenovy, Vice-Chairman of the Far Eastern Revolutionary Committee, Karakhan arrived in Mukden in late August 1923 when Peking pulsed in the turmoil of a presidential election.[29] After a lengthy discussion with Marshal Chang, who had released from jail all those who had been arrested for membership in Communist trade unions in Manchuria, Karakhan, accompanied by M. Davtian, entered Peking on September 2[30] to be greeted by a crowd of more than a thousand, including public officials. As the author of the two Soviet declarations of 1919 and 1920, Karakhan had gained the confidence of Chinese students and intellectuals. On the day after his arrival, he issued the Third Declaration on behalf of the Soviet Government. This document stated that based on the spirit of the former declarations, the Soviet Government would assist China to the best of its ability.[31]

[23] V. K. Wellington Koo, *Reminiscences of Wellington Koo*, III. Service in China, G. Questions Arising in My Terms of Office as Foreign Minister, 1923-1928, 6. Negotiations with Soviet Russia, 1922-1924, a & b.

[24] *Cheng-fu kung-pao*, CIX, Nos. 2543 & 2571.

[25] *Tung-fang tsa-chih*, XXI:13 (July 1924), p. 39.

[26] *Wu P'ei-fu hsien-sheng nien-p'u*, p. 26.

[27] American Vice Consul (Taylor) at Mukden to the Secretary of State (May 3, 1923). *Internal Affairs of China, 1910-1929*, Reel No. 33, 893.00/5013.

[28] *The North China Herald*, September 22, 1923, p. 819.

[29] American Consul (G. C. Hanson) at Harbin to the Secretary of State (September 14, 1923). *Internal Affairs of China, 1910-1929*, Reel No. 34, 893.00/5224.

[30] *Ibid.*, 893.00/4225.

[31] *Tung-fang tsa-chih*, XXI:8 (April 1924), pp. 129-32.

Foreign Minister Koo and C. T. Wang officially received him on September 4. The Koos had arrived in Peking from London via Suez on May 23, after stopping at Singapore to visit Madame Koo's family and at Shanghai to visit Koo's family.[32] On September 15 at a banquet given by Shao P'iao-p'ing, editor of *Ching Pao* (Peking Daily), Karakhan clarified his position on several issues by asserting that the Chinese Eastern Railway was a concern of the Soviet Union and China to the exclusion of any third party. He acknowledged that Outer Mongolia formed a part of Chinese territory and that China's recognition of the Soviet Government should precede Sino-Soviet negotiations.

As for Wang's principles, he detailed them to Marshal Chang Tso-lin on his visit. They included statements that the White Russians should be repressed, that Red Russia should be recognized, and that a commercial agreement should be established with Red Russia.[33] Wang preferred to follow, in regard to the Chinese Eastern Railway, the pattern of the Sino-Japanese settlement over the Tsinan-Tsingtao line, i.e., to purchase from Russia the railway and all properties attached to it and put them under Chinese authority. According to his estimates, the annual income of the railway was around forty million silver dollars, and expenditures for purposes other than the maintenance of the railway, which included costs of Russian schools, churches, and cemeteries, were more than twenty million. With the elimination of all these irregular expenditures, the capital balance on the railway could be paid within twenty years.[34]

Wang's program for Sino-Soviet negotiations of the Manchurian questions included recovery of land attached to the Chinese Eastern Railway; restoration of the Land Office of the Chinese Eastern Railway; Sino-Russian navigation on the Sungari and Amur rivers; compensation for the massacre of Chinese citizens by Russians at Chita, Amur, Khabarovsk, and Manchouli; cessation of Russian intrusions from Chita into Chinese territories; reimbursement by Russian authorities for the costs borne by the Chinese Government for the care of White Russian refugees; compensation for losses resulting from Russian paper rubles and Sino-Russian commerce. Wang's program for discussion with Russia about Manchuria paralleled the program of Marshal Chang Tso-lin of Manchuria.[35]

However, aside from the most significant questions, Sino-Soviet negotiations moved slowly for several reasons: (1) the diplomatic corps in Peking opposed China's acceptance of Soviet credentials, (2) the Cabinet refused

[32] Koo Hui-lan, *No Feast Lasts Forever*, pp. 144-49, 150-56.

[33] *Tung-fang tsa-chih*, XX:19 (October 1923), p. 4.

[34] *Ibid.*, XX:12 (June 1923), p. 11.

[35] *Ibid.*, XX:19 (October 1923), p. 4.

Karakhan's demand of recognition preceding negotiation,[36] and (3) Karakhan's underhanded dealings with Japan seemed to indicate a lack of integrity on his part. The preliminary meeting on September 18 between Wang and Karakhan ground to a halt over the dispute which had started during Joffe's service in China whether recognition should precede the negotiations. Consequently, the formal meeting scheduled for September 24 did not take place because Wang was "sick" and hospitalized.[37] Sun Yat-sen's silence, Marshal Wu P'ei-fu's strong support, and Marshal Chang Tao-lin's active participation strengthened Wang's ability to confound Karakhan's strategy of "separate dealings" with various warlords. In order to vitiate Karakhan's strategy of using Japan against China, Wang traveled to Japan on November 26 to investigate alleged "injuries to Chinese during the earthquake."[38] Karakhan did not hesitate to retaliate by stating two days later:

> Never and nowhere could I have said that all the rights on the Chinese Eastern Railway belong to China. . . . On the assumption that rights of property on the railway as a commercial enterprise belong to the Soviet Union, I am willing to discuss at the Conference any proposition of yours. . . .[39]

Koo's Ministry of Foreign Affairs quieted the suspicions of the diplomatic corps by repeated statements that "Sino-Russian relations remained of a *de facto* character. M. Karakhan had come in place of M. Joffe. His reception did not involve *de jure* recognition."[40] Dr. Koo, who retained his position as Foreign Minister under warlord President Ts'ao K'un after the latter's notorious election on October 10, 1923, did not forget to reassure the conservative Chinese factions; he sent them a telegram on November 6 warning the provinces against "the possible activities by a group of Chinese who had just returned from Moscow and were spreading the principles of Bolshevism."[41] The Chinese Government became dissatisfied at the lack of progress, and the negotiations collapsed as the year ended after Karakhan had reiterated on December 25 his principle that the previous Soviet declarations did not carry any article pledging the return of the Chinese Eastern Railway to China.[42] On December 15, the Rosta News Agency revealed a private interview with Dansan Bagatad, Chairman of the Central Committee of the People's Revolutionary Party in Mongolia, that reported ". . . the small Russian unit, stationed at Urga, is leading a most peaceful life. . . . They don't interfere in the least with the

[36] *Hua-kuo yüeh-k'an*, No. 3 (September 16, 1923), p. 9.
[37] *Tung-fang tsa-chih*, XX:20 (October 1923), p. 4.
[38] *China Year Book, 1924*, p. 876.
[39] *The North China Herald*, November 24, 1923, p. 529; December 8, 1923, p. 661.
[40] *Ibid.*, September 22, 1923, p. 824.
[41] *Ibid.*, November 10, 1923, p. 376.
[42] *Tung-fang tsa-chih*, XX:24 (December 1923), p. 122.

internal life of the Mongolian people. . . ."[43] Dr. Koo sent another note to Karakhan on January 3, 1924 requesting Soviet withdrawal of its Red Amy from Mongolia and Mongolia's restoration to China.[44]

The international scene suddenly changed in February 1924 when two great Powers in Europe, England and Italy, accorded the Soviet Government recognition, an act which made the Soviet insistence on China's recognition before negotiations unnecessary.[45] More than forty professors of the prestigious National Peking University, as well as many congressmen and other public officials, urged Foreign Minister Koo and Director General Wang to follow the British and accord recognition before negotiation.[46] Furthermore, the activities of M. M. Borodin, a Soviet "trade representative" in Canton, were so successful that Karakhan declared he was leaving Peking for the South to establish relations with the Kuomintang regime.[47] Consequently Wang rushed back from Shanghai in order to stop Karakhan's trip to the South. From Moscow, following the failure of M. Joffe's negotiations with Japan came reports that Soviet diplomacy was now threatening Japan by forming an alliance with China.[48] Between February 21 and March 1, an extensive exchange of views between the two sides produced a compromise to the effect that China would accept the Soviet request for recognition of the Soviet regime before commencement of the formal meetings. Karakhan and Wang agreed that a preliminary meeting to determine general principles for the settlement of the disputed questions between China and the Soviet Union would take place as soon as China had explicitly stated her intention of recognition.[49]

Finally, on March 3, 1924, Wang submitted his draft agreements and Karakhan's final revised agreements to the President. At the meeting of the State Council on March 6, Wang was present to explain the revised draft agreements of both sides. Wang appeared again on March 13 before the State Council to report on corrections to the draft suggested by Ministers of the Cabinet at the last Council meeting. That same evening Wang secured Karakhan's consent to two corrections suggested by the Cabinet: (1) all previous Sino-Russian treaties should be abolished prior to any new Sino-Soviet agreement, and (2) China's guarantee to prohibit the Whites' activities

[43] American Consul (Samuel Sokobin) at Kalgan to Secretary of State (January 3, 1924). *Internal Affairs of China, 1910-1929*, Reel No. 35, 893.00/5342.

[44] *Tung-fang tsa-chih*, XXI:4 (February 1924), p. 153.

[45] *Ibid.*, XXI:13 (July 1924), p. 39.

[46] *Ibid.*, XXI:13 (July 1924), p. 40.

[47] *The North China Herald*, November 14, 1923, p. 449.

[48] *Ibid.*, September 1, 1923, p. 601.

[49] *Tung-fang tsa-chih*, XXI:7 (April 1924), p. 155.

should be revised so as to be a responsibility of both China and Russia.[50] On March 14, 1924, in order to mark the close of negotiations between the Soviet Representative Karakhan and the Director General of Sino-Russian Affairs Wang, both signed the draft agreements and attached papers, which included the draft Agreement on General Principles for the Settlement of the Questions between the Republic of China and the Union of Soviet Socialist Republics of fifteen articles, the draft Agreement for the Provisional Management of the Chinese Eastern Railway of eleven articles, and seven declarations and notes.[51]

The articles of the draft Wang-Karakhan Agreement on General Principles for the Settlement of the Questions between China and the USSR included the following points:

1. Upon the signing of the Agreement, normal diplomatic and consular relations between China and the USSR would be reestablished, and the Chinese Government would take steps to transfer the former Russian Legation and Consular buildings to the USSR.

2. Within one month after signing the Agreement, a Sino-Russian Conference would be held to carry out detailed arrangements and would be completed within six months.

3. At the Conference both states would annul all conventions, treaties, agreements, and contracts concluded between China and the Tsarist Government and would replace them with new treaties and agreements on the basis of equality, reciprocity, and justice, and the spirit of the three previous Declarations.

4. The USSR declared that all treaties and agreements concluded between the former Tsarist Government and any third party or parties affecting the sovereign rights or interests of China were null and void.

5. The USSR recognized that Outer Mongolia was an integral part of China, and the complete withdrawal of Russian troops would be effected as soon as the conditions for the withdrawal, i.e., the time-limit of the withdrawal and the measures to be adopted in the interests of the safety of the frontiers, were agreed upon at the said Conference.

6. Both pledged themselves not to permit the existence and activity of any group against the other and not to engage in such propaganda.

7. Problems of navigation on the bordering rivers and lakes would be regulated on the basis of equality and reciprocity.

8. The Chinese Eastern Railway was declared a purely commercial enterprise, and all other civil, military, judicial, municipal, tax, and land matters,

[50] *Ibid.*, XXI:9 (May 1924), p. 132.
[51] *Wai-chiao kung-pao*, No. 36, June 1924, Special Documents, pp. 13-22.

with the exception of lands required by the said railway, should be administered by China; the USSR agreed to the redemption of the line by China with Chinese capital, and the future of the line was to be determined by China and the USSR alone.

9. The USSR renounced and relinquished all special rights and privileges to all concessions, the Russian portion of the Boxer Indemnity, the rights of extraterritoriality, and consular jurisdiction.

10. The custom tariff in the Sino-Russian Commercial Treaty would be drawn up in accordance with the principles of equality and reciprocity.

11. At the aforementioned Conference, both agreed to discuss questions relating to the claims for the compensation of Chinese losses during the Russian Revolution.[52]

According to the Agreement for the Provisional Management of the Chinese Eastern Railway,[53] the Board of Directors would be composed of ten persons, of whom five, including the President of the Board, would be appointed by China, and five, including the Vice-President of the Board, by the USSR. Seven persons would constitute a quorum, and all decisions of the Board would require the consent of not less than six persons. The President and the Vice-President would jointly manage the affairs of the Board, and both would sign all the documents of the Board. The Railway would establish a Board of Auditors to be composed of five persons, two Chinese, including the Chairman of the Board of Auditors, appointed by China and three Russians appointed by the USSR. The Railway was to have a manager who would be a Russian, and two assistant managers, one to be Chinese and the other Russian. The said officers would be appointed by the Board of Directors, and such appointments were to be confirmed by their respective Governments. The chief and assistant chiefs of the various departments of the Railway would be appointed by the Board of Directors. If the Chief of Department were a Chinese, the Assistant Chief of Department would be a Russian and vice versa. The employment of persons in the various departments would be in accordance with the principle of equal representation between nationals of China and the USSR. The present Agreement would become inoperative as soon as the question of the Railway was settled in the aforementioned Conference.

In the declarations of the Draft Wang-Karakhan Agreements, the Chinese Government promised to take immediate steps to transfer the property and buildings of the Russian Orthodox Mission at Peking and elsewhere to the Soviet Government. The Russian share of the Boxer Indemnity would, after

[52] *Ibid.*, pp. 1-9.
[53] *Ibid.*, pp. 10-16.

the satisfaction of all prior obligations secured thereon, be appropriated in its entirety to create a fund for the promotion of education among the Chinese people. A special commission to be established for purposes of administering and allocating the fund would consist of three persons, two of whom would be appointed by China and the other by the USSR.[54]

KOO-KARAKHAN AGREEMENTS[55]

Nevertheless, the draft Agreements at the meeting of the State Council on March 15 met strong opposition from Dr. V. K. Wellington Koo, Minister of Foreign Affairs, Lu Chin, Minister of Army, and Wang K'e-min, Minister of Finance.[56] Their objections centered on three issues:

1. In the pledge made by the Soviet Government to declare null and void all treaties, agreements, etc., concluded by the former Tsarist Government and any third party or parties affecting the sovereign rights of China, the Treaty of Friendship between the USSR and the Mongolian People's Republic concluded in Moscow on November 5, 1921 was not mentioned.[57]

2. The Soviet Government's promise to withdraw her troops from Outer Mongolia depended upon agreement on the time-limit for the withdrawal of such troops as well as the measures to be adopted in the interests of the safety of the frontiers.

3. The Soviet request for immediate transfer of all the buildings and landed properties of the Russian Orthodox Mission to the Soviet Government would, if agreed upon, establish a precedent which other Powers might follow and use sometime in the future in the hinterland of China.[58] The Cabinet instructed Dr. C. T. Wang to seek further revision with Karakhan, but the Soviet representative refused to make any changes.

The refusal of the Cabinet to approve the draft agreements and on March 13, a note from France concerning its claims over the Chinese Eastern

[54] *Ibid.*, p. 21-22.

[55] V. K. Wellington Koo, *Reminiscences of Wellington Koo*, III. Service in China, G. Questions Arising in My Terms of Office as Foreign Minister, 1922-1928, 6. Negotiations with Soviet Russia, 1923-1924, c.

[56] *Tung-fang tsa-chih*, XXI:7 (April 1924), p. 157.

[57] By the Treaty of Friendship, Outer Mongolia and the USSR recognized each other as the only legal government in its respective territory without any reference to Chinese interests in Mongolia. Eudin and North, *Soviet Russia and the East, 1920-1927: A Documentary Survey*, pp. 126-27.

[58] Ministry of Foreign Affairs to Soviet Representative (April 1, 1924) and the State Council to the various provinces (March 20, 1924). *Wai-chiao kung-pao*, No. 36, June 1924, Special Documents, pp. 36-39.

Railway[59] moved Karakhan three days later to send an ultimatum to C. T. Wang, warning him that if the Chinese Government did not recognize the draft agreement within the next three days, the Soviet representative would not consider himself bound by the agreements.[60] Karakhan visited Premier Sun Pao-ch'i without result on March 17 and on that same day, the State Council instructed Dr. Wang that:

> . . . while the negotiation was not completed, and since you had not received any government instruction to sign formally, the Government was surprised to learn that the Soviet representative sent a note concerning the limit of time to sign the draft instruments. This would not only be in disagreement with his reiterated principles and spirit for friendship with China, but also would increase the obstacles for the relations between China and the Soviet Union.

Dr. Wang received directions to settle these problems with Karakhan.[61]

On March 19, Karakhan sent notes to the Ministry of Foreign Affairs and Director General Wang stating that the Soviet Government considered formal negotiations with the duly designated representative of China as complete; accordingly, the Soviet Government refused to reopen talks on issues involved in the signed agreements. As soon as the three-day limit expired the Soviet Government would not consider itself bound, and Karakhan asserted, unless formal Sino-Soviet relations were restored unconditionally, the Chinese Government would not be permitted to reopen negotiations with the Soviet Government.[62] Karakhan pointed out in his note to Director General Wang that the "foreign policy of the Chinese Government was basically the policy of the Powers against the Soviet Union, and the sudden overturn of all completed results was caused by the French warning of March 12."[63]

Director General Wang also expressed his unwillingness to carry the burden of reopening the negotiations. Wang's reluctance compelled the State Council to decide on March 20 that the Administration of the Director General for Sino-Russian Affairs should be abolished and the negotiations shifted to the Ministry of Foreign Affairs.[64] Premier Sun Pao-ch'i and Foreign Minister Koo signed the mandate of change that followed the Council decision.[65] Additionally, Dr. Koo moved formally at the meeting to have the Council punish Dr. Wang severely; however, this motion was not carried because of the

[59] *Ibid.*, XXI:7 (April 1924), p. 156.

[60] Director General Wang to the State Council (March 16, 1924), *Wai-chiao kung-pao*, No. 36, Special Documents, pp. 22-23.

[61] The State Council to Director General Wang (March 17, 1924), *ibid.*, pp. 23-24.

[62] Soviet Representative to Ministry of Foreign Affairs (March 19, 1924), *ibid.*, pp. 24-25.

[63] Soviet Representative to Director General Wang (March 19, 1924), *ibid.*, pp. 25-30.

[64] *Tung-fang tsa-chih*, XXI:6 (March 1924), pp. 2-3.

[65] *Cheng-fu kung-pao*, CXIV, No. 2873.

opposition of President Ts'ao K'un.[66]

Two days later, on March 22, the Foreign Minister sent Karakhan a second note stating that Director General Wang had signed the draft agreements without previous instruction from the Government; Koo maintained that the credentials of plenipotentiary Wang from the Chinese Government granted him powers of negotiation only, not official signature and ratification. Furthermore, the Foreign Minister asserted that the Chinese Government conducted its foreign affairs without any intervention, thus discounting Soviet suggestions of French manipulation. Simultaneously, the Soviet representative was informed that the Ministry of Foreign Affairs would direct all negotiations with the Soviet Government henceforth.[67]

In a third Soviet note dated March 25, Karakhan argued that Dr. Wang had been granted the power to make the final resolutions and to sign the said instrument; the Chinese Government could only accept or reject the agreement without further revision. The negligence of the Chinese Government to request an extension of the three-day limit subsequent to receiving the Soviet note implied that Chinese officials had already refused such agreement and that Sino-Soviet negotiations stood at the original position because of the rejection by the Chinese Government of the agreed instruments. Furthermore, Karakhan firmly refused any further negotiations.[68]

The Chinese Ministry of Foreign Affairs responded to Karakhan in a third note of April 1. Koo declared that Karakhan had exploited incidents during the negotiations in order to avoid settling differences in Sino-Russian relations. No request for an extension of the time limit had been requested by the Chinese Government because it did not recognize the Soviet representative's authority to impose time limits upon the Chinese Government during negotiations for the restoration of relations. Dr. Koo added that the Chinese Government would be prepared to sign and ratify the agreements if questions concerning the abrogation of the Soviet-Mongolian Treaty, the unconditional withdrawal of Soviet troops from Outer Mongolia, and the improper request for transfering buildings and properties of the Orthodox Mission to the Soviet Government could be settled satisfactorily.[69]

Koo's strategy to bypass Karakhan and negotiate directly with the Soviet Government failed when Moscow refused to permit Li Chia-ao, who had been

[66] *Tung-fang tsa-chih*, XXI:6 (March 1924), p. 3.

[67] Ministry of Foreign Affairs (Koo) to the Soviet Representative (March 22, 1924), *Wai-chiao kung-pao*, No. 36, Special Documents, pp. 30-31.

[68] Soviet Representative to Minister of Foreign Affairs Koo (March 25, 1924), *ibid.*, pp. 31-35.

[69] Ministry of Foreign Affairs to the Soviet Representative (April 1, 1924), *ibid.*, pp. 35-38; *The North China Herald*, March 27 and 29, 1924, pp. 474, 478.

appointed Chinese Representative to Moscow by a Presidential directive on October 6, 1923,[70] to establish an office[71] and open direct negotiations with the Soviet Ministry of Foreign Affairs.[72] The Soviet-Japanese negotiations resumed between Karakhan and Yoshizawa,[73] the Japanese Minister in Peking. Noting these activities, the State Council resolved on March 27 that Sino-Russian negotiations be adjourned temporarily and both Premier Sun and Foreign Minister Koo became "ill" and excused themselves from regular governmental activities. The Sino-Russian negotiations appeared to be stalemated, perhaps irretrievably.[74]

No other international problem since the May Fourth Movement in 1919 had created such concern among the Chinese public as the break in Sino-Soviet negotiations. Within the short period from March 18 to March 26, Marshal Wu P'ei-fu, the powerful general of the Chihli Clique, sent six telegrams to the Cabinet urging ratification.[75] Wu's opinions mirrored those of many military generals of the various provinces, including Hsiao Yao-nan, Military Governor of Hupei, Liu Chen-hua, Commander-in-Chief of the Chen-Sung Army, and Sun Ch'uan-fang, Military Governor of Fukien.[76] Nine public bodies in Shanghai, including the Chung-hua chiao-yü kai-chin she (Chinese Society for Educational Improvement) charged that the Government based its policy upon the directions of the Powers and asserted that the Chinese people should urge the Government to recognize the Soviet Union immediately and unconditionally.[77] In a declaration made by the faculty of the National Peking University, the diplomatic authorities of the Peking Government were urged to recognize the USSR immediately and unconditionally and to request Karakhan to retain the draft Wang-Karakhan Agreements as the basis of a formal Sino-Russian Conference.[78] On April 1, four leading institutions of higher learning in Peking, the Peking Teachers University, the Peking Engineering University, Teachers College for Girls, and the College of Fine Arts, declared their support of a student demonstration and a declaration by the Peking Student Union condemning the Cabinet and Dr. Koo. They urged the Soviet Union to continue the negotiations on the basis of the principles

[70] *Wai-chiao kung-pao*, No. 30, Institutes, p. 1.

[71] *Cheng-fu kung-pao*, CV, No. 2898. Also, Allen Whiting's *Soviet Policies in China, 1917-1924*, p. 225. Whiting described the failure of Li Chia-ao's Moscow mission in detail.

[72] *Tung-fang tsa-chih*, XXI:6 (March 1924), pp. 3-4.

[73] *Ibid.*, XXI:12 (June 1924), p. 153.

[74] *Ibid.*, XXI:21 (November 1924), p. 3.

[75] *Ibid.*, XXI:9 (May 1924), pp. 135-36.

[76] *Ibid.*, XXI:13 (July 1924), p. 41.

[77] *Ibid.*, XXI:9 (May 1924), pp. 137-38.

[78] *Ibid.*, XXI:9 (May 1924), pp. 138-39.

of their previous declarations.[79]

To the surprise of almost everyone, Chinese and foreign, a Presidential mandate appeared on May 30, 1924 that affirmed the Sino-Russian Agreement on General Principles and attached papers had been properly prepared by both sides. V. K. Wellington Koo received the appointment as plenipotentiary with full powers to sign accordingly.[80] The next day another mandate stated that the Sino-Russian Agreement on General Principles for the Settlement of the Questions between China and the USSR, the Agreement for the Provisional Management of the Chinese Eastern Railway, and seven Declarations and two exchanged Notes had been duly signed by Foreign Minister Koo and Karakhan; Sino-Russian relations returned to normalcy.[81]

Two days later on June 2, the Chinese Government established the Chung-O hui-i pan-shih ch'u (Office for the Sino-Russian Conference)[82] according to its organic law with Liu Ching-jen as the Secretary General.[83] He was sworn in on June 23.[84] On June 27, Dr. Koo appointed T'ang Tsai-chang, Chang Yü-ch'üan, Shih Shao-ch'ang, Chou Ch'uan-ching, Wang Yen-chang, Ch'ien T'ai, Fan Ting, Chi Ching, and Wei Wen-pin as the Special Commissioners of the aforementioned office.[85] President Ts'ao K'un received Karakhan as first Soviet Ambassador to China at an official audience before his full credentials arrived on July 31, 1924.[86]

This unusual turn of the Sino-Soviet negotiations may be attributed to several factors. First, the repeated efforts of Li Chia-ao, Chinese Representative in Moscow, to contact the Soviet Ministry of Foreign Affairs had threatened the position of Karakhan. Second, the report of Davtian, Councilor and Deputy Representative of Karakhan at Moscow, had influenced the course of the Soviet foreign policy. Third, Karakhan had failed in his strategy to deal with various rival governments in China, particularly the Nationalist Government under Dr. Sun at Canton. Fourth, the death of Cheptsun, the last living Buddha of Urga, in June 1924 had started a rapid change in Outer Mongolia. Fifth, the intervention of France, Japan, and the United States in regard to the Chinese Eastern Railway and the French intervention in the Russian Concession at Hankow had added more complications to the

[79] *Ibid.*, XXI:9 (May 1924), pp. 139-41.

[80] Presidential Directive No. 882 to Foreign Minister Koo (May 30, 1924), *Cheng-fu kung-pao*, CXV, No. 2944, June 1, 1924.

[81] *Cheng-fu kung-pao*, CXV, No. 2945, June 2, 1924.

[82] Presidential Directive No. 990 to Foreign Minister Koo (June 2, 1924), *ibid.*, No. 2962, June 21, 1924.

[83] *Cheng-fu kung-pao*, CXV, No. 2963, June 21, 1924.

[84] *Ibid.*, No. 2967, June 25, 1924.

[85] *Ibid.*, No. 2971, June 29, 1924.

[86] *Ibid.*, CXVI, No. 3003, August 1, 1925.

Sino-Russian negotiations. Sixth, China had compromised with the Soviet regime by granting Sinkiang authority to sign a commercial treaty with the Soviet Union. Finally, the Chinese public, as well as the warlords, had exerted tremendous pressure upon the Government. It was widely believed that Marshal Wu P'ei-fu held Dr. Koo responsible for the successful conclusion of the Sino-Russian negotiations;[87] however, it was Chu Ho-hsiang, Councilor of the Ministry of Foreign Affairs, who contributed substantially to the success. He made more than twenty secret trips within ten days to Karakhan's residence under the instruction of Foreign Minister Koo to hasten revision of the draft Agreement. And, under the pretext of mediating cabinet disputes, the Cabinet met in special session at Koo's home to approve the final draft Koo-Karakhan Agreements.[88]

DISCUSSION

The principles proposed in the Agreements were fair and reciprocal. These principles included the annulment of former treaties and replacement by new agreements on the basis of equality, reciprocity, and justice, the transformation of the Chinese Eastern Railway from a line with political and military reasons for existence into a strictly commercial enterprise, the renunciation of the rights and privileges relating to all concessions and consular jurisdiction, a custom tariff in accordance with the principles of equality, and abrogation of the Boxer Indemnity. After the Great Revolution of 1917, Russia was no longer in a position to enjoy whatever rights or privileges it had held in China before the World War, and China had reclaimed all these rights and privileges during the period of the aforementioned Revolution.

After a careful examination of the Sino-Russian Agreements in their entirety, a unilateral advantage for Russia appears to emerge on many points, particularly in the case of the Chinese Eastern Railway and the problem of Outer Mongolia. According to Articles II and III of the Agreement for the Provisional Management of the Chinese Eastern Railway, the Russians had a majority both on the Board of Auditors and in the Management.[89] As a result, both the finances and operations of the line were under Soviet control. Furthermore, although the distribution of chiefs, vice-chiefs, as well as all employees in the various departments of the line, were to be carried out in accordance with the principle of equal representation between the nationals of China and the Soviet Union as designated in Articles IV and V, the status

[87] *Tung-fang tsa-chih*, XXI:12 (June 1924), p. 3.

[88] *Ibid.*, XXI:13 (July 1924), p. 42.

[89] *Wai-chiao kung-pao*, No. 36, pp. 12-13.

quo of the Soviet Union's absolute dominance over the Chinese Eastern Railway was maintained by Article VII of the said Agreement, which read as follows:

> The Government of China and the Government of the USSR . . . agree, in explanation of Article V of the Agreement . . . which provides for the principle of equal representation in the filling of posts by citizens of China and those of the USSR, that the application of this principle is not to be understood to mean that the present employees of Russian nationality shall be dismissed for the sole purpose of enforcing the said principle. It is further understood that . . . the posts shall be filled in accordance with the ability and technical, as well as educational qualifications of the applicants.[90]

Since Russians predominated in the most highly paid posts of the Railway and only Russia could provide applicants with technical and educational qualifications, the principle of equal representation was practically void.

China's sole declaration in regard to the Russo-Mongolian Treaty of Friendship and the withdrawal of Russian troops from Outer Mongolia was that "China will not and does not recognize as valid any treaty or agreement concluded between Russia since the Tsarist regime and any third party or parties, affecting the sovereign rights and interests of China." This statement did not affect in any sense the actual relations between the USSR and Outer Mongolia. The indefinite postponement of the Sino-Russian Conference would made discussion of any "conditions" or questions, such as the time limit for the withdrawal of troops and the measures to be adopted to provide for the safety of the frontiers, impossible. Any prolonged military occupation or rights of military intervention reinforced by political indoctrination and economic domination would cause Outer Mongolia to gravitate from its traditional ties with China to dependence upon the Soviet Union. The notes exchanged on August 14, 1945 between Dr. Wang Shih-chieh, Minister of Foreign Affairs of Nationalist China, and V. M. Molotov, the People's Commissar of Foreign Affairs of the USSR, included the declaration that:

> In view of the desire repeatedly expressed by the people of Outer Mongolia for their independence, the Chinese Government declares that after the defeat of Japan should a plebiscite of the Outer Mongolian people confirm the desire, the Chinese Government will recognize the independence of Outer Mongolia with the existing boundary as its boundary.[91]

This position was a surprise only in the facts that it had taken Russia more than twenty years after the Sino-Russian Agreements of 1924 to legalize the

[90] *Ibid.*, pp. 28-29.

[91] Ministry of Foreign Affairs, Republic of China, ed., Treaty of Friendship and Alliance between the Republic of China and the USSR (August 14, 1945). *Treaties between the Republic of China and Foreign States, 1927-1961*, pp. 510-11.

de facto occupation of Outer Mongolia and that Outer Mongolia, which had not been bargained away by a warlord government, was signed away by the Nationalist Government, an entity ostensibly devoted to the principle of nationalism.

The Koo-Karakhan Agreements were identical with the Wang-Karakhan Agreements except for a few insignificant points which were literary adjustments rather than substantive changes. The new agreements fell short of the original objectives of Dr. Koo and the Cabinet, for whom the original Wang-Karakhan Agreements had not been acceptable. This attitude had led to the abrupt termination of Dr. C. T. Wang's conduct of the negotiation.

Dr. Koo had other significant reasons for signing the similar agreements after the failure of the desired revision. Nationalism played a large role in his decision. The Sino-Russian Agreement on General Principles for the Settlement of the Questions between China and the USSR was the first significant equal treaty China had signed since 1871 without participating in an unpredictable war. The abolition of extraterritoriality, return of the Boxer Indemnity, exchange of representatives on the rank of ambassador, and relinquishment of the concessions symbolized this status of equality with a great European Power. The Agreements could establish a model for the other Powers to follow. Another reason influencing Koo's decision to sign was the latent threat of Soviet recognition of the Canton Government. Although Koo was aware of the Soviet flirtation with the rival government, the effect of an official recognition and alliance between the Soviet Union and the Canton regime as advocated by Dr. Sun Yat-sen would be detrimental to the unstable "Central" Government.[92] The situation was particularly acute in early 1924 when M. M. Borodin arrived in Canton as the "representative of the Soviet Government and the personal representative of L. Karakhan."[93]

Article IV in the Wang-Karakhan Agreement on Principles and the Koo-Karakhan Agreement on Principles were identical:

> The Government of the USSR, in accordance with its policy and Declarations of 1919 and 1920, declares that all Treaties, Agreement, *et cetera*, concluded between the former Tsarist Government and any third party or parties affecting the sovereign rights or interests of China, are null and void.[94]

The supplementary Declaration proposed by Koo and his Cabinet as a revision of the above article read that "the Government of the USSR declares that all

[92] Chang Kuo-t'ao, "Wo-te hui-i" (Memoir of Chang Kuo-t'ao), *Ming-pao yüeh-k'an* (Ming-pao Monthly), starting Volume I, No. 5, p. 64. Chang possibly presented the most detailed and personal description concerning the relations between the Comintern, the Chinese Communist Party, and the Kuomintang.

[93] Allen S. Whiting, *Soviet Policies in China, 1917-1924*, p. 244.

[94] *Wai-chiao kung-pao*, No. 36, Treaties, p. 3.

Treaties, Agreements, *et cetera*, concluded between the Soviet Government and any third party—namely Outer Mongolia—affecting the sovereign rights or interests of China, are null and void."[95] In the new Koo-Karakhan Agreement, a Declaration (III) was added:

> The Government of the Republic of China and the Government of the USSR jointly declare that it is understood that with reference to Article IV of the Agreement on General Principles between the Republic of China and the USSR of May 31, 1924, the Government of the Republic of China will not and does not recognize as valid any treaty, agreement, *et cetera*, concluded between Russia since the Tsarist regime and any third party or parties, affecting the sovereign rights and interests of the Republic of China. It is further understood that this expression of understanding has the same force and validity as a general declaration embodied in the said Agreement on General Principles.[96]

This joint declaration by both the Soviet Government and the Peking Government increased the validity of the Declaration. Nevertheless, the unilateral objection of China to the Treaty of Friendship between Soviet Russia and the Mongolian People's Republic would not annul its effectiveness as far as the two contracting parties were concerned. It did, however, preserve for China a right to future claims of political and diplomatic sovereignty over Outer Mongolia.

Furthermore, in a telegram to the State Council on March 23,[97] Wang said that Karakhan did not request China's sovereignty in the Wang-Karakhan Agreement on General Principles (Article V). Consequently, the Treaty of Friendship between the Soviet Union and the Mongolian People's Republic was annuled automatically. Because the treaty had never been approved by the Government of China, Outer Mongolia remained an integral part of Chinese territory, and Soviet Russia had to respect the sovereignty of China in Outer Mongolia. The ineffectiveness of the treaty and the question of its termination required no verbal illustration.

Both Chinese agreements with Karakhan were identical in regard to the second point of dispute between Wang and Koo, namely, that portion of Article V concerning the withdrawal of Soviet troops from Outer Mongolia and except that the word "conditions" in the draft Wang-Karakhan Agreements was replaced by "questions" in the Koo-Karakhan Agreements, changes were few. The revised Article V of Koo and the Cabinet[98] read as follows:

> The Government of the USSR declares that as soon as the "questions" for the withdrawal of all the troops of the USSR from Outer Monglia—namely, as to the

[95] *Ibid.*, Special Documents, p. 22.

[96] *Ibid.*, Treaties, pp. 20-21.

[97] Chengting T. Wang to the State Council (March 23, 1924), *Tung-fang tsa-chih*, XXI:8 (April 1924), p. 133.

[98] *Wai-chiao kung-pao*, No. 36, Special Documents, p. 22.

> time-limit of the withdrawal of such troops and the measures to be adopted in the interest of safety of the frontiers—are agreed upon at the Conference as provided in Article II of the present Agreement, it will effect the complete withdrawal of the troops of the USSR from Outer Mongolia.[99]

As a matter of fact, the difference between the word "conditions" of Wang and the word "questions" of Koo meant little. As Wang argued in his second telegram to the State Council on March 23,[100] even with elimination of the word "conditions," the withdrawal of the Soviet troops from Outer Mongolia was not unconditional and remained contingent to the settlement of problems of the time limit for the withdrawal of such troops and the measures to be adopted in the interests of the safety of the frontiers at the Sino-Russian Conference. Therefore, the difference between the revised Article and the Wang-Karakhan version was one of words, not substance; the revised Article, like the original draft, provided no realistic solution to the problem of withdrawal of Soviet troops. Indeed, under Koo's revised format, Soviet troops in Outer Mongolia did not withdraw until 1925 after the Mongolian People's Republic had become "independent."

The third point of dispute between Wang and Koo involved the buildings and land of the Russian Orthodox Mission. The original declaration in the draft Wang-Karakhan Agreement read as follows:

> The Government of China declares that upon the signing of Agreement of General Principles for the Settlement of the Questions between the Republic of China and the USSR of March 1924, the Chinese Government will take steps to immediately transfer the buildings and properties of the Russian Orthodox Mission at Peking and elsewhere to the Soviet Government. . . .[101]

In a note from the Ministry of Foreign Affairs to the Soviet representative on April 1, Koo sought to delay such a transfer by stating that:

> Since the list of the buildings and properties of the Russian Orthodox Mission in China (sizes, nature, numbers, and locations) has not yet been handed over by the Soviet Government to the Government of China, the exchange of notes concerning such transfer of properties of the Orthodox Mission to the Soviet Government should be postponed pending further discussions in detail in the said Conference. I find that the acquisition of real estate in China by alien governments and nations has never been permitted. It is certainly subject to further consideration.[102]

Earlier in a telegram from the State Council to the various provinces on March 20, Dr. Koo stated that the Government feared that if this precedent

[99] *Ibid.*, Treaties, pp. 3-4.

[100] *Tung-fang tsa-chih*, XXI:9 (May 1924), pp. 133-34.

[101] *Wai-chiao kung-pao*, No. 36, Special Documents, p. 21.

[102] *Ibid.*, p. 37.

were established, it would be followed by other countries to acquire real estate inland.[103] He informed the press on March 23, 1924 that the request of the Russian Government that its properties be handed over to it was improper.[104]

In a telegram[105] to the Council of State on March 23, Chengting T. Wang argued that under Tsarist Russia all religious affairs were the concern of the national administration, i.e., appropriations to build churches came from the national treasury. After the establishment of the Soviet Government, all the buildings and properties of the Russian Orthodox Mission continued to be the property of the state. It was a matter of course and conduct of reciprocity that all state properties should be handed over to a newly recognized government in accordance with international practice. Wang held that the possibility other countries might utilize such a precedent to acquire real estate in China's hinterlands was a needless worry because Russia was the only nation where churches were the property of the state. Furthermore, in case the Powers did follow the Russian example and demand acquisition of real estate within the Chinese interior, China could cite the precedent of the Agreement between China and the Soviet Union and demand that the Powers renounce and relinquish all their rights in China such as consular jurisdiction, negotiated tariff rates, concessions and leased territories, the Boxer Indemnity, and all treaties and agreements which prejudiced the sovereign rights and interests of China.

In summary, the collapse of the Sino-Soviet negotiations in March 1924 and the opposition of Koo and his Cabinet members to the draft Wang-Karakhan Agreements arose from a personal dispute and rivalry rather than a confrontation of policy.[106] The seeds of suspicion and rivalry were laid at the Paris Peace Conference over the dispute concerning seniority, and they bore fruit four years later during the Sino-Russian negotiations.

The Sino-Soviet Agreements of 1924, though imperfect, represented a greater diplomatic success for Koo, Wang, and the Peking Government of warlord China than did the Sino-Soviet Treaty of 1945 for the Nationalist Government, an ally of the Soviet Union during World War II and a victor in that war.

[103] *Ibid.*, No. 36, pp. 38-39. State Council to the Various Provinces (March 20, 1024).

[104] *The North China Herald*, March 27, 1924, p. 474.

[105] Chengting T. Wang to the State Council (March 23, 1924), *Tung-fang tsa-chih*, XXI:9 (May 1924), pp. 133-34.

[106] Whiting, *Soviet Policies in China, 1917-1924*, p. 224. The author's statement that "Wang was made the scapegoat for errors of judgment within the Ministry of Foreign Affairs," was inaccurate. Whiting did not offer any evidence for such an assumption.

CHAPTER VI

Koo and the Manchurian Incident, 1931-1933

THE CASE OF THE MANCHURIAN INCIDENT[1] AT GENEVA

At a little past ten in the evening of September 18, 1931, an explosion near Liu-t'iao-kou station of the Southern Manchurian Railway, which damaged 31 inches of railway track, yet did not delay the 10:40 Changchun-Mukden train from arriving at Mukden on schedule, activated the well positioned Japanese Kwantung Army. Within eight hours, the whole of Mukden, including the North Grand Barracks, the arsenal, the entire Northeastern Air Force as well as all public institutions and properties were under the control of the Kwantung Army without any organized resistance from the defending Tung-pei chün (Northeastern Army[2]). "The Japanese militarists who planned and executed the Manchurian operations of September, 1931, will probably be regarded by history as the first active aggressors of World War II," said former U. S. Secretary of War, H. L. Stimson. "The road to World War II is now clearly visible; it has run its terrible course from the railway tracks near Mukden to the operations of two bombers over Hiroshima and Nagasaki."[3] The national emergency created in China made national unity the only alternative for national survival, and it also offered Wellington Koo an opportunity to come back to the diplomatic scene under the former opponent Nationalist government.

Shortly after the disputed 1924 Sino-Russian Agreements, Koo was forced to resign his acting premiership and fled to a foreign concession in Tientsin when Marshal Feng Yü-hsiang took his troops back to Peking from the Jehol front and arrested the warlord President Ts'ao K'un. Yet Feng's dominant position in Peking was shortlived and the Manchurian warlord Chang Tso-lin soon drove Feng's Kuominchün out of Peking and into the northwestern desert. Emerging from political isolation, Koo returned to Peking in May

[1] Jung Chen, Chief of Staff of the Tung-pei chün, "Report on the Manchurian Incident," *Ko-ming wen-hsien*, XXXIV:879-83.

[2] Wang T'ieh-han, "Tung-pei chün-shih shih-lüeh" (A Brief History of the Northeastern Army), *Chuan-chi wen-hsüeh*, XVIII:5, pp. 5-12; 6, pp. 34-38.

[3] Henry L. Stimson and McGeorge Bundy, *On Active Service in Peace and War*, p. 220.

to become the Finance Minister under Premier W. W. Yen, and later, acting Premier and Minister of Foreign Affairs of Marshal Chang, Commander-in-Chief of the Ankuochün (National Pacification Army). Chang's raid on the Soviet embassy in April 1927, however, provided Koo with the opportunity to resign, and he returned to the Western Hills. Too prominent in previous rival governments, Koo was on the namelist of political criminals wanted by the victorious Chiang Kai-shek and left for a "fishing trip" in Canada and France until 1929, when he returned to China and joined Young Marshal Chang Hsüeh-liang in Mukden.

When Jung Chen, chief of staff of the Young Marshal, and Wang Yi-che, commander of the 7th Brigade stationed at the North Grand Barracks, near Mukden, called the Young Marshal who was recuperating in the German Hospital in Peking for instructions that night, the Young Marshal early in the morning of September 19, 1931, summoned Koo who had just returned from the sea shore resort of Pei-tai-ho. Shocked at the audacity of the Japanese Kwantung Army, Koo went to the Young Marshal immediately and recommending two steps to him: (1) To report the incident to Nanking at once and to ask the government to make an urgent appeal to the League of Nations in Geneva in accordance with the Covenant of the League; and (2) To at once dispatch an emissary acquainted with the Japanese military leaders, to see the commanding general of the Kwantung Army to find out what was his real intention and how far he was to push his aggressive plan.[4]

The Nanking government's Japan policy of non-resistance and appeal to the League of Nations for world opinion and deterrent force concurred with the policy of the Young Marshal. Chiang's principles that "pacification of the interior must go before the expulsion of the external enemy and that resisting against the foreign humiliation could only be done by a united nation" are well known and often quoted.[5] This policy coincided with the Young Marshal's views in his telegram to the Northeastern Political Commission on July 6, 1931 that:

> If we wage a war against Japan at this moment, our side would certainly lose, and the Japanese side would demand cession of territory, indemnity and the Northeast would be sunken into a myriad hell and could never be recovered. It is absolutely necessary to avoid strifes and we should deal with them by justice.[6]

---

[4]Koo Hui-lan, *Autobiography*, p. 270.

[5]Chiang Kai-shek, "Chiang chu-hsi tui Ku Wei-chün chiu-jen wai-chiao-pu-chang hsün-t'zu" (Chairman Chiang Kai-shek's Instructions to Acting Foreign Minister Wellington Koo), November 30, 1931. *Ko-min wen-hsien*, XXXV:7936, p. 1270.

[6]Bureau of Police Affairs of Kwantung Administration to Deputy Foreign Minister, July 31, 1931: Record of the Japanese Ministry of Foreign Affairs.

As a result, appeals to the League of Nations for justice were sent by Foreign Minister C. T. Wang to Alfred Sze, chief Chinese delegate at the League, and government protests were handed to Japan. Wellington Koo was recommended to the central government in Nanking by the Young Marshal. On October 1, he sent Koo to Nanking by his personal airplane to present the case to the newly formed Kuomintang Special Foreign Affairs Commission of the Central Political Committee under Tai Chi-t'ao and T. V. Soong.[7] After Koo's arrival in Nanking on October 1, he began a series of activities with the various circles including an interview with Chiang Kai-shek and a visit to the Sun Yat-sen mausoleum. By the end of November, Koo was brought to Nanking again and was appointed officiating Minister of Foreign Affairs succeeding C. T. Wang who resigned as a result of student attacks for "his" policy of non-resistance and "his" failure to persuade the League of Nations to take forceful actions.

While in Geneva, on September 25, Alfred Sze, chief Chinese delegate, informed the 65th session of the Council that China had placed her trust in the League, that the Kwantung Army should withdraw back to the railway zone, and that a neutral commission be sent to Manchuria as the only way of knowing the truth. On the other side, Kenkichi Yoshizawa, Japanese delegate, replied that Japanese operations were in the nature of self-defense and that most of the Japanese troops had already withdrawn into the South Manchurian Railway Zone; he ignored the Council's suggestion to send an informal commission to Manchuria, and insisted that the dispute be left to direct negotiation between China and Japan.[8] The Council resolved that both sides should try to restore normal relations without adopting the inquiry plan. Due to the economic crisis of the British abandoning the gold standard on the same day as the Manchurian Incident, and the reluctant attitude of Secretary Henry L. Stimson, who did not wish to do anything to hinder Prime Minister Kijūrō Shidehara's restraining influence over the military and thereby to "play into the hands of any nationalist agitators," the League failed to reach any definitive agreement in the first round.[9]

Upon the request of China after the Kwantung Army bombed Chinchou, the last base of the Chinese Northeastern Army in Manchuria, the Council was reconvened on October 13, 1931. Japan demanded direct Sino-Japanese negotiation and the establishment of agreement before the withdrawal of the Kwantung Army. Japan also condemned the Chinese boycott of Japanese goods. On the other hand, China insisted that any direct Sino-Japanese negotiations should be conducted after the date for withdrawal of Japanese

[7] *Ta-kung pao*, October 2-5, 1931.
[8] *New York Times*, September 26, 1931.
[9] Henry L. Stimson and McGeorge Bundy, *op. cit.*, pp. 227-30.

troops had been set, that such negotiations should be assisted by neutral powers and the United States, and that Sino-Japanese problems should be settled under the principles of the League of Nations Covenant, the Treaty for the Renunciation of War and the Nine Power Treaty. Since Occidental "interests in the Orient were not worth a war," both President Hoover and British Foreign Minister Lord Reading were against economic sanctions against Japan, Stimson was left alone to push the Briand-Kellogg Treaty for the Renunciation of War at Geneva, through the American observer, Ambassador Charles G. Dawes without success.[10]

On November 16, 1931, the Council was reconvened in Paris with American Ambassador to England, Charles G. Dawes as its representative. On November 21, Yoshizawa, under the pressure of the world diplomatic front in general and Stimson in particular, proposed that "the League of Nations should send a Commission of Inquiry to the spot . . . but this Commission would not be empowered to intervene in the negotiations which may be initiated between the two parties, or to supervise the movements of the military forces of either."[11]

While Sze was in Geneva pressing a withdrawal of Japanese troops, saying, "the creation of a commission should in no way furnish an excuse for a delay in beginning and progressively carrying out in the shortest possible time the complete withdrawal of the Japanese troops." Koo in Nanking called on the American Minister in China, Johnson, on the same day to inform him of the Chinese objection that "it was vague in its terms, it provided no time limit for evacuation, and it provided no method of bringing China and Japan together for a general settlement of outstanding questions."[12] Koo said the principal features of the Chinese counterproposal which was adopted by the Special Foreign Affairs Commission, are immediate cessation of hostilities and evacuation of occupied territory within a fixed period under the supervision of neutral powers, to reaffirm by both China and Japan the principles of respect for treaty obligations, and to convene a conference of interested powers to be jointly convoked by the United States and the League to discuss and settle all questions between China and Japan relating to safeguarding peace in the Far East and promoting economic development of Manchuria through international cooperation.

While Briand and his colleagues at Geneva were pressing Sze to accept the

[10] *Ibid.*, pp. 233-40, 243-44.

[11] Westel W. Willoughby, *The Sino-Japanese Controversy and the League of Nations*, p. 172.

[12] The Chargé in France (Shaw) to the Secretary of State, Paris, November 21, 1931; The Minister in China (Johnson) to the Secretary of State, Nanking, November 22, 1931. *Foreign Relations of the United States, 1931*, III:526-29, 533.

League's formula on the Commission, reports current as to imminent Japanese action at Chinchou were becoming more alarming which further complicated the task of the League. Against popular feelings and students' pressure in China, Dr. Koo, Acting Foreign Minister, on November 4, tentatively and informally proposed to the Ministers of United States, France and Britain in Nanking to establish the Chinchou neutral zone in order to block the next advance of the Kwantung Army. This strategy won Stimson's sympathy:

> In order to avoid any clash China is prepared as a temporary measure pending a general settlement of the Manchuria question, if Japan insists on withdrawal of troops in the Chinchou area to do so up to Shanhaikwan, provided Japan gives guarantees satisfactory to Great Britain, the United States and France, not to go into that zone leaving the Chinese civil administration intact including police.[13]

And in a later conversation between Dr. Koo and Johnson, on November 25, 1931, in Nanking, Koo expressed the fear that:

> By the time any commission reaches Manchuria from Europe, Japan will have been in undisturbed occupation there long enough to encourage the organization of an independent government prepared to recognize the position of Japan in Manchuria. . . .[14]

However, due to the Chinese public opinion, the Chinese government was unable to agree to the withdrawal of troops south of the Great Wall, as Koo later telegraphed Sze, thus upsetting the discussion of a neutral zone status.[15]

The Drafting Committee, on December 1, 1931, completed for submission to the Committee of Twelve, the final text of the resolution taking account to the greatest possible degree the changes suggested by both the Chinese and Japanese on December 10. After lengthy debates and exchanges of opinion among the powers and the disputants, the Council unanimously adopted the resolution without amendment, as follows:

> [The Council] decides to appoint a Commission of five members to study on the spot and to report to the Council on any circumstance which, affecting the international relations, threatens to disturb peace between China and Japan, or the good understanding. . . . The governments of China and Japan will each have the right to nominate one accessor to assist the Commission. . . . Should the two parties initiate any negotiations these would not fall within the scope of the terms of reference of the Commission, nor would it be within the competence of the Commission to interfere with the military arrangements of either party.[16]

---

[13] The Minister in China (Johnson) to the Secretary of State, Nanking, November 24, 1931. *Foreign Relations of the United States, 1931*, III:558.

[14] *Ibid.*, p. 562.

[15] The Chargé in France (Shaw) to the Secretary of State, Paris, December 5, 1931. *Foreign Relations of the United States, 1931*, III:621-22.

[16] Westel W. Willoughby, *The Sino-Japanese Controversy and the League of Nations*, p. 177-78.

In accepting the resolution, Dr. Sze made the following reservations (a) immediate cessation of hostilities, (b) termination of the Japanese occupation of Manchuria within the shortest time possible, (c) neutral observation and reporting upon all developments from then on, and (d) a comprehensive inquiry into the entire Manchuria situation on the spot by a commission appointed by the Council.[17] Right after the resolution had been passed, the Japanese cabinet under Wakatsuki fell due to the Manchurian affair, as Debuchi told Secretary Stimson, on December 11. On December 15, President Chiang of the Chinese national government also resigned due to popular sentiment and students' demonstrations for a stronger policy against Japan. When the new cabinet under Sun Fo and the southern leaders was formed by the end of the year, Dr. Koo was replaced by Eugene Chen as Minister for Foreign Affairs. Meanwhile, on December 22, the Japanese Kwantung Army announced the dispatching force of 2nd Division and 39th Brigade to begin its drive on Chinchou despite Dr. Koo's warnings and appeals directly or through his agent in Washington and Paris, and Stimson's reminder to the Japanese through Ambassador Cameron Forbes that a Japanese advance on Chinchou would have unfavorable effects upon world opinion.[18] By January 3, the Kwantung Army announced that the Muro brigade had occupied Chinchou early that morning. Accordingly, Stimson restated his nonrecognition doctrine in identical notes to both Japan and China on January 7.[19] Dr. Koo's insistance upon a conference of the Nine Power Treaty to deal with the Manchurian emergency under the United States was considered not opportune by Stimson pending further development of the situation and the Nationalist leadership. While in Manchuria preparations for establishing a new state were completed under the Kwantung Army in cooperation with the provincial warlords, the Commission of Inquiry was declared formally constituted on January 14, and was holding preliminary meetings under its newly elected chairman Lord Lytton.[20]

When new year's day arrived, the reinforced Kwantung Army under the new Minister of War, Araki Sadao, occupied Chinchou, and the last symbol of authority of the Chinese government in Manchuria was eliminated, despite the repeated warnings of the British, French and the United States.[21] Secretary

[17]The Chargé in France to the Secretary of State, Paris, December 10, 1931. *Foreign Relations of the United States, 1931*, III: 672.

[18]The Minister in China (Johnson) to the Secretary of State, Peiping, December 21, 1931. *Foreign Relations of the United States, 1931*, III: 696-96.

[19]Memorandum by the Secretary of State, Washington, January 7, 1932. *Foreign Relations of the United States, 1932*, III: 7.

[20]The Consul at Geneva (Gilbert) to the Secretary of State, Geneva, January 14, 1932. *Foreign Relations of the United States, 1932*, III: 30.

[21]Furuya Keiji, *Chiang Tsung-t'ung mi-lu* (The Secret History of President Chiang Kai-shek), VIII, pp. 123-30.

Stimson's famous nonrecognition statement failed to rally the Western powers. In the meantime, the Japanese navy utilized the boycott movement against Japanese goods as its pretext and sent 49 warships to Shanghai to start the war on January 28 to match the army's aggression in the north ignoring the peace policy with the nationalist Government and Foreign Minister Koo.[22] Amidst the war clouds in China, the 66th session of the Council began in Geneva on January 25. Upon the request of China, the 12-member committee of the Council agreed that the case of the Sino-Japanese dispute be removed from the Council to a special congress where China expected more sympathy from the small powers who had less interest in the Far East and more concern with the system of collective security.

While the Shanghai war was expanding as the Japanese brought more reinforcements, American Minister in China, Nelson T. Johnson, called on Koo for a possible arrangement of mutual withdrawal of forces at the front. Koo reflected the view of the Chinese government and the 19th Route Army who were guarding their own territory against invaders that the distance for the 19th Route Army to withdraw should be in terms of meters rather than in miles, and that the Japanese should assure the Chinese that they would not occupy the ground evacuated by the Chinese. Koo also proposed that a meeting of the representatives from the interested powers be held to settle the Shanghai question and at the same time to work out an agenda for a conference of all interested powers on all questions affecting the Far East.[23] Koo also tried to solicit American financial or material support without result. A secret conference took place on H.M.S. *Kent* between Matsuoka and Nomura on the Japanese side, and Koo and Gaston Wong representing China, on February 28. However, no agreement was made on 20-kilometer zone due to the resistance of both Japan and China. The determined resistance from the Chinese 19th Route Army and the 5th Army stalemated the war until March 2, which greatly softened the Japanese demands for cease-fire talks with the Western envoys in Shanghai. On May 5, the "Agreement between China and Japan Providing for an Armistice and the Withdrawal of Japanese Forces from Shanghai" was finally signed by Vice Minister of Foreign Affairs Quo Tai-chi and the Japanese representative M. Shigemitsu in their respective hospitals

[22] Koo Wei-chün, "Chung-hua ming-kuo cheng-fu tsai hu-an kai-shih shih chueh-ting ho-ping cheng-ts'e chih shui-t'ieh" (A Statement on the Policy of Peace of the Chinese Government at the Beginning of the Shanghai Conflict), July 2, 1932. *Ko-min wen-hsien*, XXXVI, 8075, pp. 1409-12.

[23] American Minister in China (Johnson) to Secretary of State, Shanghai, February 13, 14, 22, 29, 1932. *Foreign Relations of the United States, 1932, Far East*, III: 327-28, 415, 474.

amidst the news that Lord Lytton and his Commission was on their way to Shanghai.[24]

LYTTON COMMISSION OF INQUIRY IN CHINA

After lengthy agonizing by the Council to determine the personnel and to obtain acceptance to serve from those invited to membership upon it, the commission crossed the American continent in early February and did not land in Yokohama until February 29. The members of the Commission included Count Aldrovandi (Italian), General de Division Henri Claudel (French), the Right Hon. The Earl of Lytton (British), Dr. Heinrich Schnee (German), and Major-General Frank Ross McCoy (American). Japan appointed Mr. Isaburo Yoshida, Ambassador to Turkey, and China appointed Dr. Wellington Koo to serve as assessors. The Secretary-General of the League designated M. Robert Hass, a director in the secretariat of the League, to serve as secretary-general of the Commission.[25] After a 12-day visit in Japan including a royal banquet with the Emperor, the Commission left Kobe and sailed for Shanghai aboard the steamer *President Adams* on March 11.[26]

When the Lytton's Commission arrived in Shanghai in the evening of March 14, they were welcomed and entertained by Chinese dignitaries including Vice-Foreign Minister Quo Tai-chi, Mayor of Shanghai Wu Te-chen (Wu T'ieh-ch'eng), and Dr. Koo. Koo accompanied the Commission inspecting the war-torn areas in Shanghai and scenic Hangchow for a few days.[27] On March 26, he accompanied them aboard the steamer *Te-ho* and arrived in Nanking, the Nationalist capital, the next morning. A series of official entertainments were given by the Chinese officials including Chairman Lin Sen of the Nationalist Government, President Wang Ching-wei of the Executive Yuan, Foreign Minister Lo Wen-kan and General Chiang Kai-shek. The Chinese government through Koo handed the Commission some of the essential documents concerning (1) Sino-Japanese relations prior to the Sino-Japanese War in 1894; (2) Sino-Japanese disputes since that time; (3) the general analysis of the railway system in Manchuria; (4) the origin and story of the Manchuria Incident; (5) the origins and story of the January 28 incident in Shanghai; (6) the peace negotiations in Shanghai; and (7) the position of the Chinese

[24] Furuya Keiji, *Chiang Tsung-t'ung mi-lu*, VIII, pp. 143-73.

[25] Westel W. Willoughby, *The Sino-Japanese Controversy and the League of Nations*, pp. 200-1.

[26] *New York Times*, February 29 and March 12, 1932.

[27] *New York Times*, March 15, 1932.

government.[28] During the welcoming banquet in Shanghai, Koo emphasized in his speech the "similarities of fundamental principles and spirit between the League of Nations and China," "restoring Chinese territorial and sovereign integrity" and "respecting the dignity of the Kellogg-Briand Peace Pact and the Washington Nine Power Treaty."[29] He repeated the ideas in the following days in either official speeches or in talks with the press corps on board the steamer *Te-ho* in Nanking, Hankow, Peiping, Tientsin. . . .

After the last official contact with the Chinese government officials in the modern dormitory of the Department of Railways, the Commission took the steamer *Lung-ho* sailing for Hankow in the evening of April 1 in the company of Koo and Yoshida. Three days later, the group arrived in Hankow. Among the welcoming crowd of local leaders were Ho Ch'eng-chün and Hsia Tou-yin, who were chiefly involved in war against the 60,000 Red Army under General Ho Lung.[30] On its way back to Nanking Koo again accompanied the Commission paying a visit to Foreign Minister Lo Wen-kan and all took a Special Blue Express Train for Peiping via Tientsin. In Peiping, the Commission was entertained by the Young Marshal and Koo's families, and the Commission interviewed a series of officials, including Jung Chen, chief of staff of Young Marshal and acting commander of the Headquarters of the Manchurian forces in Mukden during the Manchurian Incident. The Commission also interviewed various groups of all classes, including Chinese and Foreign professors in Peiping, representatives of the Manchurian people in Peiping, leaders of the Manchus and Mongols, as well as representatives of cultural institutions.[31] Between April and August of 1932, Koo edited and submitted to the Commission the Memoranda, which contained three hundred documents concerning a historical survey of the Japanese aggression since 1871.

The first warning against Koo's trip to Manchuria was forwarded by the Italian ambassador in Japan to Count Aldrovandi who in turn warned Madame Hui-lan Koo.[32] On April 4, the Japanese Consul at Changchun, the new capital of the puppet Manchukuo, also reported that the Manchurian government would not allow Koo to enter Manchuria with the League Commission of Inquiry on the ground that his presence would be likely to cause commotion because people might assume that the Young Marshal would return. When asked by a Japanese reporter, Lord Lytton answered, "The Commission is an indivisible body and its action follows the resolutions of the League of Nations. Therefore, opposition to any single person is like opposition to the

[28] *Ta-kung pao*, March 26-30, 1932.
[29] *Ta-kung pao*, March 17, 1932.
[30] *New York Times*, April 8, 1932.
[31] *Ta-kung pao*, April 17, 1932.
[32] Hui-lan Koo, *Autobiography*, p. 273.

whole Commission and the League of Nations."[33] The Chinese government in Nanking also refused to accept the official telegram of opposition of Manchukuo to Koo's trip from its Foreign Minister Hsieh Chieh-shih and repeatedly instructed Koo to make the trip with the Commission. Koo himself also asserted strongly that he would definitely go to Manchuria and would be willing to make all sacrifices despite the threatened danger from the Manchurian authorities.[34]

Under the pressure of the Commission, the Japanese government eventually announced that the Japanese authorities in Manchuria were willing to protect Koo while Koo visited Manchuria. However, the Manchukuo authorities did not withdraw their threat to arrest him if Koo left the Japanese zone.[35] Meanwhile, the Chinese government changed its mind and no longer insisted that the Commission go to Manchuria via the land route, the war-torn area between Mukden and the Great Wall.[36] Eventually, the Commission was divided into two groups to go to Manchuria. On April 19, the American and Italian commissioners took the Special Blue Express to go via the land route to Mukden, and the others with Koo's company took the Chinese warship *Hai Ch'i* via Ch'in-huang tao to Dairen.[37] Both groups rejoined in Mukden on April 21. After a series of visits and interviews with the foreign community and the Japanese Kwantung Army authorities, including General Honjō, Commander of the Kwantung Army, Koo accompanied the commission to Changchun on May 2, where the Commission interviewed officials of the puppet Manchukuo, including the Chief Executive Ai-hsin-chüeh-lo Pu-yi, the last Manchu Emperor of China and the Japanese officials in that puppet regime, Premier Cheng Hsiao-hsü and Governor Hsi Hsia of Kirin. The Commission also interviewed Japanese consuls in Mukden, Changchun and Harbin. Nevertheless, the Russian and Manchukuo authorities refused the Commission permission to interview General Ma Chan-shan, a hero in the war of resistance in North Manchuria conducted by volunteers.[38]

After the inspection tours in Southern Manchuria, including Dairen Port and the steel-city, Anshan, Koo and the Commission left Mukden in the morning of June 4 and arrived at the Great Wall at seven in the evening where they were met by the welcoming group from Peiping, including Madame Koo. After spending a night with the Commission at the resort Pei-tai-ho, Koo had

[33] *Ta-kung pao*, April 17, 1932.

[34] *Ta-kung pao*, April 6 and 15, 1932.

[35] *New York Times*, April 13, 19, 24, 29, and May 7, 1932.

[36] *Ta-kung pao*, April 20, 1932.

[37] The Minister in China (Johnson) to Acting Secretary of State, Peiping, April 22, 1932. *Foreign Relations of the United States, 1931*, III: 710–11.

[38] *Ta-kung pao*, April 20, 1932.

a talk with reporters the next morning. He briefed them on their Manchurian trip and, said sadly, "All fellow workers were heart-broken when we witnessed the suffering of our 30 million fellow country men and the lost territory, abundant in natural resources. We should look farther, any personal opinion is small and any matter can be sacrificed. But if we fail in diplomacy, we all would perish. . . . people who came to talk to us usually disappeared the next day."[39] Koo was allowed only three secretaries on his tour and was not allowed to go to the bathroom unaccompanied, throughout the days in Manchuria. On the other hand, he did not even have time to unpack his bullet-proof vest ordered from Shanghai by Madame Koo before his Manchurian trip.[40] Lord Lytton also regretted that the Commission failed to interview General Ma Chan-shan, the leader of the resistance in North Manchuria, due to the lack of cooperation of the Manchurian and Russian authorities. As a matter of fact, so many guards and plain clothes men were reinforced to spy so "obviously and crudely" that no Chinese was able to reach the members of the Commission without the approval of the Japanese and Manchukuo authorities.[41]

When Koo arrived in Peiping on June 6, he again reiterated his view: (1) the sufferings of the Manchurian people are beyond the imagination of people in China proper. Without liberal and healthy mass organizations during peace time, there is no effective power in case of war. (2) Generals Ting Ch'ao and Li Tu, leaders of the volunteer resisters, face a strong enemy without effective support from the rear and without control of the communication system. This is a kind of great sacrifice and China's days in Manchuria are numbered. (3) All high schools and above are occupied as military barracks. All elementary school texts and curricula have been revised by the Japanese authorities. A decade later, Manchurian youth will not know anything about China. (4) The Manchurian government is actually in the hands of several Japanese advisers. The Chinese are used as window dressing for public opinion. The resources of Manchuria are used to nourish a Manchurian Army which would be the spearhead of the future invasion in China proper. (5) Self-help is the only alternative left for China. It is necessary for us to help ourselves first before we look for any help from other countries. Without self-help, there is no chance to recover the lost territory, solely relying on other's assistance. Strength is still the absolutely essential factor in world affairs. Only with strength can the force of reason be effectively exerted.[42]

[39] *Ta-kung pao*, May 19, June 1, 4, 5, and 8, 1932.

[40] Hui-lan Koo, *Autobiography*, p. 276.

[41] The Consul General at Mukden (Myers) to the Acting Secretary of State, Mukden, May 3, 1932. *Foreign Relations of the United States, 1932*, III: 747-51.

[42] *Ta-kung pao*, June 7, 1932.

Again before he left Peiping for Tsinan and Tsingtao in Shantung province, Koo told the reporters of Reuters that the Japanese military machine was furthering its large-scale movement of control and conquest. The Japanese utilized a method of threat and terror to coerce prominent Chinese in Manchuria to serve as puppets. This offered a great deal of explosive material in the general situation of East Asia . . . in the nearest future, there would be an immense explosion which would not only endanger the peace of the Pacific but also other parts of the world, and could not be avoided unless we could settle it through respecting international treaties and justice to China.[43] After accompanying the Commission to Shantung, Koo himself flew to Nanking, reporting to President Wang Ching-wei on June 12, Koo reported to Chiang Kai-shek in the mountain resort Lu Shan on June 14, urging that national unification for the national emergency was the only alternative for national survival. And he promised to serve as minister to France and concurrently delegate to the League of Nations, in case his appointment were granted. In Nanking, Koo also tried to impress on the nation that "the League was only an agency of arbitration and not an agency of enforcement . . . it was a mistake to depend on the League to settle disputes . . . the League for justice, . . . we must depend on our own strength to survive in national disaster . . . united, we survive and divided, we perish. All internal disputes could be forgotten for. . . ." After a brief presence at the Shanghai Bankers' Association's banquet, Koo flew back to Peiping with Premier Wang, Foreign Minister Lo Wen-kan and T. V. Soong, on June 18.[44]

As soon as they arrived in Peiping, a meeting was held between the local leaders and the members of the Commission. Again Koo's palace home was used on June 19 to entertain the entire group including both the Young Marshal, the Commission and the government leaders from Nanking, such as Wang Ching-wei, President of the Executive Yuan, T. V. Soong, Minister of Finance, Lo Wen-kan, Minister of Foreign Affairs, who had arrived the previous day. Wang indicated to the Commission that the Chinese government would be prepared to grant a considerable degree of autonomy to Manchuria using a number of foreign advisers, and was prepared to consider the demilitarization of Manchuria through the instrumentality of a nonaggression pact involving Russia, Japan, and China. The Nanking group and the Young Marshal all agreed with the Lu Shan resolution that Koo would not accompany the Lytton's Commission to go to Japan due to Japan's objections. Therefore, when the Commission left Peiping for Japan on June 28, there were no Chinese in the party.[45]

[43] *Ta-kung pao*, June 10, 1932.

[44] The Minister in China (Johnson) to the Secretary of State, Peiping, June 22, 1932. *Foreign Relations of the United States, 1932*, IV: 97-98.

[45] *New York Times*, June 19, 1932.

It was July 17 when Koo met the ill Lord Lytton on a stretcher in Tsingtao, and then escorted the Commission back to Peiping on July 20. The final report was signed by all five members of the Commission on September 4 at the Peking Hotel. Next day, the Commission said good-bye to the Young Marshal and proceeded to Shanghai, and boarded the S. S. *Yü Chih* for Europe on September 4 amidst Japanese threats to withdraw from the League of Nations.[46]

By August 13, the rumor that Koo was going to be Chinese minister to France and one of the three Chinese delegates at Geneva together with W. W. Yen and Quo Tai-chi was confirmed by the National government in Loyang.[47] After a brief stay in Pei-tai-ho, Koo flew to Nanking to consult with Wang Ching-wei and then to Hankow to consult with Chiang Kai-shek. Back in Shanghai, Koo had consultations at T. V. Soong's residence with Wang Ching-wei, Lo Wen-kan and Hsü Mo in the evening of September 3. The next morning, Koo boarded the S. S. *Yü Chih* sailed for Hong Kong with members of the Commission. Before the ship steered out of the Whangpu River, and in the presence of Wang Ching-wei, the Shanghai Mayor Wu T'ieh-ch'eng, and other dignitaries who had come to see him off, Koo said to reporters that "he would try his best to struggle for national glory at the League of Nations, and in the meanwhile, hoped that the country would be united to back up the diplomacy."[48] Several weeks later, Madame Koo followed Koo to Paris sailing on an Italian ship.[49] While Koo was at sea, the Japan-Manchukuo Protocol of September 15 was signed by General Nobuyoshi Muto and the puppet Prime Minister Cheng Hsiao-hsü and Manchukuo's security and existence was put under the protection of Japan by allowing the Kwantung Army to be stationed in Manchukuo.[50]

THE SINO-JAPANESE ARGUMENTS ON LYTTON REPORT

As the Great Powers understood that there was nothing for them to do but accept the Lytton Report, and Japan was granted a lengthy period to "study" the Report against the wishes of the impatient Chinese Delegation so that "wiser counsel would prevail in Japan and go along with Lytton's suggestions

[46] *New York Times*, June 29, 1932.

[47] *Ta-kung pao*, August 12, 13, 14, 1932.

[48] *Ta-kung pao*, September 5 and 6, 1932.

[49] Koo Hui-lan, *Autobiography*, p. 279.

[50] General Nobuyoshi Muto was concurrently governor general of the Kwantung Leased Territory, Commander of the Kwantung Army, and Japanese Ambassador to Manchukuo. *Foreign Relations of the United States, 1932, Far East*, IV: 253-54.

for the final settlement of the Manchurian Incident.[51] Consequently, the Council did not discuss the Lytton Report until its fifth meeting, held on November 21, 1932, when the Japanese representative, M. Matsuoka, opened the discussion by remarks his government had communicated to the League on the Report. At the sixth meeting of the Council, held on the same afternoon, the Chinese representative on the Council, Dr. Koo, stated the Chinese views on the Lytton Report.[52] After having paid high tribute to the members of the Lytton Commission for their conscientious work, Koo then referred to certain obstructions the Kwantung Army had put in the way of the visit of the Chinese Assessor and his staff in Manchuria. He referred to the Japanese plots and interventions blocking the unification of the Chinese Republic in order to realize the Japanese continental policy. He defended the present Chinese boycott of Japanese goods as a legitimate and peaceful method of self-defense against aggression. He mentioned that there was no anti-foreign sentiment in China except against Japan as a natural consequence of Japanese policy to "control and conquer China." He condemned the Japanese invasion in Manchuria and the puppet Manchukuo, as the Lytton Report stated:

> An explosion undoubtedly occurred on or near the railway between 10 and 10:30 p.m. on September 18th, but the damage, if any, to the railway did not, in fact, prevent the punctual arrival of the south-bound train from Changchun, and was not in itself sufficient to justify military action. The military operations of the Japanese troops during this night, which have been described above, cannot be regarded as measures of legitimate self-defense.
>
> It is clear that the independence movement, which have never been heard of in Manchuria before September, 1931, was only made possible by the presence of the Japanese troops. A group of Japanese civil and military officials, both active and retired, conceived, organized and carried through this movement, as a solution to the situation in Manchuria as it existed after the events of September 18th . . . the two which, in combination, were most effective and without which, in our judgment, the new state could not have been formed, were the presence of Japanese troops and the activities of Japanese officials, both civil and military.[53]

Koo concluded by reasserting that the settlement of the Manchurian question must conform to the League Covenants, Pact of Paris and Nine Power Treaty; that China must not suffer, or Japan benefit, by the latter's aggression; that China was entitled to claim damages; and that Japan must withdraw its troops.

[51]The Ambassador in Great Britain (Mellon) to the Secretary of State, London, October 28, 1932. *Foreign Relations of the United States, 1932, Far East*, IV:317.

[52]Koo, V. K. Wellington, China's Representative on the Council of the League of Nations. *A Statement of the Views of the Chinese Government on the Report of the Commission of Enquiry of the League of Nations* (Geneva: Chinese Delegation to the League of Nations, December 1932).

[53]*Report of the Commission of Enquiry of the League of Nations*, p. 97.

And, he urged the League to take prompt and effective action.[54]

At the seventh meeting of the Council, held on November 23, the Japanese representative, M. Matsuoka, denied all the Chinese accusations. He asserted that the Japanese government had neither advance military plans in Manchuria nor a plan for continental expansion. He characterized the Chinese boycott, endorsed by the Chinese government, as being as bad as actual war, if not worse. He denied that Japan had violated the League Covenant or any other international treaties and was not responsible for China's disorganization. Through the secret Treaty of 1896, between Russia and China, China had made the Russians wage war on Japan.[55] Koo answered Matsuoka by comparing the Manchurian Affair with the presentation of the Twenty-one Demands in 1915. When Japan was pressed for confirmation, she persistantly denied the fact. Koo said that "what Japan has done in the past in denying the authenticity of certain of her deeds, she may be doing again today." During the eighth meeting of the Council, Koo also defended China's secret treaty with Russia:

> ... With Russia alone, Japan made a secret treaty in 1907 ... and followed up with secret treaties in 1910, 1912, and 1916, all for the purpose of dividing Chinese territory with Russia ... His words of criticism on this point might have been more convincing if his own country had been less adept in the conclusion of secret treaties and alliances.[56]

At the ninth meeting of the Council, on November 25, Matsuoka communicated a memorandum listing four specific contentions that the work of the Commission had terminated when the report was presented to the Council; that any explanation from the Commission should only apply with regard to passages in the report which are not clear and distinct; that Japan could not admit the competency of the Commission to comment on the observations presented by the Japanese government to the Council or on the statements made by the Japanese representatives at the Council; and that Japan objected to any change in the report by the Commission after hearing observations and statements.[57] Since Lord Lytton declined to make changes, the President interrupted the Sino-Japanese debate by proposing this dispute to the

[54]V. K. Wellington Koo, *A Statement of the View of the Chinese Government on the Report of the Commission of Enquiry of the League of Nations* (Geneva: Chinese Delegation to the League of Nations, December 1932), pp. 36-41.

[55]The Consul at Geneva (Gilbert) to the Secretary of State, Geneva, November 23, 1932. *Foreign Relations of the United States, 1932, Far East*, IV:363-65.

[56]W. W. Willoughby, *The Sino-Japanese Controversy and the League of Nations*, p. 423.

[57]The Consul General at Geneva (Gilbert) to the Secretary of State, Geneva, November 26, 1932. *Foreign Relations of the United States, 1932, Far East*, IV:370-71.

Assembly as soon as possible, because it would not be fruitful for the Council to make further efforts, under Article XI of the Covenant, to resolve the controversy and there was no hope for any measure of agreement between the two governments in dispute. Once again Matsuoka urged the League to seek "peace based on realities," and to recognize the state of Manchukuo. And once again Koo countered, "Are we here to deal with realities alone and brush aside law and justice and the common interests of the peace of the world? Is this an organization which recognizes nothing but realities and which does not wish to uphold the principles of peace, law and justice upon which it is founded? . . ."[58]

At the tenth meeting of the Council, held on November 28, the resolution to transmit the Report of the Commission of Inquiry to the Assembly was voted and adopted unanimously (Japan abstaining) and the decision taken to refer the Sino-Japanese dispute to the Assembly. Koo filed a document on December 3 defending the Chinese position against Japanese observations on the Lytton Report, stating that the vast country of China was a relatively orderly and moral state under a young republican government and there was no reason to expect the fall of the central government; and that on the contrary there existed a reign of terror, financial stress, unrest and military domination in Japan; that the real menace to the peace of the Far East and the world was Japan's traditional policy, the so-called continental policy, of expansion and conquest on the Asiatic mainland; that the popular movement in China to emancipate her from one-sided restrictions on her political, administrative, and jurisdictional freedom was characterized by singular restraint and moderation without anti-foreignism; that China's sovereignty over Manchuria was evidenced by the facts that Japan never questioned it in the Washington Conference and that it was to the Chinese government that Japan directed her proposal for settlement; that Japan's claim to a special position in Manchuria was a mere cloak for her traditional policy of expansion and conquest on the mainland of Asia; that the Lytton Report showed that the State of Manchukuo owed its origin to the Japanese, and not to any spontaneous movement on the part of the inhabitants of Manchuria. Koo concluded by remarking that China was in full accord with the principle laid down by the Lytton Commission that any settlement of the Sino-Japanese controversy should conform to the provisions of the Covenant of the League of Nations, the Pact of Paris, and the Nine Power Treaty of Washington.

On December 6, the Assembly held its ninth meeting, the Sino-Japanese discussion was opened by Dr. W. W. Yen, calling attention to four important findings of the Lytton Commission: that the Japanese claim of 300 outstanding

[58]W. W. Willoughby, *op. cit.*, p. 430.

cases between the two countries and that peaceful methods for settling them had been exhausted cannot be substantiated; that the military operations of the Japanese troops during that night cannot be regarded as measures of legitimate self-defense; that the Japanese continued their advance in Manchuria and ended with the occupation of the whole of Manchuria; that Japan conceived, organized and carried through the independence movement, resulting in what is known as the state of Manchukuo. Yen requested that:

> (1) That the Special Assembly, based on the findings of the Commission of Enquiry, declare that Japan has violated the Covenant of the League of Nations, the Pact of Paris and the Nine Power Treaty of Washington;
>
> (2) That the Special Assembly call upon Japan to put into execution forthwith the Council Resolutions of September 30th and December 10th, 1931, so that all Japanese troops will be withdrawn into the so-called Railway Zone . . . ;
>
> (3) That the Special Assembly . . . declare that it will not recognize the said Manchukuo Government and will not enter into any relations therewith;
>
> (4) That the Special Assembly make and publish before a definite date and within the shortest time a report for the final settlement of the dispute . . .[59]

Relying on collective security for their own protection, all the small powers had sympathized with the victim of aggression. At the tenth plenary meeting, on December 6, Mr. Connoly, representing the Irish Free State urged his colleagues "to stand definitely with courage and determination behind the Covenant and its own decisions," and refuse to recognize the "State of Manchukuo." M. Benes, representing Czechoslovakia, declared himself in favor of the adoption of the Commission's Report and said that the military operations of the Japanese in Manchuria and the bombardment at Shanghai were not acts of legitimate self-defense and the creation of Manchukuo was not due to the spontaneous action on the part of the Chinese population of Manchuria and was fundamentally opposed to Article X of the Covenant and the Nine Power Treaty. Representatives from other small powers, including M. Undén of Sweden, M. Lange of Norway, and M. de Madariaga of Spain followed suit. Among the great powers, M. Paul-Boncour of France said, "Except in the case of an express stipulation in treaties in force, the Covenant does not authorize a state, however well-founded its grievances against another state, to seek redress by method other than the pacific methods set forth in Article XII of the Covenant." He declared the Lytton Report an extremely clear, substantiated and impartial report and urged its adoption. The speeches of Sir John Simon of Great Britain, Baron Aloisi of Italy, and Baron von Neurath of Germany were relatively colorless.[60]

[59] The Consul at Geneva (Gilbert) to the Secretary of State, Geneva, December 6, 1932. *Foreign Relations of the United States, 1932, Far East*, IV:391-93.

[60] W. W. Willoughby, *op. cit.*, pp. 443-54.

The general debate was concluded at the 15th plenary of the Assembly, December 8 by the vigorous and plain-speaking Quo Tai-chi, Chinese representative at the Assembly and Commissioner of Foreign Affairs in Shanghai during the Shanghai Armistice. Having praised the judgment of the Lytton Report, he denied there was any semblance of justification between the British landing of troops in Shanghai and the Japanese Manchurian Incident, the British did not launch any large-scale attack, nor aerial or navar bombardment on thickly populated towns and defenseless institutions, nor did they occupy Chinese territory outside of the International Settlement. He emphasized the common obligation of every nation to play its part in preventing aggressive war and the solid resistance of the Chinese people against wrongs done to them. He remarked that China could not enter negotiations on the basis of recognition of Manchukuo, nor could the Assembly, in view of its Resolution of March 11. In reference to the ten principles laid down in Chapter IX of the Commission's Report, Quo said:

> China is ready to take these principles as a basis of discussion provided the resolutions of September 30th and December 10th, 1931, are enforced, provided the principles of the report are taken as a whole and provided they are all interpreted in the light of the third principle; namely, that any solution must conform to the provisions of the Covenant, the Pact of Paris and the Nine Power Treaty. . . .[61]

This was followed again by M. Matsuoka's defense of the event on September 18, his denial of Japan's violation of international treaties and agreements, and his condemnation of the disorder of the Chinese government. He warned members of the Assembly that were Japan to be weakened by the League or by any other institution or powers, they might be sure that Sovietism would soon reach the mouth of the Yangtze.

Among the rumors of Pu-yi's being installed as the emperor of a Manchu-Mongol empire, Secretary Stimson began a series of contacts and behind-the-scene pushes with the Great Powers through his office in Washington, D. C., his representatives in Geneva, and elsewhere. On December 6, he achieved understanding with the Canadian Minister, Herridge, that it was in the interest of the entire world that the peace treaties be maintained and that the special interests of the Western Powers in the Pacific lay in the Nine Power Treaty. These peace articles and alignments of nations would forestall Japan's adventure in Manchuria. By declaring nonrecognition, the League would be put on the same footing as the United States.[62] A similar understanding was

[61] W. W. Willoughby, *op. cit.*, pp. 456-59.

[62] Memorandum by the Secretary of State of a conversation with the Canadian Minister, December 6, 1932. *Foreign Relations of the United States, 1932, Far East*, IV: 388-90.

reached with Sir John Simon through the American Ambassador to France, Edge,[63] as well as with the French Government.[64]

In order to study the report of the Commission of Inquiry, the observations of the parties and the Assembly, and to draw up proposals with a view to the settlement of the dispute, a resolution proposed by the representatives of Switzerland and Czechoslovakia was adopted at the 15th plenary meeting of the Assembly, held on December 9, to set up a Special Committee from members of the Committee of Nineteen which was the main organ to deal with Sino-Japanese disputes at the Assembly. The endeavors of the Special Committee to conciliate the parties also failed due to the Japanese objections to the proposed resolution of the Special Committee that the United States and Soviet Union should participate and that there be exclusion of the recognition of the independence of Manchukuo from any settlement. Since a settlement of the Sino-Japanese controversy by conciliation proceedings would be futile, the Committee of Nineteen began to prepare a report which was circulated to the members of the Assembly on February 16, 1933 amidst the conflicting influences of great powers emphasizing conciliation, and the smaller powers interested in finding a basis for conciliation which would be consistent with the terms of the Covenant.[65]

The Japanese Delegation found the report unacceptable. In its Observations on the Report, they went on to assert once more that Japan had acted in self-defense; that the support of Manchukuo as an independent state was necessary for the maintenance of peace in the Far East; that Jehol was a part of Manchuria; that the Covenant, the Pact of Paris and the Nine Power Treaty set forth only general principles which, in practical application, needed to be related to the realities of the situation; that there was no central government in China strong enough to fulfill the requirements of the proposals made in the report; that the soverignty of Manchuria did not belong to China but to the people of Manchuria; that should Japanese troops be withdrawn, life and property in Manchuria would be in danger; that Japan opposed the non-member states, the United States and Russia, on the proposed committee of conciliation; and that non-recognition of the Manchurian government would be an obstacle to good understanding and friendly relations between these nations.[66] At the Assembly, Matsuoka criticized the Report and declared that

[63]The Ambassador in France (Edge) to the Secretary of State, Paris, December 14, 1932. *Foreign Relations of the United States, 1932, Far East*, IV:420-23.

[64]The Department of State to the French Embassy, Washington, D. C., December 6, 1932. *Foreign Relations of the United States, 1932, Far East*, IV:390-91.

[65]The Minister in Switzerland (Wilson) to the Secretary of State, Geneva, December 12, 1932. *Foreign Relations of the United States, 1932, Far East*, IV:414-15.

[66]W. W. Willoughby, *op. cit.*, p. 511.

it was a fiction to deal with China as a sovereign state; that the majority of the people of Manchuria were distinctly different from those of China; that the Jehol invasion had been necessitated by Chinese action; that Manchuria was regarded by Japanese as a matter of life and death, like the Panama Canal Zone for Americans, and Egypt for the British. He opposed any attempt by the League to adopt the Report.

This draft report was adopted by the Assembly by a unanimous vote except for the single dissenting voice of Japan, as the Assembly Report of February 24, 1933 on the Sino-Japanese Dispute. It represents the mature verdict of the League toward the dispute. The Report is divided into four parts. Part I stated that the Assembly adopted as part of its own report the first eight chapters of the Report of the Commission of Enquiry. Part II is entitled "Development of the Dispute before the League of Nations," which included the historical background of the controversy, the texts of the Assembly and the Council resolutions, and the development of the situation in Manchuria and at Shanghai while the controversy was being dealt with at Geneva. Part III is entitled "Chief Characteristics of the Dispute," which recognized China's sovereignty in Manchuria, and that the ties binding Manchuria and the rest of China were growing stronger, that national reconstruction in China had achieved considerable progress, that a group of Japanese civil and military officials conceived, organized, carried and still controlled the Manchurian independence movement, that the Japanese had greatly aggravated the situation created on the night of September 18, by their military operation, and the creation of Manchukuo and the recognition by its government. Part IV, the final part, is entitled "Statements of Recommendations," including that the settlements should observe the provisions of the peace articles as well as the Assembly resolutions, such as the evacuation of the Japanese troops, that the Japanese rights and interests be respected, such as autonomous Manchurian administration under the Chinese sovereignty, and finally it contains the details of Sino-Japanese negotiation to carry out the above-mentioned Assembly resolution under the assistance of third powers. When the President of the Assembly declared that the Report was unanimously adopted, the entire Japanese Delegation withdrew from the Assembly hall amidst the applause of the observers, including Madame Koo. Subsequently, the Japanese government sent a note to the League formally withdrawing from the international organization, which was received on March 27.

Shortly after the vote, Dr. Koo, speaking for China, made some concluding remarks saying that although the requirements of justice could be considered to have been met by the fact that the Report had been adopted by the Assembly, the principal object of the League's existence, the maintenance of peace, remained yet to be fulfilled, as evidenced by the Japanese attack upon

Jehol in pursuance of her fixed policy of territorial aggrandizement on the mainland of Asia. Koo asked the delegates not to adjourn its present session without making an effort to deal adequately with the grave situation in the Far East. "Shall they stand together to circumscribe, to control, and speedily end it or shall they, drifting and disunited, be dragged one by one into what so easily might become a spreading whirlpool of disaster?" China was by no means satisfied that the League had taken more than a step toward dealing adequately with the situation which Japan had created by her attacks and the policy of aggression which she was still pursuing toward China. He urged the delegates to take the next steps to the sanctions provided for in Article XVI of the Covenant. On the eve of the Assembly meeting which adopted the Report, the Japanese army, no doubt as a reply to the League's pronouncement, and in disregard of the League Covenant under Articles XII and XV, attacked and occupied Jehol Province, and declared it a part of the "State of Manchukuo."[67]

[67]The Minister in China (Johnson) to the Secretary of State, Peiping, March 5, 6, 7, and 10, 1933. *Foreign Relations of the United States, 1933, Far East*, III: 223-30.

CHAPTER VII

Koo in the League of Nations and the Sino-Japanese War, 1937-1941

FROM HUMILIATING AGREEMENTS TO NATIONWIDE WAR

The guns on the bridgehead of Lukouchiao (Marco Polo Bridge) finally opened China's nationwide War of Resistance against Japan on July 7, 1937, and forced Japan to replace her policy of stealthy encroachment with full military operation. After the Manchurian occupation, the Japanese Kwantung Army continued their push into Jehol province. Following the famous battles along the Great Wall with the Chinese 29th Army under Sung Che-yüan (Marshal Feng Yü-hsiang's Northwest Army remnants) in March 1933, the situation came to a standstill. Through the efforts of Huang Fu, Chairman of the Peiping Political Affairs Council, the T'angku Truce was signed in May 1933 by Hsiung Pin and General Okamura, then Deputy Chief of Staff of the Kwantung Army, putting the triangular area between Peiping, Tientsin and the Great Wall under the local security force. As the Kwantung Army withdrew to the Great Wall, Sung's army went further south of the line between Peiping and Tientsin.[1]

Among the settlements reached after numerous incidents prior to the nationwide Sino-Japanese War, the best known are the Ho-Umezu Agreement[2] and the Ch'in-Doihara Agreement.[3] The former was concluded on June 10, 1935, by the Chinese Defense Minister Ho Ying-ch'in and Lieutenant General Umezu Yoshijirō, the commander of the Japanese North China Garrison in Tientsin. This agreement committed the Chinese to withdraw Yü Hsüeh-chung's Manchurian units and two divisions under Huang Chieh and Kuan Lin-cheng, belonging to Chiang Kai-shek, out of Hopei province; and to abolish all anti-Japanese activities in north China, including Kuomintang party organs, the political training department of the Peiping branch of the Military Affairs Commission, and the Blue Shirts. The latter accord was negotiated by Ch'in Te-ch'un, acting governor of Chahar and deputy commander of the 29th Army, and by General Doihara Kenji, head of both the

[1] Ch'in Te-ch'un, *Hai-shih t'an-wang* (Memoir of Ch'in Te-ch'un), p. 58.

[2] Furuya Keiji, *Chiang Tsung-t'ung mi-lu*, X, pp. 34-35.

[3] Ch'in Te-ch'un, *Hai-shih t'an-wang*, pp. 60-64.

Kwantung Army's special service organ and North China Garrison's special service organ, and was accepted by the Chinese Government on June 27, 1935. By using the second Chang-pei incident as the pretext, when four Japanese military personnel were detained overnight due to their lack of travel permits, Doihara exacted from Ch'in terms such as punishment of the officers responsible, dissolution of Kuomintang party organs and the Blue Shirts from Chahar, and the withdrawal of the 29th Army from regions east of the extension of the T'angku Truce line and north of the northern Great Wall line. Then Doihara was able to proceed with the next stage of aggression by creating an autonomous government in north China's five provinces. In view of the lack of support for Doihara's "autonomous manifesto" from north China leaders, including Shantung Governor Han Fu-ch'ü, Hopei Governor Shang Chen and 29th Army commander Sung Che-yüan, war seemed the only alternative for the frustrated Japanese militarists to take over north China.[4]

The Japanese premeditated attack at Lukouchiao ignited the Sino-Japanese War, under the pretext of searching for a missing soldier after an illegal maneuver at Lukouchiao, ten miles south of Peiping in the early hours of July 7.[5] When they were refused entry to the city of Wan-ping to search for the missing soldier by the garrison regiment commander, Chi Hsin-wen of the 29th Army, the Japanese began to bombard the Wan-ping city at the north end of the bridge.[6] Soon the war spread to other cities and to Shanghai, where the Japanese naval authorities provoked an incident on August 9, [7] concentrating thirty warships and thousands of marines in Shanghai within forty-eight hours. The Japanese naval forces, using the International Settle-

[4] Alvin D. Coox and Hilary Conroy (eds.), *China and Japan: Search for Balance since World War I* (Santa Barbara, California: ABC-Clio, 1978), pp. 184-92.

[5] The Ambassador in China (Johnson) to the Secretary of State, Peiping, August 17, 1937. "Regardless of the accuracy of these versions, the responsibility for the outbreak rests with the Japanese for the reasons that (1) the Japanese were unnecessarily holding maneuvers at night in close proximity to a regularly stationed Chinese garrison at a time when a tense political situation existed, (2) the Japanese authorities knew well that the Chinese troops concerned were a part of the reputedly anti-Japanese 37th Division, and (3) the Japanese claim that they had a right to maneuver in that area under the terms of the Protocol of 1901 was ill-founded as the area lies well outside of the zone delimited in the Protocol for the movement of foreign troops." *Foreign Relations of the United States, 1937, Far East,* III: 432-33.

[6] Liu Ju-ming, *Liu Ju-ming hui-i lu* (Memoir of Liu Ju-ming), pp. 113-14.

[7] August 13 Incident. One Japanese naval officer and one Japanese seaman attempted to approach the Chinese airport in the suburb of Shanghai on August 9 when they were stopped by a Chinese guard. A clash took place in which the two Japanese and a member of the Chinese Peace Preservation Corps were killed. The Japanese attack, both ashore and afloat, began four days later.

ment as their base of operation, attacked the Chinese districts despite the total acceptance of the Japanese demands by Shanghai authorities.

KOO APPEALS TO LEAGUE OF NATIONS

Koo had been raised to the rank of ambassador after returning to Paris in April 1936 when the news of the Lukouchiao Incident reached him. He was made Chinese chief delegate to the League of Nations after the Incident. Following instructions from the home government, Koo began to explore the powers' opinion concerning China's invoking Article 17 of the Covenant of the League of Nations, so that the Council of the League could "institute any inquiry into the circumstances of the dispute and recommend such actions as may seem best and most effectual in the circumstances," including diplomatic, economic and military sanctions. Koo also suggested Article 10 or 11 of the Covenant as the alternative in case Japan refused to accept any intervention by the League.[8] Article 10 called for the "members of the League to undertake to respect and preserve as against external aggression the territorial integrity and existing political independence of all Members." Article 11 said "any war or threat of war . . . is hereby declared a matter of concern to the whole League, and the League shall take any action that may be deemed wise and effectual to safeguard the peace of nations."

To coordinate their strategies, Finance Minister H. H. Kung, who was the chief Chinese delegate to the coronation of King George VI, called a conference in London. It was attended by Wellington Koo, Quo Tai-chi, Chinese Ambassador to the Court of St. James, and T. F. Tsiang (Chiang Ting-fu), Chinese Ambassador to Moscow. The conference was based on the assumption that the Chinese Government would have to fight. T. F. Tsiang believed that the Soviet Union would preserve neutrality during the first few months and that if the war should be protracted, the Soviet Government, provided it could obtain assurances of support from either England, France, or the United States, would intervene despite the warnings from Germany and Italy of their intention to take the side of Japan. Quo was of the opinion that Great Britain would do nothing. Koo believed that the great powers, particularly France, were loath to take any action with regard to matters in the Far East due to European troubles and that they were convinced that the Japanese, after butchering various Chinese armies, would be able to take over China as far as the Yellow River and set up another Manchukuo. In any case France would

[8]The Ambassador in France (Bullitt) to the Secretary of State, Paris, July 13, 1937. *Foreign Relations of the United States, 1937, Far East*, III: 152-53.

be prepared to act only in concert with Great Britain and the United States.[9] The envoys jointly suggested to their government to win Soviet military cooperation and material support from the Western powers for the War of Resistance.

China sent her first note on the Sino-Japanese incident to the League secretariat on August 30 as a first step toward a future appeal.[10] Since joint action of the Western powers against Japan was nil, and the joint efforts of the powers for peace produced no result among the belligerents, China decided to carry the case to the League of Nations, despite the reluctance of the Western diplomats, who believed that the League would be unable to refuse to take up the matter but that the impotence of the League would once more be demonstrated. On September 13 when the League of Nations Assembly was opened by Dr. Juan Negrin, Premier of war-torn Spain, the League faced China's formal appeal, presented the previous day, against Japan under Articles 10, 11, and 17 of the Covenant. The next of China's appeal, signed by Dr. Koo as her chief delegate, stated that Japan's continued aggression in China invoked action under Article 10, which guarantees the territorial integrity of members; Articles 11, which provides that the League may take action in a controversy; and Article 17, which provides that a nonmember can be summoned to answer charges.[11]

Before the 18th Assembly of the League of Nations, China's chief delegate Koo gave a touching speech inviting the powers' attention to a situation of the gravest kind.[12] He first provided the Assembly with information about the Japanese invasion force of 300,000 men, equipped with the most deadly instruments of war. He then condemned the Japanese air bombings against Chinese civilians and cultural and educational institutions, including the famous Nankai University; and he accused the Japanese of using the International Settlement in Shanghai as a base of operation. Despite China's readiness for peaceful settlement, the Japanese continued their attacks, occupied Peiping and Tientsin, and invaded Shanghai with the sole purpose of domination and conquest. He refuted Japan's overpopulation argument because there were hardly 300,000 Japanese living in Manchuria, where Japan

[9]The Ambassador in France (Bullitt) to the Secretary of the State, Paris, July 28, 1937. *Foreign Relations of the United States, 1937, Far East*, III: 288-89.

[10]The Consul General at Geneva (Everett) to the Secretary of State, Geneva, August 31, 1937. *Foreign Relations of the United States, 1937, Far East*, IV: 8-9.

[11]*New York Times*, September 14, 1937, p. 1.

[12]Speech by His Excellency Dr. V. K. Wellington Koo, First Delegate of China to the XVIIIth Assembly of the League of Nations, September 15, 1937. *Japanese Aggression and the League of Nations, 1937*, I, published by the Press Bureau of the Chinese Delegation, Geneva.

had exercised a predominant influence for more than a quarter of a century. He also refuted Japan's war materials argument because most of her needs were supplied not from China but principally from other countries, such as cotton from the United States, oil from America and the Netherland Indies, and iron from India and Malaya. Since Japan was in the grip of the war party, its continental policy would eventually become a menance to European and American interests. "Peace is indivisible," Koo argued, "the principle of collective security . . . is beyond question the only logical and sound basis for any system of organized peace in the world."

Great Britain and other League members favored referring the Chinese appeal against Japan to the Advisory Committee on the Far East which the Assembly had established in 1933 to deal with the Sino-Japanese conflict. That Committee enjoyed a freedom not enjoyed by the League members because the United States was included.[13] The position of the United States was significant because the application of the U. S. Neutrality Act or failure of the U. S. to cooperate would have very deplorable effects on the League and, practically, on all hope for China there. At the beginning of the war on July 16, Chinese Vice-Minister of Foreign Affairs Hsü Mo had already appealed to Johnson, United States Ambassador in Nanking, that there "would be no early application of the law [U. S. Neutrality Act] because the law would bear more disadvantageously on China as the weaker contestant since Japan did not need, as China did, access to financial and material resources."[14]

The League Council, on September 16, referred to the Advisory Committee on the Far East the difficult task of examining the Sino-Japanse conflict. The Committee invited China, Japan, Germany and Australia to send delegates. Contending that "a just, equitable and practical solution" of the Sino-Japanese questions could be found by themselves, both Japan and Germany declined. On September 27, Koo presented another speech before the Committee. He informed them that the Japanese army of invasion had increased to 350,000 men, that Japan's real intention was the subjugation of China, and that her policy violated international law and treaty obligaton. Koo stated that if the League "cannot enforce international law and the principles of the Covenant, it can at least denounce it, it can at least make it known that it has not abandoned them." Koo urged the Committee to condemn the indiscriminate aerial warfare, by quoting Cordell Hull's speech that "the government of the United States holds that any general bombardment of an extensive region in which a large civil population resides is

[13] *New York Times*, September 16, 1937, p. 9.

[14] The Ambassador in China (Johnson) to the Secretary of State, Peiping, July 16, 1937. *Foreign Relations of the United States, 1937, Far East*, III: 182-83.

unjustifiable and contrary to legal and humanitarian principles." And he urged the Committee to act speedily and effectively to take concrete and feasible measures to aid China.[15] Koo's efforts were also supported by his colleagues in Europe, including Quo Tai-chi, Chinese Ambassador to Britain, Tsien Tai, Chinese Ambassador to Belgium, and Wunsz King, Chinese Minister to the Netherlands.

On September 27, 1937, Koo won his first battle when the delegates of the twenty-two other nations on the Committee adopted the Resolution Against Aerial Bombardment of Open Towns and Noncombatants. The Resolution declared that "no excuse can be made for such acts which have aroused horror and indignation throughout the world," and the Committee "solemnly condemns them."[16] The Resolution was adopted by the Assembly the following day. On September 29 the American representative read before the Committee a statement that the American Government "holds the view that any general bombing of an extensive area wherein there resides a large populace engaged in peaceful pursuits is unwarranted and contrary to the principles of law and humanity."[17]

During these decisive days, Koo intensified his efforts and presented China's case in several speeches before the Advisory Committee on September 29 and October 1, respectively. He and his colleagues, such as Tsien Tai, Wunsz King, and Minister Hoo Chi-tsai, also spoke before the various committees of the Assembly. Koo even broadcast to the United States from Geneva on September 26 that China "has a special modeling on the United States democracy," that the United States' traditional policy towards China "has been of friendship and helpfulness" from Anson Burlingame to Charles Evans Hughes, who made possible the conclusion of the Nine-Power Treaty of Washington, that Japan "threatened the peace of the Pacific and the well-being of the United States," and that China needed moral support and material aid to enable her to cope successfully for her national existence and the cause of general peace.[18] On October 1 Koo moved without success to adopt a resolution condemning the Japanese violations of international law and illegal

[15] Speech by His Excellency Dr. V. K. Wellington Koo before the Far East Advisory Committee on September 27, 1937. *Japanese Aggression and the League of Nations, 1937*, II, pp. 7-15.

[16] Resolution Against Aerial Bombardment of Open Towns and Non-Combatants, September 27th-28th. *Japanese Aggression and the League of Nations, 1937*, II, p. 17.

[17] V. K. Wellington Koo, "The Problem of the Pacific and Collective Security." An address at a meeting of the Academy of Diplomacy, December 17, 1937, Paris. *Japanese Aggression and the League of Nations, 1938*, III, Annex, pp. 37-38.

[18] Speech by His Excellency Dr. V. K. Wellington Koo, Broadcast to the United States of America from Geneva, on September 26, 1937. *Japanese Aggression and the League of Nations, 1937*, II, pp. 82-86.

blockade of the Chinese coasts.[19]

Koo's work finally bore fruit as the Advisory Committee on October 5 adopted a report and passed a resolution condemning Japan, both of which were adopted by the Assembly next day. After listing the main developments of events from the days of the Protocol of 1901, the Report offered both the Chinese and Japanese versions concerning the Lukouchiao Incident and the Shanghai Incident. The Report discussed the three treaties and Japan's breach of them, namely the Final Protocol of September 7, 1901, the Nine-Power Treaty signed at Washington in 1922, and the Pact of Paris of 1928. In conclusion, the Report stated:

> It cannot, however, be challenged that powerful Japanese armies have invaded Chinese territory and are in military control of large areas, including Peiping itself; that the Japanese Government has taken naval measures to close the coast of China to Chinese shipping; and that Japanese aircraft are carrying out bombardments over widely separated regions of the country.
>
> ... The Committee is bound to take the view that the military operations carried on by Japan against China by land, sea and air are out of all proportion to the incident that occasioned the conflict; that such action cannot possibly facilitate or promote the friendly cooperation between the two nations that Japanese statesmen have affirmed to be the aim of their policy; that it can be justified neither on the basis of existing legal instruments nor on that of the right of self-defense, and that it is in contravention of Japan's obligations under the Nine-Power Treaty of February 6th, 1922, and under the Pact of Paris of August 27th, 1928.[20]

Together with the Report, a resolution was also adopted by the Committee and accepted later by the Assembly. It proposed that the signatory powers of the Nine-Power Treaty should hold a conference. In conclusion, it stated:

> The Assembly ... expresses its moral support for China, and recommends that Members of the League should refrain from taking any action which might have the effect of weakening China's power of resistance and thus of increasing her difficulties in the present conflict, and should also consider how far they can individually extend aid to China.[21]

The League resolution was echoed immediately by President Roosevelt at Chicago on October 5, and was also formally supported by a statement

[19]The Minister in Switzerland (Harrison) to the Secretary of State, Geneva, October 1, 1937. *Foreign Relations of the United States, 1937, Far East*, IV: 49.

[20]The First Report, Adopted by the Advisory Committee on October 5th and by the Assembly on October 6, 1937. *Japanese Aggression and the League of Nations, 1937*, II, pp. 41-53.

[21]Resolution of the Assembly. *Japanese Aggression and the League of Nations, 1937*, II, pp. 57-62; The Minister in Switzerland (Harrison) to the Secretary of State, Geneva, October 5, 1937. *Foreign Relations of the United States, 1937*, IV: 58.

from the State Department the next day.[22] The statement repeated American principles governing international relations, including abstinence by all nations from the use of force in the pursuit of policy and from interference in the internal affairs of other nations, adjustment of problems in international relations by process of peaceful negotiation and agreement, respect by all nations for the rights of others, observance by all nations of established obligations, and the upholding of the principle of the sanctity of treaties. The statement concluded that "the action of Japan in China is inconsistent with the principles which should govern the relationships between nations and is contrary to the provisions of the Nine-Power Treaty regarding principles and policies to be followed in matters concerning China and to those of the Kellogg-Briand Pact."

In the resolution of the Assembly, it not only approved the Report but also requested its President "to take necessary actions with regard to the proposed meeting of the Members of the League which are Parties to the Nine-Power Treaty of Washington." Invitations were sent to the parties, and Chinese Foreign Minister Wang Chung-Hui accepted immediately, hoping the powers concerned "will lose no time in proceeding with such consultation as is contemplated and adopt most useful and effective measures to put an immediate end to the conflict."[23]

THE NINE-POWER TREATY CONFERENCE AT BRUSSELS

It may be recalled that on October 7, 1937 the Advisory Committee adopted two reports: the first report denounced Japan as the treaty violator; and the second report suggested that the League should invite "those members of the League who were parties to the Nine-Power Treaty to initiate at the earliest possible moment the consultation and full and frank communication provided for by that treaty." The Nine-Power Treaty of Washington, 1922, provided that the contracting powers agreed "to respect the sovereignty, the independence, and the territorial and administrative integrity of China" and "to provide the fullest and most unembarrassed opportunity to China to develop and maintain for herself an effective and stable government."[24] The powers

[22] The Secretary of State to the Minister in Switzerland (Harrison), Washington, October 6, 1937. *Foreign Relations of the United States, 1937, Far East*, IV: 62.

[23] China' Reply Accepting the Invitation, Nanking, October 8th, 1937, by Wang Chung-Hui. *Japanese Aggression and the League of Nations, 1937*, II, pp. 58, 60.

[24] "The Problem of the Pacific and Collective Security," an address by Dr. V. K. Wellington Koo at a meeting of the Academy of Diplomacy, December 17, 1937. *Japanese Aggression and the League of Nations, 1938*, III, Annex, pp. 33-34.

also pledged "to refrain from taking advantage of conditions in China in order to seek special rights or privileges." The idea of the Nine-Power Treaty Conference was well supported by League members because it would involve the United States, a member of this Treaty, in more active participation and because Japan might be willing to attend since she was no longer a member of the League and would not attend any League meetings.

Due to the unripe opinion at home and the doubtful prospects of such a conference, both the United States and British Governments did not want to be the host country. At the American suggestion, the British successfully persuaded the Belgian Government to be the host.[25] On October 16 invitations were sent to all the signatories of the Nine-Power Treaty, including Great Britain, the United States, France, Italy, China, Japan, the Netherlands, Portugal, and the adhering countries (Bolivia, Sweden, Denmark, Norway, and Mexico). At the British suggestion, and in accord with the accepting powers, invitations were also sent to Germany and the USSR. All accepted except Japan and Germany. Japanese public opinion, such as editorials in *Asahi Shimbun*, doubted that the purpose of the conference was to sit in judgment of Japan.[26] The Japanese Government declined because the League, in the report adopted on October 6, had declared the Japanese military operations in China were a violation of the Nine-Power Treaty, and because the Assembly had even gone to the length of assuring China of its moral support and of recommending to its members to abstain from any action that might weaken China's power of resistance, and to study how they might individually give aid to China, Japan also believed that a gathering of so many powers, whose interests in East Asia were of varying degrees, would only complicate the situation.[27] Germany—a partner of the Germany-Italy-Japan anti-Communist triangle—did not want to offend Japan.

THE DECLARATION OF NOVEMBER 15

Under the chair of the host country, Foreign Minister Spaak, the Conference was finally opened on November 3, after postponement, Dr. Koo again represented China as its chief delegate and was helped by Tsien Tai, Chinese

[25]Memorandum by the Adviser on Political Relations (Dunn) of a Trans-Atlantic Telephone Conversation with the Chargé in the United Kingdom (Johnson), Washington, October 8, 1937. *Foreign Relations of the United States, 1937*, IV: 67-68.

[26]The Ambassador in Japan (Grew) to the Secretary of State, Tokyo, October 8, 1937. *Foreign Relations of the United States, 1937*, IV: 67.

[27]The Ambassador in Japan (Grew) to the Secretary of State, Tokyo, October 27, 1937. *Foreign Relations of the United States, 1937*, IV: 112-13.

Ambassador to Belgium. After speeches given by Eden and Litvinov, Koo presented China's case to the delegates from 19 countries, including Norman Davis of the United States. Koo spoke of the continued armed aggression by more than a half-million Japanese soldiers in China, and the puppet regimes set up by the Japanese militarists in all occupied provinces. Koo condemned Japan's violation of the articles and spirit of the Nine-Power Treaty and urged peace "that will render justice to China."[28] Wishing that China would receive more aid from the powers after the failure of mediation, Koo circulated a memorandum pointing out the vulnerability of Japan's financial and economic situation and the possible effects of economic restrictions by the powers.

Since the Western powers only wanted mediation, and mediation required the presence of both parties, the Conference decided to send Japan a second invitation on November 7, with a much more conciliatory tone without mentioning anything which might insult Japan. Inasmuch as the Japanese Government objected that a "gathering of so many powers would only serve to complicate the situation," the Conference asked whether Japan would only dispatch one or more representatives to exchange views with representatives of a small number of powers to be chosen for that purpose. Again, Japan refused the invitation on November 12, stating that the opinion of participating powers was insufficient to persuade her to modify her previous views, and that Japan could not participate in a meeting based on a resolution which accused her of being the violator of the treaty.

At the November 7 meeting, discussing Japan's second refusal, Koo presented his views:

> The refusal of the Japanese Government is more resolute and absolute than ever, and both the language and tone of its reply seem to indicate clearly that all the painstaking efforts of the Conference to secure her collaboration have been taken as a sign of weakness and served apparently only to inspire insolence. The claim that Japan's present action in China is resorted to as a measure of self-defense is not only a deliberate distortion of the meaning of the time-honored term, it could in no way justify her claim that the matter lay outside the scope of the Nine Power Treaty. The "full and frank communication" envisaged in Article 7 of the Treaty is intended for just such a situation. Now that the door of conciliation and mediation has been slammed in your face by the latest reply of the Japanese Government, will you not decide to withhold supplies of war materials and credit to Japan and extend aid to China? It would be a modest way in which you can fulfill your obligation of helping to check Japanese aggression and upholding the treaty in question.[29]

---

[28]Tsien Tai, *China and the Nine Power Conference at Brussels in 1937*, p. 5.
[29]*Ibid.*, pp. 9-10.

As an atmosphere of despair in Brussels prevailed due to the absence of the British and French foreign ministers, the criticism within the United States, and the abstention of the Scandinavian countries, Koo maintained the Chinese stand of refusal of direct negotiation to avoid more Japanese demands, the acceptance of legitimate mediation for a just peace, China's determination to continue resistance to the end, and the powers' extension of aid to China and imposition of financial and economic restrictions on Japan in case of the failure of mediation. Koo urged a London-Washington-Paris axis to serve as a realistic foundation for worldwide peace. He addressed the Academy of Diplomacy in Paris, December 17, 1937:

> I am tempted to think that a most effective triangle in defense of liberty and peace would be that of Great Britain, the United States and France. United by a community of ideals and blessed with unlimited resources of military and economic power at their disposal, Great Britain, the United States and France, acting concertedly or even parallelly, provided they act, will prove, I believe, to be an anchor-sheet in the present stormy world, and with them acting together, other peace-loving countries will not be slow to associate themselves in the common task of safeguarding law and order, peace and security in the world.[30]

Much upset by the Japanese attitude, the delegates at Brussels adopted on November 15 a declaration which first rejected the Japanese view that the conflict concerned only the two countries directly involved, and insisted it was of concern to all parties to the Nine-Power Treaty and the Pact of Paris. It concluded that "the states represented at Brussels must consider what is to be their common attitude in a situation where one party to an international treaty maintains the views against the views of all the other parties that the action which it has taken does not come within the scope of the treaty which the other parties held to be operative in the circumstances."[31] Italy cast the only negative vote due to her anti-Communist triangular relations with Japan. The Scandinavian countries, under the shadow of the mighty German fleet, abstained, saying that they were sympathetic to the principle of the declaration, but their political interests in the Far East would not justify their signature. Then the Conference adjourned for a week so that the delegations could consult their governments on the next steps.

[30] V. K. Wellington Koo, "The Problem of the Pacific and Collective Security," an address at a meeting of the Academy of Diplomacy, December 17, 1937, with M. Henry-Berenger, President of the Foreign Affairs Commission of the French Senate in the chair. *Japanese Aggression and the League of Nations, 1938*, III, Annex, p. 48, Also *New York Times*, December 19, 1937, p. 37.

[31] Koo, *Reminiscences*, IV, p. 837.

REPORT OF THE CONFERENCE, NOVEMBER 24, 1937[32]

The Conference resumed after nine days and only adjourned on November 24 after adopting a report and a declaration, drafted by the U. S. and the United Kingdom, at its final session despite Italian opposition. This report of twelve sections contained a summary of the Conference, including some previously published reports and correspondence between the Conference and Japan. The text of the declaration by the Conference was no more than a reaffirmation of certain general principles of the Nine-Power Treaty as Koo later commented. It stated that "force by itself can provide no just and lasting solution for disputes between nations," and that "a satisfactory settlement cannot be achieved by direct negotiation between the parties to the conflict alone and only by consultation with other powers principally concerned can there be achieved just and durable terms." The Conference urged that hostilities be suspended and that peaceful processes be returned to. The Conference was supposed to be called again by its chairman or two of its members. However, it never was reconvened.

In short, the Brussels reports did not even go as far as the League report of October 6. No great power was ready for a showdown with Japan. Great Britain and France's preoccupation with the Spanish conflict and Nazi Germany and Italy, the fear of war within the United States due to her heavy trading with Japan,[33] the withdrawal of the purge-weakened Soviet Union from the Conference after her exclusion from certain committees, and the Scandinavian countries' fear of the German fleet were obvious causes of the death of the Conference. Added to these was the deterioration of the Chinese military situation, particularly after the fall of Shanghai into the hands of Japan on November 9, as Tsien Tai has analyzed.[34] Wunsz King wrote: "The Brussels Conference reminds one strikingly of La Fontaine's famous fable at the meeting held by the rats to face their common foe Rodilard, the only difference being that at the international gathering nobody even dared to make the suggestion to bell the cat."[35]

[32]The Report of the Brussels Conference, November 24, 1937. Appendix V to William L. Tung's *V. K. Wellington Koo and China's Wartime Diplomacy*, pp. 147-60.

[33]Shih Kuo-kang, "Pi-ching hui-i chih-hou" (After the Brussels Conference), *Tung-fang tsa-chih*, XXXIV:20-21 (November 1937), pp. 2-3.

[34]Tsien Tai, *China and the Nine Power Conference at Brussels in 1937*, pp. 18-19.

[35]Wunsz King, *China and the League of Nations: The Sino-Japanese Controversy*, pp. 88-89.

REAFFIRMATION OF LEAGUE RESOLUTION OF OCTOBER 6, 1937

Despite the debacle in Brussels, Koo was by no means giving up his effort to inform the powers of the expansion of Japanese military aggression in central and southern China, and the increased threat to western territorial and economic rights in East Asia, condemning the Japanese war of indiscriminate bombing and the use of gas. He kept pressing the powers for sanctions against Japan and for material and moral assistance to China. As early as January, Koo had already worked out, with Anthony Eden, Yvon Delbos, and Maxim Litvinov, a tentative resolution to be submitted to the League of Nations Council regarding the Sino-Japanese War. The draft resolution recommended not only generally that League members aid China, but reminded them specially of certain things that they might do, without committing them to act, including the reconvening of the Nine-Power Treaty Conference or the Advisory Committee as a prelude to a proposal for imposing sanctions on Japan.[36]

Due to British unwillingness to act, the draft resolution was greatly watered down when it was sent to Washington for support.[37] On February 2 the League of Nations session closed with the Council's adoption of the resolution reaffirming the League position as expressed in its Resolution of October 6, 1937 in favor of China. Dr. Koo declared that the resolution of February was "inadequate."[38] In accepting the resolution he said that he did so confidently, believing that greater effect than heretofore would be given to the terms of the Assembly resolution and that the proposed examination would be pursued with energy and promptness. He reserved the right to ask the League to adopt positive measures under the Covenant and further stated that his acceptance was also based upon the understanding that the Council remained apprised of the appeal of the Chinese Government invoking Articles 10, 11, and 17 of the Covenant.

Koo's continued pressures through his many effective speeches appealing to the League on behalf of China, such as his general speeches before the 101st session of the League Council on May 10 and May 14, and his communications to the League regarding Japanese indiscriminate bombing of Chinese noncombatants and the use of poison gas, resulted in a secret session

[36] *New York Times*, January 29, 1938, p. 6, and January 30, 1938, p. 1.

[37] The Chargé in the United Kingdom (Johnson) to the Secretary of State, London, January 4, 1938. *Foreign Relations of the United States, 1937, Far East*, III: 489-90.

[38] *New York Times*, February 3, 1938, p. 3.

of the Council on May 13.[39] Next day the Council in public session passed a resolution unanimously (Poland abstaining):[40]

> The Council: 1. Earnestly urges members of the League to do their utmost to give effect to the recommendations contained in previous resolutions of the Assembly and Council in this matter, and to take into serious and sympathetic consideration requests they may receive from the Chinese in conformity with the said resolution;
>
> 2. Expresses its sympathy with China and her heroic struggle for the maintenance of her independence and territorial integrity, threatened by the Japanese invasion, and with the suffering which is thereby inflicted on her people.
>
> 3. Recalls that the use of gases is a method of war condemned by international law, which cannot fail, should resort be had to it, to meet with the probation of the civilized world; and requests the governments of states who may be in a position to do so to communicate to the League any information that they may obtain on the subject.

APPLICATION OF ARTICLE 17 OF THE COVENANT

Lacking assured assistance from the great powers and offering an opportunity to the United States to back up the action of the League by parallel actions,[41] Koo requested the League Council to give immediate effect to Article 17 of the Covenant on September 11, 1938, precisely one year after he had invoked Articles 10, 11, and 17 against the Japanese invasion.[42] In the meantime, Quo Tai-chi and C. T. Wang were also instructed by the Chinese Government to solicit the support of London and Washington.

On September 16 Koo delivered a forceful speech before the fifth meeting of the 19th Assembly. First he reviewed the year-long Japanese aggression and the League's resolutions of October 6. Then he described Japan's intensified aggression, the Nanking massacre, the indiscriminate aerial

[39] Koo, Speech before the Second Meeting of the 101st Session of the Council of the League of Nations, May 10, 1938; Speech before the 8th Meeting of 101st Session of the Council on May 14, 1938; Communication of the Chinese Delegation to the League on May 5, 1938, regarding indiscriminate bombing of Chinese noncombatants and other outrages committed by the Japanese invaders; Communication from His Excellency Ambassador V. K. Wellington Koo to the League on May 9, 1938, regarding the use of poison gas by the Japanese invaders. *Japanese Aggression and the League of Nations, 1938*, IV, pp. 5-23.

[40] The Consul at Geneva (Bucknell) to the Secretary of State, Geneva, May 14, 1938. *Foreign Relations of the United States, 1938, Far East*, III: 505.

[41] The Ambassador in China (Johnson) to the Secretary of State, Chungking, September 22, 1938. *Foreign Relations of the United States, 1938, Far East*, III: 511.

[42] Application of Article 17 of the Covenant. *Japanese Aggression and the League of Nations, 1938*, V, pp. 9-10.

bombardment, the poison gas warfare, the naval blockade, and the harmful effects on foreign rights and interests in China. After condemning the Platonic resolutions, he stated that "peace is indivisible. Aggression in one region, however remote, if not effectively checked by collective action, encourages similar aggression in other parts of the world." Finally he asked the League (1) to apply Article 17 of the Covenant, (2) to implement the various resolutions of the Assembly and of the Council by recommending an embargo against the aggressor, encompassing arms, munitions, aeroplanes, oil and essential raw materials for her industry, as well as financial credits for her war coffers, and by adopting measures of financial and material aid to China, (3) to take effective measures to deter Japan from continuing to apply such barbarous methods of warfare as the use of poison gas and the indiscriminate aerial bombing of undefended towns and civilian populations.[43]

On September 19 Koo again spoke before the 4th meeting of the 102nd session of the Council, declaring that "so long as the Covenant is not amended, the obligations as well as the rights of the Member States as provided in its Articles must remain valid. China has a right to ask for everything which can be done collectively by the League as an entity. By virtue of the various resolutions of the League, China has a right to ask for everything that can be done by each Member State in its individual capacity."[44] During the next day's speech before the meeting of the Third Committee of the League, he presented practical measures for the protection of civilian noncombatants against air bombing, including an International Commission of Inquiry on the spot, embargoes of oil and planes against Japan, and a general conference of members and nonmembers to discuss all the relevant questions.[45]

The Council agreed to telegraph an invitation to the Japanese Government in accordance with paragraph 1 of Article 17. However, due to "the measures envisaged by the Council which would not serve to bring about a just settlement," the Imperial Japanese Government again would not accept the invitation.[45] The Council on September 30 adopted a report drafted by Russia, Great Britain, France, and Greece, declaring that "in view of Japan's refusal of the invitation extended under Article 17 and of the fact that the Assembly had already found Japanese military operations in China to be illicit, Article 16 is applicable."[47] The League members now were entitled not only to act

[43]Koo, Speech before the Fifth Meeting of the 19th Assembly on September 16, 1938. *Japanese Aggression and the League of Nations, 1938*, V, pp. 11-23.

[44]*Ibid.*, pp. 31-33.

[45]Koo, Speech before the Third Committee held on September 20, 1938. *Ibid.*, pp. 74-77.

[46]The Consul at Geneva (Bucknell) to the Secretary of State, Geneva, September 22, 1938. *Foreign Relations of the United States, 1938, Far East*, III: 511.

[47]*Ibid.*, September 30, 1938, III: 517.

as before on the basis of the findings, but also to adopt individually the measures provided for in Article 16. Before the 103rd session of the Council on September 30, Koo, although disappointed by the League's failure to adopt his practical measures, urged that the member states "do their utmost to carry out individually the provisions of Article 16."[48] Litvinov believed that "such measures can be effective when they are coordinated and taken collectively." He said that his government was ready to take part in such coordination.

During the following years until June 10, 1940, when Koo led his embassy staff to Bordeaux, following the French Government, he kept pressing the powers and the Council also to adopt resolutions reaffirming the resolutions previously adopted. These actions included the Council Resolution of January 20, 1939, rejecting the Japanese claim to establish a new order in the Far East,[49] appealing to world opinion to oppose the creation in Nanking of a puppet government under Wang Ching-wei,[50] and the Council Resolution of May 27, 1939, inviting the government of the states represented on the Council and on the Far East Advisory Committee having official representatives in China to furnish the League cases of bombing by Japanese aircraft of civilian populations.[51] Koo was also successful in winning some financial assistance from the United States and Great Britain for China and in reopening the Burma Road in 1940.

While Koo was occupied in Geneva, Madame Koo was busy organizing war relief charities. Among many donors were her Chinese servants who voluntarily offered 10 per cent of their salaries for the duration of the war and a French girl who, having no money to give, sent her engagement ring to sell.[52] Under Hitler's bombs and gunfire, the Koos and the embassy staff entered Portugal temporarily. Soon Koo left for Vichy in occupied France, where Madame Koo visited him occasionally, driving through the war ruins after the armistice. After the Vichy government had acceded to the Japanese demands in Indo-China, there was little for Koo to do in France. He was instructed by Chiang Kai-shek to become Chinese Ambassador to the Court of St. James, replacing

[48]Koo, Speech accepting the Report, before the Second Meeting of the 103rd Session of the Council on September 30, 1938. *Japanese Aggression and the League of Nations, 1938*, V, pp. 9-10.

[49]Resolution adopted by the 104th Session of the Council, on January 20, 1939. *Japanese Aggression and the League of Nations, 1939*, VI, p. 26.

[50]Statement by Koo before the Second Meeting of the 107th Session of the Council of the League of Nations on December 14, 1939. *Ibid.*, pp. 7-15.

[51]Resolution adopted by the 105th Session of the Council at its 4th Meeting, on May 27, 1939. *Ibid.*, pp. 24-25.

[52]Koo Hui-lan, *Autobiography*, pp. 328-29.

Quo Tai-chi who was promoted to Minister of Foreign Affairs.[53]

Despite Koo's repeated failures in Geneva and Brussels, he worked ceaselessly for collective security and urged the League to adopt concrete measures, economic, diplomatic or military, against the Japanese aggressor. He succeeded in that the League adopted resolutions condemning Japan as the violator of existing treaties of peace, viewing Japan's military operations as being out of proportion to the incident, expressing its moral support for China, and sanctioning individual states to extend aid to China. Moreover, he was the first statesman to publicly advocate a London-Washington-Paris triangle serving as a center for the peace-loving countries in the common cause against world-wide aggression, the very first step to build the United Nations.[54]

[53] *Ibid*., pp. 340-61.

[54] For details of Koo's Mission at Geneva and Brussels, see his *Reminiscences*, IV. Mission to France (Preliminary draft).

CHAPTER VIII

Koo and the United Nations, 1938-1966

During the last decade of Koo's diplomatic career, he devoted most of his energy to a few significant issues, foremost among which were organizational activities at the United Nations, negotiation of the Japanese Peace Treaty, the Sino-American Mutual Defence Treaty,[1] and preservation of the Nationalist Government's seat at the General Assembly and on the Security Council. Koo performed his duties well and to the satisfaction of his own government as well as his American hosts in Washington.

FORMATION OF THE UNITED NATIONS

In a speech delivered at the Academy of Diplomacy in Paris in December 1937 after the ill-fated Brussels Conference, Koo, then Ambassador to France, urged the establishment of a new collective security system to cope with Japanese aggression in the Pacific. The League of Nations, Koo asserted, was only half collective and offered no security. He believed that

> A most effective triangle in defence of liberty and peace would be that of Great Britain, the United States and France. United by a community of ideals and blessed with unlimited resources of military and economic power at their disposal . . . they will prove to be an anchor-sheet in the present stormy world.[2]

Koo's ideas of collective security did not become part of official Chinese foreign policy until, coinciding with the reelection of President Franklin D. Roosevelt in November 1940, Generalissimo Chiang Kai-shek summoned American Ambassador Nelson T. Johnson to present a formal version of the concepts. Chiang asked Foreign Minister Quo Tai-chi to read a document entitled "Sino-American Plan of Cooperation" that detailed Chinese

[1] Due to lack of English and Chinese official documents concerning negotiation details at the time of this author's writing, no special section on this treaty is included in this chapter.

[2] "The Problem of the Pacific and Collective Security," an address by Dr. V. K. Wellington Koo, Chinese Ambassador at Paris, at a meeting of the Academy of Diplomacy, December 17, 1937. *Japanese Aggression and the League of Nations, 1938*, III, p. 48.

thoughts about security. Under this proposal, China and Great Britain were to "conclude an alliance and to secure the adherence of the United States; and, in the absence of such adherence, to secure the approval and support of this alliance by the United States." Additionally the plan also included concrete measures of mutual assistance, such as loans and warplanes from the United Kingdom and the United States to China. Chiang also verbally promised Johnson that upon the recovery of Chinese ports from Japan the said ports would be open for the use of the American and British navies for a period of 10 to 20 years.[3] France was not included because Vichy had signed a Franco-Japanese Agreement under German dictation and had submitted to the Japanese demands by stopping the flow of war materials through Indo-China to China.[4]

On the evening of December 8, after Pearl Harbor, Chiang again summoned both the American Ambassador Gauss and the Soviet Ambassador Alexander S. Panyushkin and stressed the necessity for unity, "for effective and successful prosecution of war, Chinese Government considers essential conclusion of a military alliance between Soviet Russia, United States, Britain, Australia, New Zealand, Canada, Holland and China" under the Inter-Allied War Council in Washington against every member of the Axis group, and that an agreement be concluded among countries above-mentioned not to sign separate peace.[5] President Roosevelt responded favorably. Twenty days later, the President informed Chiang that a supreme command was being established, a supreme command for all British, Dutch and American forces in the Southwest Pacific theater. He suggested that Chiang assume the command of all forces of the United Powers operating in the Chinese theater. The nucleus of the future United Nations was being formed.

As soon as Koo arrived in London, he began a series of speeches to convince the British public that China's determination to defeat the enemy remained "inflexible as ever" despite the grave reverses she had suffered. He utilized every instance of Japanese aggression to promote the formation of the American, British, Chinese and Dutch front, later referred to as ABCD. Commenting on reports that Japanese reinforcements had been sent to Indo-China, Koo remarked that "if Japan decides to pounce on another victim, it would be just as well if the democracies should avail themselves of the opportunity to remove once for all this constant menace to the safety of the

[3]The American Ambassador (Johnson) to the Secretary of State, Chungking, November, 7, 1940. *Foreign Relations of the United States, 1940, Far East*, IV: 689.

[4]Koo, *Reminiscences*, IV, Sections 13-18.

[5]The Ambassador in China (Gauss) to the Secretary of State, Chungking, December 8, 1941. *Foreign Relations of the United States, 1941, Far East,* IV: 736.

freedom-loving countries of the Far East."[6] When his pressure on British authorities, particularly Foreign Minister Anthony Eden, to relinquish British special rights in China, acquired through the unequal treaties after the Opium War, yielded concrete results, he was able to take a "sojourn" at home, the first one in ten years, to prepare the "Sino-British Treaty for the Abolition of Extraterritoriality and Related Rights in China."[7] He arrived in Chungking, the wartime capital of China, in October 1942 in time to host the British Parliamentary Goodwill Mission headed by Lord Ailwyn. On January 11, the said treaty was formally signed between British Ambassador Horace J. Seymour in China and Chinese Foreign Minister Tse Vung Soong, and China thus ended de jure her era of second class citizenship in the family of nations. However, Koo's plan of a Sino-British alliance did not have immediate results.[8] On his way back to London he was received by Secretary of State Cordell Hull on April 1 in Washington, and he was showered with tributes and speeches in the British Parliament and by the public when he arrived.[9]

DUMBARTON OAKS CONFERENCE

As the war drew to an end, U. S. Under Secretary of State Edward R. Stettinius came to London to complete his preliminary contact with representatives of the Big Four Allied Governments. Koo and Stettinius met secretly on April 18 to pave the way for the Dumbarton Oaks Conference.[10] In early August, Stettinius announced that the Four-Power Conference on Security Organization for Peace in the Post-War World would open on August 14 with the first group sessions between the U. S., Great Britain and the Soviet Union to be followed by similar sessions between U. S., Great Britain and China. Koo received appointment as chairman of a Chinese delegation which also included Chinese Ambassador in Washington Wei Tao-ming, Vice-Minister for Foreign Affairs Victor Chi-tsai Hoo, and Chief of the Military Mission in Washington Shang Chen.[11] On August 25, former American Ambassador to Japan, Joseph

[6] *New York Times*, Koo's speech on the defence of Burma, November 17, and speech on ABCD Front on December 7, 1941, on China's continuing the war on May 28 and on June 19, 1942, Koo's Message to British Public, July 7, 1942.

[7] *New York Times*, Koo's negotiation with Eden on June 18, July 26, 1941; June 5, 1942.

[8] Chinese Ministry of Foreign Affairs, *Treaties between the Republic of China and Foreign States, 1927-1957* (Taipei: The Commercial Press, 1958), p. 589.

[9] *The Times*, London, February 5, March 11, April 1, May 21, June 1, July 8, 1943.

[10] *New York Times*, April 19, 1944.

[11] *New York Times*, August 25 and 26, 1944; *The Central Daily*, August 19, 1944.

Grew, met Dr. Koo when he arrived on a Pan American clipper at the Marine Terminal of La Guardia Field North Beach, Queens. As soon as he arrived in Washington on August 28, he again presented the Chinese collective security plan to the United States and United Kingdom. Chiang Kai-shek's pressure on President Roosevelt and Secretary Hull stressed the necessity of China being represented at the conference because, as the Chinese leader argued, "without the participation of Asiatic peoples, the conference will have no meaning for half of humanity."[12]

Based on a proposal of the semi-official People's Foreign Relations Association in Chungking, the Chinese plan detailed the provisions for the use of force to repress future aggressors but emphasized that security could not be attained by force alone. Differences among nations that contributed to two world wars should be eliminated by creating six commissions to deal with economic, territorial, social, cultural, international law and international court problems. The function of the Economic Commission would be to draft international conventions for economic cooperation, supervise their execution, formulate and execute plans for economic sanctions against aggressors and to compile and study statistics, then report on world economic conditions. The proposed Territorial Trusteeship Commission was to administer or supervise territories as would be placed under the trusteeship of the international organization, or should be internationalized for strategic reasons of protection and welfare of the local population and to promote their self-government and independence. The Social Welfare Office was to promote and supervise the various projects relating to the manufacture and sale of opium, suppress traffic in women and children, prevent and control the spread of disease, and introduce measures of social relief and insurance. The Cultural Relations Office dealt with the basic problems of educating the peoples, to prepare publications, school texts and research works calculated to promote international understanding and friendship, encouraging international peace movements, and removing possible causes of international ill-feeling in the fields of radio braodcasts, films, theater, and literature. The plan also included an International Law Codification Commission and an International Court of Justice.[13]

Furthermore, the Chinese proposal included a suggestion for a world federation of states, in which the voting power would be proportional to national population. The organization would possess an international police force drawn from the great powers under the direction of the Security Council, and more authority assigned to small powers and peoples under trusteeship.

[12]Generalissimo Chiang Kai-shek to President Roosevelt, Chungking, June 2, 1944. *Foreign Relations of the United States, 1944, China*, VI: 94.

[13]*New York Times*, October 3, 1944.

When the Russian phase of the Dumbarton Oaks Security Conference ended, the Chinese phase began on September 29. A month of waiting was over for Koo and his staff and, blessed by Secretary Hull and Deputy Premier H. H. Kung in an atmosphere of victory after the liberation of Paris and Belgrade from the Axis, negotiations began. Cooperation between Chairman Stettinius and Koo was extremely good, and the session lasted only a week or so, mainly compromising opinions of the Chinese delegates and the draft of the first stage. By October 7, Koo and Stettinius were able to make their closing speeches, leaving a set of agreed and disagreed proposals in preparation for the general framework of an international organization.[14] "The set of agreed proposals," Koo remarked, "will constitute a most valuable instrument for consideration and adoption by all the interested powers at a general conference."[15] After an audience with President Roosevelt, Koo departed for London.

SAN FRANCISCO CONFERENCE ON INTERNATIONAL ORGANIZATION

Koo was in Chungking when President Roosevelt's telegram of March 15, 1945 reached Chiang Kai-shek on March 22 through the American embassy in Chungking. As suggested by President Roosevelt, Chiang appointed a Chinese delegation of ten members from diverse political parties to attend the United Nations Conference on International Organization at San Francisco.[16] In addition to Dr. Koo, the Delegation included Foreign Minister and acting President of the Executive Yuan T. V. Soong and Wei Tao-ming, Chinese Ambassador in Washington. Six were members of the People's Political Council. Of the six, three, Dr. Wang Chung-Hui, Secretary General of the Supreme Council for National Defense, Dr. Wu Yi-fang, President of the Jinling College, and Li Hwang, founding member of the Nationalist Youth Party belonged to the Presidium of the People's Political Council. The three ordinary members were Hu Lin, General Manager of the *Ta-kung pao* (newspaper), Tung Pi-wu, founding member of the Chinese Communist Party, and Dr. Carson Chang, founding member of the Chinese National Socialist Party. The Delegation also included the famous Dr. Hu Shih, and additional

[14] *New York Times*, October 6, 1944.

[15] *New York Times*, October 7, 1944; Koo, *Reminiscences*, II. Second Mission to London, E, 1944-1945.

[16] Memorandum by the Secretary of State (Stettinius) to President Roosevelt, Washington, March 14, 1945. *Foreign Relations of the United States, 1945, Far East and China*, VII: 278.

supporting staff members.[17]

Amid the celebration of the German surrender and the end of hostilities in Europe, delegations from 54 nations assembled at the Opera House in San Francisco on April 26 to renew their pursuit of peace. However, the real conflicting interests concerning every aspect of the Charter were ironed out by the Big Four and they, as sponsoring governments, jointly presented to the Conference their agreements in the form of amendments to the Dumbarton Oaks Proposals. In its first meeting of the Big Four on May 3 Dr. Koo and T. V. Soong represented China. Koo presented the Chinese first amendment in a proposal for the insertion in Chapter VII that "if any party to a dispute fails to comply with the judgement of the International Court of Justice, the Security Council may, upon application by the other party or parties concerned, take such action as it may deem necessary to give effect to the judgement." Due to the strong opposition of Eden, Molotov and Stettinius, T. V. Soong reserved China's position with respect to this provision.[18]

In Chapter VIII, Section A, Koo proposed to add that "in the case of a non-member, it should be required to accept for the purpose of such dispute, the obligations of pacific settlement provided in the Charter." Koo explained that the purpose of the proposal was to assure that when the Organization took up consideration of a dispute involving a non-member, it could rely on the compliance of such a non-member. Both Molotov and Stettinius withdrew their previous opposition after consultation with their delegations and this amendment was therefore adopted.[19]

The third amendment pertaining to Chapter VIII, Section B, Dr. Koo proposed, was a recommendation concerning a provisional measure which might be taken by the Security Council. Koo explained that these actions were intended to facilitate the Organization's task of maintaining or restoring international peace and security. Their origins, of course, lay in the experience of the League of Nations in the case of the Manchurian Incident in 1931. The measures were designed to maintain the conditions existing at the time the disturbance occurred, in order to prevent any aggravation of the situation without prejudice to the rights, claims, or position of the parties concerned. Molotov and Eden had no objection to the provisions. Stettinius reserved the right at the meeting, but decided to support it after his conference with the

[17] *The Times*, London, March 6 and April 6, 1945; *Documents of the United Nations Conference on International Organization, San Francisco, 1945* (New York and London: United Nations Information Organization, 1945), I: 18-20.

[18] *Foreign Relations of the United States, General: The United Nations, 1945*, I: 564, 577, 585.

[19] Herbert Briggs, *The Law of Nations* (New York: Appleton-Century-Crafts, 1952), p. 1059. United Nations Charter, Chapter V, Art. 32.

United States Delegation led by Secretary of State Hull.[20]

When Stettinius informed the Big Four meeting that M. Georges Bidault had called him to express his regret at not participating in the conversations, no objections were raised among the great powers to the participation of France on May 3, 1945. Thus when the Big Four convened their next meeting four days later on May 7, it became a Five-Power Informal Consultative Meeting on Proposed Amendments. As the foreign ministers of the great powers were leaving San Francisco, the Consultative Meeting appointed their deputies to organize a Committee of Deputies to consider the amendments that had been proposed by the other nations represented at the Conference. Koo appointed himself as a member of this committee on behalf of China.[21]

Among many of Koo's contributions to the Conference, his dedication to the rights of the small powers and his pledge for colonial peoples' independence were well acknowledged. At the meeting of the trusteeship committee on May 17, Koo reintroduced the principle of the Chinese plan that the Charter agreed to "promote the development toward independence or self-government as may be appropriate to the particular circumstances of each territory and its people." Apart from Soviet Union, both Great Britain and France were in agreement with the United States that they "would oppose making a specific promise of independence as a goal for colonial peoples and would stand out against any further modification of the veto power unless the Big Five agreed."[22] Furthermore, while agreeing with the Yalta principle of great power unanimity for voting in the Security Council, Koo urged the great powers to give the smaller nations greater opportunity to review the Dumbarton Oaks proposals. Koo served at the Conference as a spokesman for the small powers as well as for China.

On June 26, the Conference finally came to a successful conclusion.[23] At the final session of the United Nations Conference, leaders of the delegations addressed the world. After Lord Halifax, Stettinius and Andrei Gromyko, Dr. Koo expressed his deep appreciation to Stettinius for his chairmanship, his thanks for American hospitality, and his recognition of "the incorporation in the Charter of the many new features not contained in the Dumbarton Oaks plan."[24] To China, first of the United Nations to suffer attack by a

[20] *Foreign Relations of the United States, General: The United Nations, 1945*, I: 567, 575.

[21] *Ibid.*, I: 629.

[22] *New York Times*, May 18, 1945.

[23] Koo, *Reminiscences*, V. Second Mission to London, E. 1944-1945.

[24] Statement of the Acting Chairman of the Delegation of China The Honorable V. K. Wellington Koo. *Documents of the United Nations Conference on International Organization, San Francisco, 1945* (London and New York: United Nations Information Organization, 1945), II, 692-93.

member of the Axis, went the honor of signing the Charter first. At noon, Koo used his country's writing brush to inscribe his name in two freshly printed and freshly bound volumes of the Charter and the Statute of the International Court of Justice.[25] He represented China on the executive committee to plan the United Nations operations in London. He also participated in the selection of the first Secretary General and promoted the principle of geographic representation in the United Nations' various committees and councils.[26]

In an effort to solve China's post-war problems, Koo succeeded Wei Taoming as Ambassador to Washington in September 1945. He left London in a B.O.A.C. Constellation plane on July 4, 1946 for the U. S. shortly after being received by the British King and giving his farewell speech over the radio.[27]

JAPANESE PEACE TREATY

As the civil war on the China mainland gradually developed into a struggle of survival for the Nationalist Government, Koo devoted more and more of his time to seeking American military, economic, and moral support for the Nationalist cause. Yet, nothing caused more embarrassment for Koo and the Nationalist Government during the last years of Koo's long diplomatic career than the Japanese Peace Treaty. The issue was first mentioned in the correspondence between General George C. Marshall and the Chinese Foreign Minister Wang Shih-chieh in October 1947. Both foresaw the difficulty of China's participation, in the event of non-participation by Soviet Union.[28] However, there seemed to be no serious exchange of opinions between the State Department and the Nationalist Government until the end of 1950, a year after the total defeat of the Nationalist Government and its withdrawal to Taiwan.

Two international events in 1950 made the Japanese Peace Treaty a high priority issue. First, the Sino-Soviet Treaty of Friendship, Alliance and Mutual Assistance in February designated Japan as the mutual enemy and created an international situation that threatened to permit the Chinese Communists to represent China in the negotiation of the Japanese Peace Treaty. Second, the Korean War erupted in June and solidified American determination for an early Japanese Peace Treaty in order to defend the disarmed Japan

[25] *Foreign Relations of the United States, General: The United Nations, 1946*, I:143, 158.

[26] *New York Times*, June 27, 1945.

[27] *The Times*, London, June 24, July 5, 1946.

[28] *Foreign Relations of the United States, The Far East: China*, VII.

from Communist advance and keep her within the camp of the Western Alliance.[29]

The shifting international balance after the outbreak of the Korean War made it difficult for Taiwan to maintain its diplomatic position. Koo returned to Taiwan for consultations. Between late July and late August 1950, his busy schedule included 130 engagements, 13 speeches, and four conversations with President Chiang Kai-shek. Koo warned the Taiwan authorities that relations between the United States and Taiwan had reached a very difficult point. The Taiwan authorities should understand that American China policy, as well as that of the Soviets, was to achieve a peaceful settlement with the Chinese Communists, instead of a third World War. Taiwan should put aside questions of prestige and pride and should seek to establish a firm, practical, and sound basis for cooperation. Against Premier Ch'en Ch'eng's policy to reduce the diplomatic and consular service abroad, Koo argued that:

> The Nationalist government, having lost the mainland and having established itself on a small island, had, as its only hope of maintaining itself as an international entity in the family of nations, to keep up its international relations and cultivate the friendship of the non-Communist world, so that when the time came for Taiwan to launch a campaign for the recovery of the mainland, we could count upon its sympathy and support. . . .[30]

On September 11, 1950, a secret memorandum on the Japanese Peace Treaty as envisaged by the United States Government was tentatively prepared by the Department of State under Secretary Dean Acheson. It was handed to representatives of the Far East Commission powers, including Koo, during the series of informal bilateral discussions of the settlement, held in New York during the autumn of 1950. The Treaty would reflect the principles:

1. **Parties**: Any or all nations at war with Japan which are willing to make peace on the basis proposed and as may be agreed.
2. **United Nations**: Membership by Japan would be contemplated.
3. **Territory**: Japan would (a) recognize the independence of Korea; (b) agree to U. N. trusteeship, with the U. S. as administering authority, of the Ryukyu and Bonin Islands; and (c) accept the future decision of the U. K., U.S.S.R., China and U. S. with reference to the status of Formosa, Pescadores, South Sakhalin and the Kuriles. In the event of no decision within a year after the treaty came into effect, the U. N. General Assembly would decide. Special rights and interests in China would be renounced.
4. **Security**: The Treaty would contemplate that, pending satisfactory alternative security arrangements such as U. N. assumption of effective responsibility, there would be continuing cooperative responsibility between Japanese facilities and U. S. and perhaps other forces for the maintenance of international

[29] Furuya Keiji, *Chiang Tsung-t'ung pi-lu*, XIV, p. 115.
[30] Koo, *Reminiscences*, VII. A, 2.

peace and security in the Japan area.

5. **Political and Commercial Arrangements**: Japan would agree to adhere to multilateral treaties dealing with narcotics and fishing. Prewar bilateral treaties could be revived by mutual agreement. Pending the conclusion of new commercial treaties, Japan would extend most-favored-nation treatment, subject to normal exceptions.
6. **Claims**: All parties would waive claims arising out of war acts prior to September 2, 1945, except that (a) the Allied Powers would, in general, hold Japanese property within their territory and (b) Japan would restore allied property or, if not restorable intact, provide yen to compensate for an agreed percentage of lost value.
7. **Disputes**: Claims disputes would be settled by a special neutral tribunal to be set up by the President of the International Court of Justice. Other disputes would be referred either to diplomatic settlement, or to the International Court of Justice.[31]

In a conversation with John Foster Dulles on December 19, 1950, Koo stated that his Government was in general accord with principles set out in the 7-point memorandum previously given him. With respect to Formosa, it was his understanding that even though the future disposition of Formosa was left unsettled, Japan would, by the treaty, renounce its own title thereto. Koo brought up the question of Chinese Communist participation and Dulles assured him that no other country had raised this as a major point yet. Nevertheless, the situation changed rapidly. On the day of Dulles' return from his trip to Tokyo, April 24, 1959, Koo was received at the State Department. He expressed his concern to Dulles that:

> Since the United States had modified its position and had now proposed instead a general renunciation by Japan of her sovereignty and rights over Formosa and the Pescadores, the Chinese Government could not see why, according to the American draft, Japan would return to Soviet Russia the southern part of Sakhalin and hand over to the Soviet Union the Kurile Islands. The disparity between the treatment accorded to those two groups of territories had created an impression of discrimination against China. . . ."[32]

Mr. Dulles said:

> Yes. . . . The United States believed that the Soviet Union would not participate in the proposed treaty and therefore the American drafts provided, in accordance with the language of the Yalta Agreement, that Japan would hand back Southern Sakhalin to Soviet Russia and turn over the Kuriles to her. . . .[33]

[31] *Foreign Relations of the United States, East Asia and the Pacific, 1950*, VI: 1296-97.

[32] Koo, Notes of a Conversation with Mr. John Foster Dulles, *Wellington Koo Collection*, Box 124-51, p. 2.

[33] Koo, Notes of a Conversation with Mr. John Foster Dulles, *Wellington Koo Collection*, Box 124-51, p. 4.

Koo also asked about the United States' stand on the British memorandum to the United States Government urging that an invitation be sent to the Chinese Communist Government to participate in the negotiations for a Japanese peace treaty and suggesting that a provision should be included in the treaty for the return of Formosa to China in accordance with the Cairo Agreement. For Koo, the case became urgent when Prime Minister Yoshida stated to the Japanese Diet that "the Japanese government would naturally be willing to negotiate and conclude the treaty with them with no objection if the Chinese Communists so proposed within three years."[34] Dulles remarked that:

> Not only the countries which had recognized Communist China opposed it, but others like Canada, Australia and New Zealand raised the same objection. In going over the Far East Commission he found there were 12 countries besides Nationalist China and of these 12, not more than two were in favor of her participation.[35]

Nevertheless, Dulles assured Koo that the American Government in its written reply to Britain stated that the "United States Government recognized only the National Government of the Republic of China and saw no reason for inviting the Peiping Regime to participate in the discussion."

Furthermore, Dulles remarked that the United States was willing to carry out the Cairo Agreement regarding Formosa and the Pescadores, but

> Since the Chinese National Government insisted that Formosa was a part of Chinese territory—a view also held by the Peiping Communist regime—if the United States had accepted this view, it could not justify its policy of stationing the Seventh Fleet in the Formosa Strait to protect it from attack by the Chinese Communists as that would constitute an act of intervention in the domestic affairs of China.[36]

For this reason in the treaty, Dulles preferred to have a simple renunciation by Japan of her sovereignty and rights over Formosa and deliberately leave the status of Formosa vague to be determined in the future. The same principle was quoted in the Chou-Nixon Shanghai Communique as a path to rapproachement with the People's Republic of China in 1972, and President Carter's Joint Communique of normalization of relations with the People's Republic of China in 1978.

Searching for a compromise formula concerning the Chinese representation, Dulles flew to London in mid-June. The subsequent agreement between Dulles and the British Foreign Minister, Mr. Herbert Morrison of the Labor Party, was forwarded in due time to Koo and to an extremely disappointed

[34] Koo, *Reminiscences*, VII. D, p. 329.

[35] *Ibid.*, VII. D, pp. 113-15.

[36] Koo, Notes of a Conversation with Mr. John Foster Dulles, 5 p.m., Tuesday, April 24, 1951, at the State Department, *Wellington Koo Collection*, Box 184, 124-51, Interviews, p. 4.

Nationalist Government in Taipei. The magic formula proposed that a number of countries would sign the multilateral treaty with Japan; Japan would decide with which China to enter into a bilateral treaty that would parallel the lines of the multilateral agreement. Dulles even assured Koo that Japan would not go with the Communists. Dr. Koo stated that "his Government would consider it as a humiliation to have Japan determine with which Government—the Nationalist Government or the Peiping regime—to conclude a peace treaty."[37] Furthermore, Japan herself did not wish to be called upon to assume this responsibility. Koo preferred that the United States and the allied powers ask Japan to sign the bilateral peace treaty with the Nationalist Government. Dulles declared that he could not ask Japan and the other allies to do so until the question of the binding force of the signature of the Nationalist Government with regard to the Chinese mainland had been answered.

Koo argued that:

> Firstly, as regards the right of the Nationalist Government to negotiate and sign a peace treaty with Japan there should be no question. It was the National Government which led the Chinese nation to resist the Japanese invasion. It remained a full-fledged ally now. It was still a member of many important international organizations. It was still recognized by a great majority of the countries of the world. It had effective control of Formosa . . . and a large number of armed forces.[38]
> . . .

Secondly, the degree of effectiveness of the National Government's signature could only arise at the time when it had been ratified and put into effect. The issue might be changed by future developments. Therefore, the question of the degree of effectiveness of the National Government's ratification could be left until the time when the treaty was implemented. Nevertheless, Dulles considered the possibility of the Nationalist Government participating in the multilateral peace treaty was remote; and despite the strong opposition of the Nationalist Government, the draft Japanese Peace Treaty was made public officially on July 12 in Washington, Tokyo and forty more countries.

At their meeting on July 6, Dulles gave Koo a copy of the draft Japanese Peace Treaty. Dulles pointed out that Southern Sakhalin and its adjacent islands as well as the Kuriles were now treated in the same manner as Formosa and the Pescadores in that Japan was called upon to relinquish her rights and all claims to these territories as suggested by Koo. Dulles also pointed out that although Article 21 did provide a list of the Allied Powers which were to

[37]Koo, Notes of a Conversation with Mr. John Foster Dulles, 11 a.m., Tuesday, July 3, 1951, at the State Department, *Wellington Koo Collection*, Box 184, 124-51, p. 7.

[38]Koo, Notes of a Conversation with Mr. John Foster Dulles, 5 p.m., Tuesday, April 24, 1951, at the State Department, *Wellington Koo Collection*, Box 184, 124-51, p. 5.

be signatories to the treaty from which China was omitted, Article 23 required Japan to pledge herself within three years to conclude a treaty on the same terms as provided in the multilateral treaty with any of the other Allied Powers which were not parties to the multilateral agreement.[39]

When he noted Dulles' determination to prevent the Nationalist Government's participation in the multilateral peace treaty, Dr. Koo changed his strategy. He pointed out contradictions in the American position in the

> Signing of the bilateral peace treaty between Japan and the National Government simultaneously with the multilateral peace treaty, in view of the Washington Declaration of January 1, 1942, to which the National Government was a signatory and under which it undertook the obligation not to make a separate peace with the common enemy.[40]

When Koo met Dulles again on July 11, he had already learned from Taipei that American Ambassador Karl L. Rankin had made the American position unequivocal when he delivered a copy of the Japanese peace treaty to Foreign Minister Yeh. Neither the signing of a bilateral document of peace between China and Japan before the conclusion of the multilateral concord nor a simultaneous ceremony involving the two treaties would be possible.[41] Nevertheless, Dr. Koo urged Dulles to arrange the immediate opening of negotiations between Japan and the Nationalist Government. Dulles insisted that the question of the inability of the Nationalist Government to enforce the treaty on the mainland be cleared for the present. Henceforth, the bilateral Sino-Japanese peace negotiations were conducted in Tokyo and Taipei as Dulles and Koo agreed.

Following the broad pattern of the San Francisco Treaty of Peace with Japan, representatives of the Republic of China and Japan hammered out peace terms between the two states. Seven months later, April 28, 1952, Foreign Minister Yeh Kung-ch'ao and Isao Kawada signed the treaty and officially ended hostilities that had begun in 1931. In Article 2, Japan simply renounced all rights, title, and claims to Formosa and the Pescadores as well as the Spratly and the Paracel Islands. In the exchange of notes of April 28 between the two envoys, the Japanese representative stated the understanding reached between the two parties that "the terms of the present treaty shall, in respect of the Republic of China, be applicable to all the territories which are

[39]Koo, Notes of a Conversation with Mr. John Foster Dulles, 2:30 p.m., Friday, July 6, 1951, at the State Department, *Wellington Koo Collection*, Box 184, 136-51, pp. 1-2.

[40]*Ibid.*, p. 6.

[41]Koo, Notes of a Conversation with Mr. John Foster Dulles, 12 noon, Wednesday, July 11, 1951, at the State Department, *Wellington Koo Collection*, Box 184, 137-51, p. 1.

now, or which may hereafter be, under the control of its Government."[42]

OTHER INVOLVEMENTS IN WASHINGTON

Besides the above-mentioned issues in which Koo played an important part, he was also involved in several other matters of significance during his last years in the Washington embassy. When the Korean War broke out, Koo suggested to Foreign Minister Yeh Kung-ch'ao of the Nationalist Government that Chiang Kai-shek's offer of 33,000 troops in response to Trygve Lie's call for aid should await consultation with the United States Government. In late June, 1950, after a White House conference called to review the Taiwan offer, both Secretary of State Dean Acheson and Dean Rusk, Assistant Secretary of State for Far Eastern Affairs, opposed the inclusion of Nationalist troops because they were eager to localize the Korean crisis and prevent its spread to the Chinese mainland. Furthermore, the officials expressed concern for the defense requirements of Taiwan itself and the possibility of Nationalist exploitation of the United States for new weapons and supplies.[43] On his way back from Taipei to Washington, Koo visited General Douglas MacArthur at the Supreme Command Allied Powers on August 18, 1950. He renewed the offer to the U. N. of 33,000 Nationalist troops; the General declined the offer this time.

Koo was also the moving force behind the defense of the Taiwan seat at the United Nations using his influence and prestige to rally the United States and the Western allies for the struggle. Chou En-lai cabled to Trygve Lie to lodge a formal complaint with the Security Council on August 24, 1950, that the United States policy in Formosa represented armed aggression against Chinese territory and a violation of the United Nations Charter. Chou declared that the Security Council was obliged to condemn the United States government and to take immediate action to compel the withdrawal of United States' forces from Taiwan. The Soviets reinforced Chou's protest when Jacob A. Malik opened the first meeting over which he presided by disqualifying the representative of Nationalist China. Koo argued effectively with Dean Acheson and Dean Rusk to take a strong stand with Bevin and Schuman in the Three Foreign Ministers Conference at New York City in early September, to get their endorsement for the American policy vis-à-vis Formosa and their support in the United Nations for a united stand against the Soviet Union and the Communist world.[44] Consequently, the Soviet proposal that a representative of Communist China be invited to participate during the Security

[42] *Treaties between the Republic of China and Foreign States, 1927-1957*, pp. 248-55.

[43] Koo, *Reminiscences*, VII. A, pp. 13, 16, 18, 28, 29.

[44] *Ibid.*, VII. A, pp. 185, 189.

Council's consideration of its complaint was defeated on September 11.

When the decision to invite a Chinese Communist representative was finally made by the Security Council on September 29, Koo made a trip to New York and convinced Dr. T. F. Tsiang, Nationalist Chief Delegate at the United Nations to propose that the discussion on the Formosan issue be confined to the question of security and peace in the Western Pacific. To avoid the embarrassing question of American military intervention, the status of Formosa would not be discussed. Koo also recommended that Tsiang suggest a committee of study, rather than a commission of inquiry to make an investigation in Taiwan.[45] The Formosan question was resolved for Koo when Dulles informed him on November 16 that the United States Government had decided to ask for a delay of the consideration of the status of Formosa until the end of the agenda of the Political Commission on the General Assembly, a postponement of the day of reckoning. The confrontation of the Chinese troops with the United Nations forces in North Korea and the passage of the U. S. draft resolution to declare China an aggressor, caused the British and Indian efforts to seat Communist China to be received less enthusiastically among the members of the United Nations. As a result, Prime Minister Attlee agreed with the United States that seating the Chinese Communists was inopportune. Thus the Western powers established a pattern which blocked Communist China's seat at the United Nations throughout all the years Koo was in Washington.

INTERNATIONAL COURT OF JUSTICE

In the face of the stepped up Chinese Communist political and diplomatic offensive, Koo resigned from his post in Washington after a short visit to Taipei in late January, 1956. Taipei authorities accepted his resignation on March 22, and Koo was appointed senior advisor to President Chiang on May 8. Koo left Washington for New York amid laudatory editorials that "he has added several brilliant chapters to his country's diplomatic history" and that "he has been our great friend and it has been a singular pleasure that he could make his home with us for so long a time."[46] After welcoming his successor, Dr. Hollington Tong, Koo planned to have a good rest and to think about his personal financial affairs for retirement, including, perhaps, a legal office of international finance and trade as well as the writing of his memoirs.

In the 1956, the death of judge Hsü Mo, a Nationalist Chinese Judge at the International Court of Justice at The Hague, prompted the Taiwan Govern-

[45] *Ibid.*, VII. A, pp. 213, 267.
[46] *New York Times*, April 7, 1956.

ment to request Koo's agreement to run for office to complete Hsü's remaining one year in 1957. Since international law had been a favorite subject of his study at the graduate school of Columbia University, Koo quickly gave his consent. At the 757th meeting of the United Nations Security Council, Koo received an absolute majority, 8 to 3. On January 10, the Assembly gave him 42 votes after an initial deadlock between Koo and the Japanese S. Kuriyama.[47] Dr. T. F. Tsiang and former ambassadors Tsien Tai and Wunsz King saw Koo off when he sailed with his newly-married wife, Juliana Young, widow of former Consul General to Manila Clarence Kuang-son Young, on the *Nieuw Amsterdam* of the Holland-American Line from Hoboken Pier in New Jersey on April 4, 1957. After the ship reached Rotterdam on the morning of April 12, Koo began a series of courtesy calls, including the Court located in the Peace Palace built by Andrew Carnegie. He also won an easy re-election for his own ten-year term on October 1, 1957.

During his ten-year tenure at the Court, there must have been more than 200 meetings including public sittings, private meetings for elaborating and draft committee meetings with the President of the Court. Koo attended every one of them. Among the many cases settled during these years at The Hague, Koo's opinions were with the majority in the cases concerning the Application of the Convention of 1902 Governing the Guardianship of Infants, 1958, Interhandel Preliminary Objections, 1959, and the Barcelona Traction Light and Power Company, Ltd., 1964. He was better known for his minority opinions on cases such as Right of Passage Over Certain Indian Territories, 1957, and the Northern Cameroons, 1962, but he was most praised for his minority opinion with Judge Lauterpacht Spender on the case of The Aerial Accident of July 27, 1955, 1959.[48] On May 9, 1964, Koo was elected Vice-President of the International Court of Justice.

On October 18, 1966, the Nationalist Government through Foreign Minister Shen Ch'ang-huan directed Koo to stand for re-election. Chang Ch'ün, Chiang Kai-shek's senior statesman, also came to persuade him to run two months later; Chang was convinced that Koo was the only person from China with enough international prestige to retain the Nationalist seat at The Hague. However, President Lyndon B. Johnson had already pledged the seat to President Ferdinand Marcos during his visit to the Philippines in April. In a quid pro quo for support of the Philippines in defense of the Nationalist seat

[47] *New York Times*, January 11 and 12, 1957.

[48] Huang Wu-chih, *Kuo-chi fa-yüan fa-kuan Ku Wei-chün ke-pieh i-chien yü fan-tui i-chien, 1957-67* (Judge V. K. Wellington Koo's Individual and Minority Opinions at the International Court of Justice). This is a work based on the author's Master Thesis at the School of Diplomacy, National Cheng-chih University.

at the United Nations, the Nationalist Government decided not to challenge the Philippinos. When his term expired on February 5, 1967, Koo returned to New York and chose an apartment on Park Avenue as his permanent residence due to its closeness to political and cultural activities, to Columbia University and to the families of his and his wife's children.[49]

REMINISCENCES OF WELLINGTON KOO

On October 5, 1963, Koo presented his diplomatic papers to Columbia University, his alma mater. Dr. Grayson Kirk, President of the University said that the Koo Collection "provides an accurate and detailed account of a career filled with significant assignments, executed in a truly effective and distinguished manner."[50] As early as May 1958, the East Asian Institute of Columbia University had already begun the project, supervised by Professors C. Martin Wilbur and Franklin L. Ho, to tape-record recollections of five Nationalist leaders of the Republic of China including Koo. Because of its great length, Koo's oral briefing spanned seventeen years, from his occasional vacations in New York from The Hague to his retirement years during the early 1970s. In the presence of President William J. McGill and Professor C. Martin Wilbur, Dr. Koo presented the completed memoir to Columbia University on May 28, 1976. The memoir contains eight volumes and 11,000 typed pages. It is the most complete and most useful autobiography ever done by a Chinese statesman in modern times.

On Koo's 90th birthday, January 29, 1977, Columbia University sponsored a grand celebration in its new auditorium at the School of International Affairs to honor his achievements. More than 400 guests attended and the Dean of the School of International Affairs was the keynoter. All three amateur Chinese opera societies in New York collaborated in presenting the Chinese opera, *Szu-lang t'an-mu* (The Filial Son's Visit to His Mother), a romance derived from the war history of the Sung dynasty.[51] The V. K. Wellington Koo Fellowship in East Asian International Relations with a principal of over one hundred thousand dollars for graduate students of Columbia University was dedicated by President McGill at a reception in honor of Dr. Koo On April 11, 1979.[52]

[49] Yuan Tao-feng, "Chi chiu-shih ch'i-su Ku Wei-chün" (Noting on Ninety Years Old Scholar Ku Wei-chün), *Tung-fang tsa-chih* (Taiwan), IX:9 (October 1, 1975), p. 70.

[50] *New York Times*, October 6, 1963.

[51] Weng Ya-nan, "Ku Wei-chün ta-shih chiu-shih shou-ch'ing" (On Ambassador Koo's 90th Birthday Celebration), *Chinese Culture Association Annuals*, No. 23, pp. 89-92. Palo Alto, California: Chinese Culture Association, 1977.

[52] *World Journal*, San Francisco and New York: World Journal Inc., April 7, 1979.

CHAPTER IX

Conclusion

ELEMENTS OF V. K. WELLINGTON KOO'S DIPLOMACY

Throughout his career, Wellington Koo labored to advance the national interest as defined by the Chinese intelligentsia and bourgeois classes in major treaty ports along the eastern and southeastern coast. The primary themes of Koo's diplomacy were derived from his traditional family background with its emphasis on classic Confucian learning, his Western education and experiences, and his nationalistic social environment. These forces found expression in Koo's diplomatic work in three significant ways: abolition of the unequal treaties, cooperation with countries led by Britain and the United States, and diplomacy above internal disputes and parties.

The cornerstone of Koo's beliefs was abrogation of the unequal treaties and equality for the Chinese people in the modern community of nations. For this principle, Dr. Koo went abroad to study international law and politics, and he dedicated his dissertation, *The Status of Aliens in China*, to it. To advance this cause, Dr. Koo returned to China to serve the Chinese Government and accepted appointment as Chinese Representative to the Paris Peace Conference and the Washington Disarmament Conference. On both occasions, Dr. Koo and his colleagues presented the problem of abolition of unequal treaties and alien rights to the major Powers. Koo accepted the Foreign Ministership of the various warlords of the Peking Government in order to maintain Chinese continuity in the face of pressures from the major Powers while China was weak and embroiled in civil war. In this official post, he greatly strengthened the international position of China.

During the period of warlord China, Dr. Koo contributed to China's recovery of significant sovereign rights, and he laid the foundation for the restoration of other essential sovereign privileges, such as tariff autonomy and the abrogation of extraterritoriality. As Chinese Ambassador to the Court of St. James in 1943, he negotiated two important pacts: (1) the Sino-British Treaty for the Abolition of Extraterritoriality and Related Rights in China and (2) the Treaty between the Republic of China and the United States of America for the Relinquishment of Extraterritorial Rights in China and the

Regulations of Related Matters.[1] From his London post as a member of the Commission of Four (Allied Powers), Dr. Koo maneuvered among the allies, Great Britain, the United States, and the Soviet Union, to help establish the United Nations. His representation of China at the Dumbarton Oaks Conversation in 1944 and the United Nations Conference on International Organization at San Francisco in 1945 is well recorded.

Even his political foes did not deny that he was a sincere patriot who dedicated his life to championing China's rights and position in the family of nations, and whose life's goal was "to put China on the map."[2] Madame Huilan Koo wrote:

> His great concern was China. He was dedicated to his country. That he never saw me as an individual is not surprising. He was an honorable man, the kind China needed, but not a husband for me.[3]

Koo's second related theme was international cooperation with the Anglo-American group. His many years of education and experience in the United States convinced him that the United States had no ambitions in China. He believed that the United States was very sympathetic toward China's aspirations and rights during the period between the two world wars. At the end of World War I, Koo felt that "China's only opportunity to throw off the burden of unequal treaties which tied her hands and feet, and develop into a first-rate modern state was the peace conference to be held on the basis of President Wilson's Fourteen Points." When the United States broke diplomatic relations with Germany over the sinking of American merchantmen by U-boats, Koo "advocated and recommended to Peking to follow the United States' lead."[4] At the Washington Disarmament Conference, his cooperation with the Department of State was so close that some Chinese intellectuals thought, facetiously perhaps, Hughes was the Superior Plenipotentiary of the Chinese Delegation. When the Sino-Soviet Agreements of 1924 were signed against the advice of the Anglo-American bloc, Marshal Wu P'ei-fu supported by strong opinion endangered Koo's political life. In this matter, Koo acknowledged the power of a fundamental principle: nationalism.

Whenever Dr. Koo was stationed abroad, his posts were at the centers of the Anglo-American bloc activity in international diplomacy. He served energetically in Washington, London, and centers of the international organizations. Koo became Chinese Minister to Washington after the Japanese issued the Twenty-One Demands and remained until the end of the Paris

[1] Ministry of Foreign Affairs, Republic of China (ed.), *Treaties between the Republic of China and Foreign States, 1927-1961*, pp. 589-659.

[2] Interview with Dr. Koo, November 26, 1966.

[3] Koo Hui-lan, *No Feast Lasts Forever*, p. 119.

[4] V. K. Wellington Koo to Chu Pao-chin, July 1, 1969.

Peace Conference in 1920. Then he was accredited to the Court of St. James until after the Washington Disarmament Conference in 1922. Following the Manchurian "Incident" of 1931, as Minister to Paris, he accompanied the Lytton Commission back to Geneva and argued the Chinese case at the League of Nations. Because the United States was not a member, the Chinese presentation occurred under the shadow of British and French interests. After Hitler conquered France, Dr. Koo remained Chinese Ambassador to the Vichy regime until his transfer back to London in 1941. In 1946 when the political center of international diplomacy in the post-World War II era shifted to the United States, symbolized by the transfer of the United Nations to New York, Koo was appointed Ambassador to Washington. One important reason for his assignment was preservation of the seat held by the Nationalist Government at the Security Council. This task he accomplished to the complete satisfaction of the Nationalist Government and retained his post as Ambassador to Washington until 1956.[5]

In 1963, Dr. Koo presented his collection of diplomatic papers to Columbia University. He chose to reside in New York, rather than Taiwan, after he retired from his post at the International Court of Justice in 1966.

The third theme related to Koo's work was that diplomacy should transcend internal politics and parties. He believed that China should always confront foreign powers as one unit and that the administrative independence and territorial integrity of China were beyond any domestic disputes and party interests. Slogans such as "working for China without reference to any political clique" and "abolishing unequal treaties is not confined to any one party" became his maxims. Koo was never identified with any party or faction, and his nonaffiliation was known even to the Communists.[6] As long as the legitimate Chinese Government was dedicated to Chinese nationalism, strong enough to perpetuate its political life, and acceptable to the Anglo-American bloc in the international arena, Dr. Koo was more than happy to participate in its foreign office.

Koo's experience in Chinese internal politics was long and varied. He acted as the English secretary for Premier T'ang Shao-i in 1912, subsequently serving President Yüan's Ministry of Foreign Affairs after T'ang split with

[5] Ch'en Chih-mai, *Chiang T'ing-fu ti chih-shih yü sheng-p'ing* (The Life of Chiang T'ing-fu). Ch'en devoted a chapter on the struggle of Chiang and Koo for the Nationalist Government's seat at the Security Council, pp. 128-39.

[6] *A List of the Various Cliques among Members of the Central Committee Elected by the Sixth Congress of the Kuomintang* (Confidential for reference only). The original biographies of Kuomintang leaders was prepared by the Communist intelligence for confidential purposes in August 1945. It was translated into English by the Committee on International and Regional Studies of Harvard University, and was published in February 1948. (Gift of Dr. Derk Bodde to the University of Pennsylvania Library, 1952.)

Yüan. As Foreign Minister of the Peking Government, Koo served under the joint operation of the victorious Chihli and Fengtien Cliques between May and November 1922 after the defeat of the Anhwei Clique under Tuan Ch'i-jui. After the first Chihli-Fengtien War he was not only Foreign Minister, but also Premier between February 1923 and September 1924 for the Chihli group. Following the second Chihli-Fengtien War between October 1926 and June 1927, Koo again headed the Foreign Ministry as well as the Premiership for the Peking Government under the domination of the Fengtien Clique. The Mukden Incident in September 1931 brought Dr. Koo into the service of the Nationalist Government. On November 23, 1931 he became Foreign Minister of the Nationalist Government, which had defeated the Fengtien Army and driven them back into Manchuria in June 1928.[7] Without interruption, Koo successfully served many Nationalist Government factions dominated by Chiang Kai-shek, Li Tsung-jen of Kwangsi, or Sun Fo of the Crown Prince clique.

Putting diplomacy above factions and parties also enabled Dr. Koo to facilitate his official functions at home or abroad while softening the hostility of his political foes. In Paris he employed the principle of Chinese solidarity against foreigners to quiet the angry demonstrators who surrounded his residence and prevented the Chinese delegates from signing the Treaty of Versailles. In Washington he utilized this principle to persuade the Chinese students and representatives of the Chinese people that he and Wang Chung-Hui should attend the Sino-Japanese negotiations of the problem of Shantung. Time and again, in a China struggling for her political independence and territorial integrity, Dr. Koo advocated the unity of all factions and parties after his return to his homeland in 1922. Near the end of World War II, Dr. Koo and President Franklin D. Roosevelt strongly recommended to the Nationalist Government the inclusion of a Chinese Communist representative in the Chinese Delegation to San Francisco. The suggestions brought Tung Pi-wu into the Chinese diplomatic group attending the organization of the United Nations in 1945.[8]

[7] *Chung-kuo wai-chiao chi-kuan li-jen shou-chang hsien-ming nien-piao*, pp. 53–64.

[8] Wu Chün-ts'ai, *Chung-Kung jen-ming lu* (A Name List of the Chinese Communists), pp. 567–68. Tung Pi-wu was born in 1886, studied in Japan in 1910, organized the first Communist cell in Hupei and attended the First Congress of the Chinese Communists in 1921. He attended the Sun Yat-sen University of Moscow in 1928, became the Chairman of the Supreme Court of the Chinese Soviet Central Government in 1932, attended the San Francisco Conference in 1945, became Chairman of the North China People's Government in 1948, President of the Supreme People's Court in 1954, and was a Vice-Chairman of the People's Republic of China in 1959. He died in 1975.

THE ANGLO-AMERICAN GROUP OF CHINESE DIPLOMATS

To a considerable extent, Dr. Koo was a model of the Anglo-American Group of the Diplomatic Clique in the Peking Government after the Paris Peace Conference and the Nationalist Government in Nanking. In addition to Dr. Koo, the prominent members of that group included Sao-Ke Alfred Sze, Chengting T. Wang, and W. W. Yen. Because they all shared the same aspirations and ideological themes as Dr. Koo, it is very interesting to note that all the members of this group fit into a remarkably corresponding pattern with similar characters and backgrounds.

1. All four of them were natives of southeastern coastal provinces. Like W. W. Yen who was born in Shanghai in 1877, Dr. Koo was born and grew to adulthood in that most Westernized Chinese city. Chengting T. Wang was born in Ningpo of Chekiang Province in 1882, while Sao-Ke Alfred Sze, born in 1877, called Chen-tse in Kiangsu Province his home.
2. They were either sons of the missionary or prosperous merchants of the Yangtze Delta.
3. During their boyhood, they all received many years of traditional Chinese education, including the Confucian classics. Like Koo, C. T. Wang "acquired the rudiments of traditional education" before he entered the Peiyang University in Tientsin in 1896. Sze pursued his traditional Chinese training between 1882 and 1887, renewing his studies in 1890 under Hu Wei-hsien at the Chinese College in Shanghai until his assignment to Washington in 1893. Yen received his "early education from home tutors and in local schools" of the traditional style until he entered the Anglo-Chinese College in Shanghai.
4. Christian schools in China provided the earliest introduction of Western knowledge to the young Chinese. Like Dr. Koo, Sze was a student of St. John's College from 1887 to 1890 under F. L. Hawks Pott. Yen studied there also as well as at the Anglo-Chinese College between 1891 and 1893. Before entering Peiyang University in 1896, Wang, too, matriculated at a Christian school.
5. Later, they sought higher education in the United States. Koo received his degree, including the Ph.D., from Columbia University. Wang earned his B.A. at Yale, graduating in 1910. Sze received his A.B. and M.A. degrees from Cornell University in 1900 and 1902 respectively, while Yen graduated from the University of Virginia in 1900 with a baccalaureate.
6. Each member of the group started his career as a secretary or teacher specializing in English rather than as a professional diplomat. Because

of his knowledge of the English language, Dr. Koo's first position was secretary to the President and the Premier of China. Wang taught English at various schools during his earlier years; indeed, upon his return from the United States, he became secretary of the Chinese Y.M.C.A. at Shanghai. Sze's first appointment was as an English interpreter to Yang Ju, Chinese Minister to Washington in 1893, and upon his return from the United States, Sze served as English secretary to Tuan Fang, Governor of Hupei Province in 1902. Yen returned to China in 1900 to become professor of English at St. John's University, accepting soon afterward the offer of the Commercial Press to serve as its English editor.

7. Additionally, the Anglo-American group served both the warlord governments in Peking and the Nationalist Government in Nanking. Dr. Koo functioned as Minister of Foreign Affairs, Minister, and Ambassador under the various regimes. Wang was Chief of Diplomatic Affairs in 1911 under General Li Yüan-hung, revolutionary commander of the Wuchang Uprising. Appointed Vice-Minister of Commerce and Industry by Yüan Shih-k'ai's Government in 1912, Wang lobbied in America in 1919 on behalf of the Canton Government for its representation at the Paris Peace Conference, although he accepted the appointment as one of the Chinese delegates by the Peking Government under the control of the An-fu Clique without the sanction of the Canton Government. Between November 1922 and January 1923, Wang was concurrently Foreign Minister and acting Premier under the coalition of the Chihli and Fengtien Cliques. He succeeded Dr. Koo as the Foreign Minister of the Peking Government under the domination of the Christian General Feng Yü-hsiang after the *coup d'état* in October 1924. Wang succeeded Huang Fu as Foreign Minister of the Nationalist Government in June 1928 after the Tsinan Incident, only to be replaced by Dr. Koo in 1931 after the Mukden "Incident." In July 1937, Wang succeeded Sze as the Chinese Ambassador to Washington. When the Sino-Japanese War erupted, ushered in by the Lukouchiao Incident, he retired from the diplomatic service after his return from Washington in 1938.

Sze's government service began under the Imperial Ch'ing as General Manager of the Peking-Hankow Railway in 1906 and Associate Manager of the Peking-Mukden Railway in 1907. The next year he was appointed *Taotai* of Harbin, entering the Ministry of Foreign Affairs in 1910 as a Junior Councilor. After the Revolution in 1911, he became Minister of Communications in T'ang Shao-i's cabinet. Between 1914 and 1921 Sze remained Chinese Minister to London until he was transferred to Washington after the Paris Peace Conference. Concluding a two-year accreditation to Washington, he returned to China and served briefly as

Foreign Minister to Chang Shao-tseng's cabinet in 1923. After the Northern Expedition of the Nationalist Government, Sze retraced his earlier diplomatic paths, first to London in 1929, and in 1932, back to his Washington post. With the elevation of the legation to embassy status in 1935, he became the first Chinese Ambassador to the United States and continued in that position until 1937, when C. T. Wang succeeded him after the Lukouchiao Incident.

W. W. Yen followed Minister Wu T'ing-fang to Washington as his secondary secretary, only to be recalled to Peking one year later to organize a press bureau. In 1911, Yen became Councilor to the Ministry of Foreign Affairs of the Ch'ing Government. After the Revolution of 1911, President Yüan Shih-k'ai appointed him Vice Minister of Foreign Affairs, an office he held between April 1912 and January 1913. As Foreign Minister, acting Premier, and later Premier of the Peking Government, he operated under the domination of the Chihli Party from August 1920 to July 1922. Dr. Koo succeeded him after the Washington Disarmament Conference. In September 1924, President Ts'ao K'un, leader of the Chihli Clique, made him Premier until after the Capital Revolution in October 1924. Chief Executive Tuan Ch'i-jui appointed Yen Minister to the Court of St. James in October 1925. Upon his return from Europe, he again became Premier and acting Foreign Minister in May-June 1926, under the coalition of Marshal Chang Tso-lin of the Fengtien Clique and Marshal Wu P'ei-fu of the Chihli Clique. After the Mukden "Incident" in 1931, the Nationalist Government appointed him Minister to Washington in October 1932. He served as one of the Chinese delegates to the League of Nations, championing China's cause against Japanese aggression in Manchuria. Because all the members of the Anglo-American group served both the Peking Government and the Nationalist Government, Alfred Sze and W. W. Yen serving the Imperial Ch'ing as well, their experiences tended to emphasize further the similarity of their characters and professional viewpoints.

8. They usually held diplomatic posts at the centers of Anglo-American diplomacy, Washington, London, or a post near the world organizations, be it Paris for the League of Nations or Washington for the United Nations. Besides Koo's posts mentioned above, Chengting T. Wang also served as Chinese Minister to Washington from 1937 to 1938. Sao-Ke Alfred Sze was Chinese Minister to London between 1914 and 1921 and Chinese Minister to Washington between 1921 and 1929. In 1929, he was sent back to London for another three years until 1932 when he was returned to Washington until 1937. W. W. Yen was the Chinese

Minister to Germany, Denmark, and later Sweden from 1913 to 1920. He was sent to the United States as Chinese Ambassador from 1931 to 1932 and sent to Moscow from 1938 to 1942.

9. As their illustrious career moved toward a close, the Anglo-American group prepared for retirement in British Hong Kong or in the United States. Chengting T. Wang stayed in Hong Kong after his retirement from the diplomatic service in 1938, residing there until his death in 1961. Sao-Ke Alfred Sze did not return to China after his wartime assignment as Deputy Chairman of Materials Supply Commission of the Chinese Government in 1941. He died in Washington in January 1958. W. W. Yen retired in Hong Kong and the Japanese military authorities took him back to Shanghai when that island fell to the Japanese. Yen could not be exploited, however. He refused to serve the Japanese regime in any capacity. He died in Shanghai after his unsuccessful peace mission to Peking in 1950 on behalf of the Nationalist Government under acting President Li Tsung-jen, leader of the Kwangsi Clique.[9]

THE DIPLOMATS, WARLORDS AND THE NEWS MEDIA

The Peking Government's foreign policy was not entirely dominated by warlords. At different times, diplomats, public opinion, and the intelligentsia shared influence and responsibility in different ways and proportions. The warlords were mainly professional soldiers. They grew up in traditional environments and were exposed to a patriotic atmosphere. Except for a few students from the Japanese military academies, many of them lacked a good education and knew little about foreign affairs. Once a warlord achieved power, he tended to delegate the complicated and dangerous foreign affairs to the professional diplomats, who were highly capable, had no popular power base, possessed no ambition, and remained devoted to their duty to guard the international position of China for whatever Chinese government they served. Whenever there was any international problem, President Ts'ao K'un would tell his staff: "Wai-chiao, tsan-men pu-tung. Wen Shao-ch'uan hao-la." (As for foreign affairs, I don't know anything about it; just ask Wellington.) Unless

[9] The sources of this section are mainly from the following works: (a) *Biographical Dictionary of Republican China*; (b) *Biographies of Prominent Chinese*; (c) *Chuan-chi wen-hsüeh* (Biographical Literature); (d) *Chung-hua ming-kuo ta-shih chi* (The Important Issues of the Republic of China); (e) *Chung-kuo wai-chiao chi-kuan li-jen shou-chang hsien-ming nien-piao*; (f) *A List of the Various Cliques among Members of the Central Committee Elected by the Sixth Congress of the Kuomintang*; and (g) *Shih Chao-chi tsao-nien hui-i lu.*

the decision was to affect their position significantly, such as the policy to join the World War on the Allied side, most warlords remained reluctant to interfere with the conduct of foreign affairs.

The ability, international reputation, and trustworthiness of the Anglo-American-group diplomats was indispensable in securing funds from foreign and domestic sources for the warlords' armies and civil wars. The summary of a six months study of China's financial difficulties revealed that Dr. Yen's Commission for the Readjustment of Finances reported to the foreign bankers in April 1924 that the total annual revenue of the Peking Government during Ts'ao K'un's presidency was $209 million silver. However, the actual sum realized by the Central Government as unappropriated funds after deductions for the service of the foreign and domestic loans secured upon the revenues and the sums retained by the provincial authorities was only seven million dollars. The amount required for administration and military expenses exceeded $123 million silver.[10] It is not surprising that, throughout this period, the payment of civil officials or diplomats was often one or two years in arrears. Because the Peking Government was always desperately pressed for money, the political life of the Minister of Finance and the Minister of Foreign Affairs depended to a great extent on their ability to bargain successfully with foreign diplomats and their governments for release of the surplus funds of the maritime customs and salt gabelle. To raise the Chinese tariff rate and to facilitate the procurement of loans from foreign sources meant long negotiations for the Chinese, not sovereign decisions. On February 9, 1924, Dr. Koo concluded and signed the Sino-German Agreement which netted the Peking Government $43 million silver.[11]

Throughout the period of Republican China, public opinion, dominated by intelligentsia such as professors and college students in Peking and Shanghai as well as professional journalists, probably exerted more pressure on the Government than at any period of Chinese history since the unification of the Warring States by Ch'in in 221 B.C. Because of their control over the news media, the intellectuals and professional journalists gained influence in the policy-making of the Chinese Government. Both the political leaders and the diplomats considered public support a significant requirement for policy-making. The pressure of public opinion shaped Dr. Koo's decision, as well as the determination of his Chinese colleagues at Paris to refuse to sign the Treaty of Versailles, in spite of Government instruction. Pro-Japanese diplomats, such as Ts'ao Ju-lin and Chang Tsung-hsiang, felt the wrath of public anger and were permanently replaced by the Anglo-American group during the May

[10] *The North China Herald*, April 26, 1924.

[11] *Wai-chiao wen-tu: Chung-Te hsieh-yüeh chi fu-chien* (The Sino-German Agreement and Annex).

Fourth Movement in 1919. Perhaps it was also the pressure of public opinion that caused Dr. Koo to sign the Wang-Karakhan Agreement in 1924 with so little change. As returned students, Dr. Koo and other Chinese diplomats usually cultivated good relations with the news media and society as a whole. Even warlords manifested considerable toleration toward members of the press, except in the later part of warlord China when Shao P'iao-p'ing, editor of *Ching Pao* (Peking Daily), was executed by Young Marshal Chang Hsüeh-liang on April 28, 1926, and Lin Pai-shui of the *She-hui jih-pao* (Society Daily) was executed by General Chang Tsung-ch'ang on August 5, 1926. These extreme cases resulted primarily from blackmail activities, however, rather than from expression of the journalists' opinion.[12]

A British newspaper columnist of the 1930s wrote of Dr. Koo, and it seems valid today:

> Few people are more typical of the new China than Dr. Wellington Koo. American by training, smooth, polished, infinitely patient and gentle, there is no diplomat of the Western world who can surpass him in poise and suavity. If you watch him in the Council of the League as he debates with the Japanese delegate, you get something of his secret. He always knows his case to the last comma. He is never angry. He understands your difficulties. He presses home his pleas despite [the difficulties] only because, after all, principles are important and he knows that, with you as with him, a zeal for the Convenant of the League is essential among men of honor.[13]

The background of the traditional family and Confucian learning, the Anglo-American education and their experience in diplomacy were great assets in the generally successful careers of the Anglo-American group as negotiators for the termination of unequal treaties and the safekeeping of China's international position during the Republican era. So long as the foreign policy of the warlords and the Nationalist Government remained pro-Anglo-American and resisted Japanese and Soviet intrusion into China, Dr. Koo and his fellow "Anglo-Americans" were indispensable. Yet, in 1949, when the tide changed, these very assets became liabilities. The "Anglo-Americans" were caught in an impossible position, which not only led to the termination of their service for new China, but also became a source of controversy in the problem of normalization of relations between China and the United States.

[12]Kung Te-po, *Kung Te-po hui-i lu*, pp. 89-91. Lin Wei-chün, daughter of Lin Pai-shui, defends her father's professional integrity in her "Lin Pai-shui hsien-sheng chuan" (Biography of Mr. Lin Pai-shui), *Chuan-chi wen-hsüeh*, XIV, No. 5, p. 44.

[13]Koo Hui-lan, *No Feast Lasts Forever*, pp. 11-12.

Glossary

Ai-hsin-chüeh-lo Pu-yi (Aisin-Gioro Pu Yi) 愛新覺羅溥儀
An-fu Clique 安福系
Ankuochün 安國軍
Anshan 鞍山
Araki Sadao 荒木貞夫
Asahi Shimbun 朝日新聞
Chang, Carson (Chang Chia-sen) 張嘉森、張君勱
Chang Chia-sen (see Carson Chang)
Chang Chih-tung 張之洞
Chang Ching-yao 張敬堯
Chang Ch'ün 張群
Chang Hsüeh-liang 張學良
Chang Hsün 張勳
Chang Kuo-t'ao 張國燾
Chang-pei 張北
Chang Shao-tseng 張紹曾
Chang Tso-lin 張作霖
Chang Tsung-ch'ang 張宗昌
Chang Tsung-hsiang 章宗祥
Chang Wen-t'ung 張文通
Chang Ying-hua 張英華
Chang Yü-ch'üan 張煜全
Changchun 長春
Chao Te-chao 趙德朝
Chao T'i 趙倜
Chefoo 芝罘（煙台）
Chen-Sung Army 鎮嵩軍
Chen-tse 震澤
Chen, Eugene 陳友仁
Ch'en Ch'eng 陳誠
Ch'en Chih-mai 陳之邁
Ch'en Ch'ung-tsu 陳崇祖
Ch'en Hsi-chang 陳錫璋
Ch'en Kuang-yüan 陳光遠
Ch'en Lu 陳籙
Ch'en T'iao-yüan 陳調元
Ch'en Yüan-yüan 陳圓圓
Cheng Hsiao-hsü 鄭孝胥
Cheng Shih-ch'i 鄭士琦
Cheng Tien-fong 程天放
Cheptsun Damba Hut'ukht'u 哲布尊丹巴呼圖克圖
Chi Ching 嵇鏡
Chi Hsin-wen 吉星文
Ch'i Hsieh-yüan 齊燮元
Chia Shih-i 賈士毅
Chia-ting 嘉定
Chiang Ching-yüan 江經沅
Chiang Chung-cheng (see Chiang Kai-shek) 蔣中正
Chiang Fu-an 蔣福安
Chiang Kai-shek 蔣介石、蔣中正、蔣志清
Chiang Meng-lin 蔣夢麟
Chiao-t'ung Clique 交通系
Ch'ien Neng-hsün 錢能訓
Ch'ien T'ai (Tsien Tai) 錢泰
Chihli-Anhwei War 直皖戰爭
Chihli Army 直軍
Chihli Clique 直系
Chin Yün-p'eng 靳雲鵬
Ch'in-Doihara Agreement 秦土協定
Ch'in-huang tao 秦皇島
Ch'in Te-ch'un 秦德純
Chinchou (Chinchow) 錦州
Chinda 珍田
Ching Pao 京報
Chinlingchen 金嶺鎮
Chou Ch'uan-ching 周傳經
Chou En-lai 周恩來
Chou Tzu-ch'i 周自齊
Chow Tse-tsung 周策縱
Chu Ch'i-ch'ien 朱啟鈐
Chu Ho-hsiang 朱鶴翔
chü-jen 舉人

Chün t'ung chü 軍統局
Chung-hsi shu-yüan 中西書院
Chung-hsing Coal Mine Company 中興煤礦
Chung-hua chiao-yü kai-chin she 中華教育改進社
Chung-kuo hsüeh-shu chu-tso chiang-chu wei-yüan-hui 中國學術著作獎助委員會
Chung-O hui-i pan-shih ch'u 中俄會議辦事處
Dairen 大連
Debuchi Katsuji 出淵勝次
Doihara Kenji 土肥原賢二
Fan Ting 樊鼎
Fangtse (Fang-tzu) 坊子
Feng-Chih War 奉直戰爭
Feng-chün 奉軍
Feng Kuo-chang 馮國璋
Feng Shao-shan 馮少山
Feng-tien 奉天
Feng Yü-hsiang 馮玉祥
Furuya Keiji 古屋奎二
Gaimushō 外務省
Hai Ch'i 海圻艦
Hamaguchi Ōsachi 浜口雄幸
Han Fu-ch'ü 韓復榘
Handa Dorji 杭達多爾濟
Hangchow 杭州
Hanihara Masanao 埴原正野
Hankow 漢口
Harbin 哈爾濱
Hei-ho 黑河
Heilungkiang 黑龍江
Hiroshima 廣島
Hioki, R. 日置益
Ho Ch'eng-chün 何成濬
Ho Feng-yü 何鋒鈺
Ho Lung 賀龍
Ho Szu-yüan 何思源
Ho-Umezu Agreement 何梅協定
Ho Ying-ch'in 何應欽
Honjō Shigeru 本庄繁
Hoo Chi-tsai 胡世澤
Hoo Wei-teh (Hu Wei-te) 胡維德
Hsi Hsia 熙洽
Hsia Chin-lin 夏晉麟
Hsia Tou-yin 夏斗寅
Hsiang Tao 嚮導週報
Hsiao Yao-nan 蕭耀南
Hsieh Chieh-shih 謝介石
Hsien-tai p'ing-lun 現代評論
hsiu-ts'ai 秀才
Hsiung Pin 熊斌
Hsü Ching-ch'eng 許景澄
Hsü Mo 徐謨
Hsü Shih-ch'ang 徐世昌
Hsü Shih-ying 許世英
Hsü Shu-cheng 徐樹錚
Hsü Shu-hsi 徐淑希
Hsüeh Chün-tu 薛君度
Hu Lin 胡霖
Hu Shih 胡適
Hu Wei-hsien 胡維賢
Hu Wei-te (see Hoo Wei-teh)
Hua-kuo yüeh-k'an 華國月刊
Huai-jen t'ang Hall 懷仁堂
Huang Chieh 黃杰
Huang Fu 黃郛
Huang Hui-lan 黃蕙蘭
Huang-p'u (see Whangpu)
Huang Wu-chih 黃武智
Jiji Shimpō 時事新報
Jinling College 金陵大學
Jung Chen 榮臻
Kajima 加島，鹿島
Kao Ling-wei 高凌蔚
Kao Tien-chün 高殿均
Kao Yin-tsu 高隱祖
Kaomi-Hsuchow Railway 高密徐州鐵路
Katō Tomosaburō 加藤友三郎
Kawada Isao 河田烈
Kawakami 河上
Kenseikai Party 憲政會
Kiaochow 膠州
Kiaochow-Tsinan Railway 膠濟鐵路
King, Wunsz 金問泗
Kirin 吉林
Kobdo 科布多
Koo Ch'ing-ch'uan 顧晴川 (see Koo Jung)
Koo Jung (Ku Jung) 顧溶
Koo Shao-ch'uan (Ku Shao-ch'uan) 顧少川
Koo Wei-chün (Ku Wei-chün, V. K. Wellington Koo) 顧維鈞
Kowloon 九龍
Kuan Lin-cheng 關麟徵
Kuang-hsü 光緒
Kung Hsiang-hsi (H. H. Kung) 孔祥熙
Kung-Hsin-chan 龔心湛

Kung Te-po 龔德柏
Kuo-min tsa-chih she 國民雜誌社
Kuo-wen chou-pao 國聞週報
Kuominchün 國民軍
Kuriyama 栗山
Kwang-chow 廣州
Li Chia-ao 李家鏊
Li Chien-nung 李劍農
Li Ching-hsi 李經羲
Li Hung-chang 李鴻章
Li Hwang 李璜
Li Tsung-jen 李宗仁
Li Tu 李杜
Li Yüan-hung 黎元洪
Liang Ch'i-ch'ao 梁啟超
Liang Ching-tun 梁敬錞
Liang Lung 梁龍
Liang Shang-tung 梁上棟
Liang Shih-i 梁士詒
Liaotung 遼東
likin (a local transit tax) 釐金
Lin Pai-shui 林白水
Lin Wei-chün 林慰君
Linch'eng 臨城
Lin Sen 林森
Liu Chen-hua 劉鎮華
Liu Ching-jen 劉鏡人
Liu Ju-ming 劉汝明
Liu-t'iao-kou 柳條溝
Liu Yen 劉彥
Lo Chia-lun 羅家倫
Lo Kuang 羅光
Lo Wen-kan 羅文幹
Lou Tseng-tsiang 陸徵祥
Loyang 洛陽
Lu Chin 陸錦
Lu Chung-lin 鹿鍾麟
Lu Yung-hua (Lü Jung-huan) 呂榮寰
Lu Shan 廬山
Lu Tsung-yü 陸宗輿
Lü-shun (Port Arthur) 旅順
Lukouchiao 蘆溝橋
Lung-Hai Railway 隴海鐵路
Lung-ho 隆和輪
Ma Chan-shan 馬占山
Ma Fu-hsiang 馬福祥
Ma Soo 馬素
Makino Nobuaki 牧野伸顯
Manchouli 滿州里
Manchukuo 滿洲國
Matsuoka Yōsuke 松岡洋右
Ming-pao yüeh-k'an 明報月刊
Minseito Party 民政黨
Mochizuki Kotaro 望月幸太郎
Muto Nobuyoshi 武藤信義
Nagasaki 長崎
Nankai University 南開大學
Nien rebels 捻匪
Ningpo 寧波
Nishihara Loans 西原借款
Nomura 野村
Obata Torikichi 小幡酉吉
Obata Yūkichi 小幡酉吉
Odagiri Masunosuke 小田切
Oei Tiong Ham 黃宗翰
Okamura Yasuji 岡村寧次
Pao Kuei-ch'ing 鮑貴卿
Paoting 保定
Pao-tu-ku 抱犢崮
Pei-tai-ho 北戴河
Peiyang Army 北洋軍
Peking-Hankow Railway 京漢鐵路
Peking-Mukden Railway 京奉鐵路
Pi Kuei-fang 畢桂芳
P'u-k'ou 浦口
Quo Tai-chi (Kuo T'ai-ch'i) 郭泰祺
San To 三多
Sasebo 佐世保
Shakou Station 沙溝站
Shang Chen 商震
Shanhaikwan 山海關
Shao P'iao-p'ing 邵飄萍
She-hui jih-pao 社會日報
Shen Ch'ang-huan 沈昌煥
Shen Yü Hang 慎裕行
Shidehara Kijūrō 幣原喜重郎
Shigemitsu Mamoru 重光葵
Shih Chao-chi (Sao-Ke Alfred Sze) 施肇基
Shih Shao-ch'ang 施紹常
Shimonoseki 馬關
Soong, Tse Vung (T. V. Soong) 宋子文
Suiyuan 綏遠
Sun Ch'uan-fang 孫傳芳
Sun Fo 孫科
Sun Fu-chi 孫福基
Sun Kuei-chih 孫桂枝 (Sun Mei-yao)
Sun Mei-yao 孫美瑤
Sun Pao-ch'i 孫寶琦

Sun Yat-sen 孫逸仙
Sun Yüeh 孫岳
Sung Che-yüan 宋哲元
Sze, Sao-Ke Alfred 施肇基
Szu-lang t'an-mu 四郎探母
Ta-kung pao 大公報
Tai Chi-t'ao 戴季陶
Tai Li 戴笠
Talien Wan 大連灣
Tan Chia (chief) 當家
T'ang Shao-i 唐紹儀
T'ang Tsai-chang 唐在章
T'ang Tsai-li 唐在禮
T'angku Truce 溏沽停戰
Taotai 道台
Te-ho 德和輪
T'ien Chung-yü 田中玉
Tientsin-Paoting Clique 津保派
Tientsin-P'uk'ou Railway 津浦鐵路
Ting Ch'ao 丁超
Ting-kuo Army 定國軍
Tokugawa Iyesato 德川家達
Tong, Hollington K. (Tung Hsien-kuang) 董顯光
Ts'an-chan an 參戰案
Tsao-chuang 棗莊
Ts'ao Ju-lin 曹汝霖
Ts'ao Jui 曹銳
Ts'ao K'un 曹錕
Tsechuan (Tzu-ch'uan) 淄川
Ts'en Hsüeh-lü 岑學呂
Tsiang, T. F. (Chiang T'ing-fu) 蔣廷黻
Tsien Tai 錢泰
Tsinan-Shunteh Railway 濟南順德鐵路
Tsinanfu 濟南府
Tsingtao 青島
Tuan Ch'i-jui 段祺瑞
Tuan Fang 端方
Tuchün 督軍
Tung-fang tsa-chih 東方雜誌
Tung-pei chün 東北軍
Tung Pi-wu 董必武
T'ung Chih-jen 童志仁
Tupan 督辦
Uchida 內田
Uliasutai 烏里雅蘇台
Umezu Yoshijirō 梅津美治郎
Wai-chiao kung-pao 外交公報
"Wai-chiao, tsan-men pu-tung, Wen Shao-ch'uan hao-la." 外交，咱們不懂。問少川好啦。
Waichiaopu 外交部
Wakatsuki Reijiro 若槻禮次郎
Wan-ping 宛平
Wang Chao-ming (Wang Ching-wei) 汪兆銘
Wang Ching-t'ing (Wang, Chengting T.) 王正廷
Wang Ching-wei 汪精衛
Wang Ch'ung-hui (Wang Chung-Hui) 王寵惠
Wang Huai-ch'ing 王懷慶
Wang K'e-min 王克敏
Wang Kuang-ch'i 王光祈
Wang Shih-chieh 王世杰
Wang T'ieh-han 王鐵漢
Wang Yen-chang 王延璋
Wang Yi-che 王以哲
Wei Suntchou (Wei Ch'en-tsu) 魏宸組
Wei Tao-ming 魏道明
Wei Wen-pin 魏文彬
Wen Shih-chen 溫世珍
Weng Ya-nan 翁雅南
Whampoa (Military Academy) 黃浦（軍校）
Whangpu (Huang-p'u) 黃浦（江）
Wu Ch'ao-shu 伍朝樞
Wu Chün-ts'ai 吳俊才
Wu P'ei-fu 吳佩孚
Wu San-kuei 吳三桂
Wu Te-chen (Wu T'ieh-ch'eng) 吳鐵城
Wu T'ing-fang 伍廷芳
Wu Yi-fang 吳貽芳
Wu Yü-lin 吳毓麟
Yang I-te 楊以德
Yang Ju 楊儒
Yang Yü-t'ing 楊宇霆
Yeh Kung-ch'ao (George Yeh) 葉公超
Yeh Kung-ch'o 葉恭綽
Yen-chou-fu 兗州府
Yen Hsi-shan 閻錫山
Yen Hui-ch'ing (W. W. Yen) 顏惠慶
Yomiuri Shimbun 読売新聞
Yoshida Isaburo 吉田伊三郎
Yoshizawa Kenkichi 芳澤謙吉
Young, Clarence Kuang-son 楊光泩
Yü Chih 于治輪
Yü Hsüeh-chung 于學忠
Yü Jih-chang 余日章
Yü-ts'ai hsüeh-hsiao 育才學校
Yüan Shih-k'ai 袁世凱
Yüan Tao-feng 袁道豐

Bibliographical Notes

Every piece of source material was counter-checked if both Chinese and English versions were available, and the more detailed and accurate form was always used. Moreover, all of the texts and theories were based upon primary source materials. An attempt has been made to avoid reliance on secondary works whenever possible in order to avoid previous prejudices and misunderstandings that would be passed on to the reader.

In regard to the personal background and significant questions concerning Dr. Koo, this writer has received invaluable help from his notes taken during interviews with Dr. Koo between 1966 and 1967, as well as from his correspondence with Dr. Koo from 1966 to 1976. These sources provide a considerable body of direct material beyond the reach of most historians. Koo's massive 11,000-page work *Reminiscences of Wellington Koo*, a Chinese Oral History Project of the East Asian Institute of Columbia University, provides the most detailed and useful source. Also helpful were the writer's interviews and correspondence with Wunsz King (Chin Wen-szu), former Chinese Ambassador to the Netherlands and Dr. Koo's life-long confidant, and those with Dr. Te-kong Tọng (T'ang Te-kang), former Director of the East Asian Library of Columbia University and editor of the early part of Dr. Koo's memoir for Columbia University. Another significant source is *Hui-laṇ Koo: An Autobiography as Told to Mary Van Rensselaer Thayer* and its new version, *No Feast Lasts Forever*, by Madame Wellington Koo. Hui-lan Koo's period of association with Dr. Koo, first as his financée at the Paris Peace Conference and later as Madame Wellington Koo from 1919 to the time when the couple separated in 1956, covered the essential period pertinent to this work. Her memoir illustrates the private side of Dr. Koo better than any source, delineating his character and ideals, his conduct of affairs, and his motives. *No Feast Lasts Forever* traces her years with Koo to 1956, when Koo resigned from his diplomatic career for the last time.

One of the most significant collections of published materials included in the present study was the *Wai-chiaọ kung-pao* (Foreign Affairs Gazette). From 1921 to 1928, this official publication of the Ministry of Foreign Affairs of the Peking Government contained treaties, communications with foreign states, and the instructions and appointments of the Ministry. It includes the major documents for the Paris Peace Conference and the Washington Conference. It was extremely useful for details of the Sino-Russian negotiations because all the official notes and memoranda exchanged among Dr. Koo, Dr. Chengting T. Wang, and Mr. Karakhan are included. Another series of diplomatic documents was *Wai-chiao wen-tu* (Diplomatic Documents), published by the Ministry of Foreign Afairs from 1919 to 1921. It contains such important items as "Hsiu-kai shui-tse an" (Tariff Revision), 1912-1915, "Ts'an-chan an" (Participation in the War), 1917, and the "Chung-Jih chün-shih hsieh-ting an" (Sino-Japanese Military Agreements). The *Cheng-fu kung-pao* (Government Gazette) of the Peking Government proved beneficial.

Another important series published by the Commercial Press was the *Tung-fang tsa-chih* (The Eastern Miscellany) which first appeared in 1904. It became one of the oldest and most respected modern journals in China, for it not only contained documentary materials of the Peking Government and the local governments, but also carried many invaluable articles by scholars in various disciplines. Many articles, indispensable to the study of Dr. Koo and warlord China's diplomacy, were contributed by authoritative scholars from the National Peking University including Chou Keng-sheng, Yen Shu-t'ang, and Wang Shih-chieh. *Hsien-tai p'ing-lun* (The Contemporary Review) was a weekly review edited by professors of the National Peking University. Notable contributors included Ch'ien Tuan-sheng, Chang Hsi-jo, and Chou Keng-sheng, professors of the National Peking University. *Kuo-wen chou-pao* (Kuowen Weekly) as well as the leading independent newspaper, *Ta-kung pao* (Ta-kung Daily), were edited by Wu Ting-ch'ang. Both *Hsien-tai p'ing-lun* and *Kuo-wen chou-pao* published influential and critical articles on China's foreign affairs and Dr. Koo's conduct of foreign policy. The *Hsiang Tao* (Guide Weekly), organ of the Central Committee of the Chinese Communist Party from 1924 to 1927, published numerous short but stimulating articles by leftist intellectuals, who presented useful views of the ideological confrontation in China.

Many biographies and memoirs provide significant and critical material from unofficial viewpoints. *Lu Cheng-hsiang chuan* (Biography of Lou Tseng-tsiang) was written by Father Lo Kuang, now Arch-Bishop of Taipei. Lo quoted extensively from material Lou, Foreign Minister and head of the Chinese Delegation to the Paris Peace Conference, dictated to him while he stayed with Lou at a convent in Belgium. The work offers valuable information concerning Lou's diplomatic career and the Twenty-One Demands, in addition to the Paris Peace Conference. Another significant work dealing with affairs in China throughout World War I is Ts'ao Ju-lin's *I-sheng chih hui-i* (Memoir of Ts'ao Ju-lin). Vice-Minister of Foreign Affairs during the discussions of the Twenty-One Demands and the negotiator of the Nishihara loans,

Ts'ao subsequently remained a confidant of Marshal Tuan Ch'i-jui, head of the An-fu Clique and leader of the war faction. The work contains vivid descriptions concerning the split of the Peking Government on the question of participation in the European War. *Wu P'ei-fu chuan* (Biography of Wu P'ei-fu), compiled by editors of the Chunghua Book Company, reveals the interesting "telegram warfare" between the Marshal and Premier Liang Shih-i on the settlement of the Shantung question. Ts'en Hsüeh-lü's *San-shui Liang Yen-sun hsien-sheng nien-p'u* (Chronological Biography of Liang Shih-i), the counterpart of *Biography of Wu P'ei-fu*, presents the opposite side of the dispute by defending the integrity of the ill-fated premier. The *Shih Chao-chi tsao-nien hui-i lu* (Reminiscences of His Early Years as Told to Anming Fu) and the *Liu Ju-ming hui-i lu* (Memoir of Liu Ju-ming) also present some useful information. General Liu was a confidant and follower of Christian General Feng Yü-hsiang after 1912 and participated in every campaign Feng led. This work is particularly helpful in regard to the conflict among the warlords themselves and between the warlords and the Peking Government over foreign policy.

Wunsz King Collection on V. K. Wellington Koo Papers provided much of the material for the chapter on the Paris Peace Conference. Wunsz King compiled this invaluable collection while he was Dr. Koo's personal secretary in Paris. Approximately a hundred pages in length, the material is primarily composed of notes of interviews and memoranda between Dr. Koo and President Wilson, Secretary Robert Lansing, and other members of the American and British Delegations at Paris with emphasis on the problem of Shantung. Since Dr. Koo's pre-1931 archive was lost in mainland China, this collection is the only part of Dr. Koo's papers from the early conferences still extant. To this date, with the exception of Mr. King himself, no other scholar has used it.

Papers Relating to the Foreign Relations of the United States: The Paris Peace Conference, 1919, published by the American Government Printing Office, is another useful collection, containing thirteen volumes on the minutes and documents of the Council of Four and the Council of Ten. *Woodrow Wilson and World Settlement*, personal materials of Wilson at Paris, was edited by Ray Stannard Baker, Wilson's spokesman at the Paris Peace Conference. Baker's work remains an excellent survey of Wilson's policies and illustrates the factors in the President's major decisions at the Conference. Robert Lansing's *The Peace Negotiations: A Personal Narrative* and Arthur S. Link's *Wilson the Diplomatist: A Look at His Major Foreign Policies* offer critical views of the President's decision concerning Shantung. Lansing was Secretary of State and delegate of the American Government to the Conference, while Link is the leading Wilsonian scholar at Princeton. *Kung Te-po hui-i lu* (Memoir of Kung Te-po) is the reminiscences of Kung Te-po, a journalist trained in Japan. He was editor and publisher of many newspapers and was an attaché of the Chinese Delegation to the Washington Disarmament Conference. His works offer critical observations of Dr. Koo's activities.

For the Washington Conference, the *Conference on the Limitation of Armament, Washington, November 12, 1921-February 6, 1922* proved to be an indispensable source of official materials of the American Government in both English and French. The documents contain minutes of the Plenary Sessions, the Committee on Limitation of Armament, and the Committee on Pacific and Far Eastern Questions. Its sister work, *Conference on the Limitation of Armament: Subcommittees, Washington, November 12, 1921-February 6, 1922*, includes the complete minutes of seven subcommittees of the Whole Committee on Pacific and Far Eastern Questions. Activities of the Subcommittee on Foreign Post Offices in China, the Subcommittee on Chinese Revenue, the Subcommittee on Extraterritoriality, and the Subcommittee on Chinese Eastern Railway were represented in the minutes; discussions and debates in these subcommittees reflect the positions and conflicts of interest of the powers. Equally useful were the *Senate Documents of the United States, 67th Congress, Second Session, 1921-1922*, No. 126, containing the account and minutes of the Washington Conference, and the official British *Documents on British Foreign Policy, 1919-1939*, edited by E. L. Woodward and Rohan Butler, recording the attitude of His Majesty's Government regarding Japanese policy toward China.

For the questions relating to Shantung and the Kiaochow-Tsinanfu (Chiao-chou-Chinan) Railway, the *Conversations between Chinese and Japanese Representatives (to Conference on Limitation of Armament) in Regard to the Shantung Question* is extremely important. It is the complete record of minutes of the thirty-six sessions of the direct Sino-Japanese negotiations on the recovery of Shantung. This 396-page volume was prepared by the Japanese delegation and published by the American Government Printing Office in English in 1922. It also contains the Treaty for Settlement of Outstanding Questions Relative to Shantung, and the Agreed Terms of Understanding Recorded in the Minutes of the Treaty for the Settlement of Outstanding Questions Relative to Shantung. It is an interesting work, revealing how Dr. Koo and his colleagues conducted negotiations. It exposes Koo's coordinated plan with his Chinese colleagues for attack and retreat at the conference table and his maneuvers to gain assistance of third powers in case of impasse.

Chia Shih-i's *Hua-hui chien-wen lu* (Reminiscences Pertaining to the Washington Disarmament Conference) is a significant work in the sense that it presents an intimate picture of the Chinese delegates. As technical member of the Chinese Delegation to the Conference, Chia reveals background activities of the Chinese delegates outside the Conference room. Wunsz King's *Ts'ung Pa-li ho-hui tao Kuo-lien* (From Paris Peace Conference to the League of Nations) and his English pamphlet, *China at the Washington Conference, 1921-1922*, were helpful. Because King was Koo's confidant and secretary at the Washington Disarmament Conference, he reflects Dr. Koo's viewpoints better than other writers, although his intimate association with Dr. Koo until his (King's) death in April 1968 may have impaired his independent judgment of Dr. Koo. The well-known *China at the Conference* by Professor Westel W. Willoughby, technical expert to the Chinese Delegation to the Conference on Limitation of Armament, was also useful.

For the Linch'eng kidnapping and international control of Chinese railway, the *Roy S. Anderson Papers on Modern Chinese History* have been discovered and consulted for the first time. Roy S. Anderson, the son of Dr. David L. Anderson, founder of Soochow (Su-chou) University, went to the bandit lair and negotiated the agreement which effected the release of both Chinese and foreign passengers. The present trustee of this collection is Roy S. Anderson, a nephew of the negotiator, who worked for many years under Tai Li, head of Chiang Kai-shek's Chün t'ung chü (Bureau of Investigation and Statistics of the Commission on Military Affairs) or secret police, until Tai's death after the surrender of Japan. Among these papers was the telegram of Ts'ao K'un, head of the Chihli Clique and President-apparent, guaranteeing terms made by Anderson with the bandits.

On the restoration of Sino-Russian relations in 1923 and 1924, the *Chung O hui-i ts'an-k'ao wen-chien* (Documents for Reference on Sino-Russian Conference) is an official collection of documents prepared by the Chinese Ministry of Foreign Affairs for the Chinese delegates at the Sino-Soviet Conference. The second part of this collection, *Chung O wen-t'i lai-wang wen-chien* (Documents and Notes Exchanged between China and Russia on the Sino-Russian Problems), was indispensable to this study. It contains all the official exchanges between the Chinese Ministry of Foreign Affairs and the representatives of the Far Eastern Republic and the Soviet Union, including Yurin and Joffe, up to the arrival of Karakhan in Peking in early September 1923.

Wai-Meng chiao-she shih-mo chi (The Complete Story of Negotiations on Outer Mongolia) is the work of Pi Kuei-fang, first Imperial Agent of Altai in 1911 and negotiator of the Tripartite Agreement of 1915, in regard to Outer Mongolia. A related work is *Chih-shih pi-chi* (Notes of Ch'en Lu) by Ch'en Lu, deputy of Pi Kuei-fang during negotiation of the Tripartite Agreement for Outer Mongolia and first Chinese Resident General at Urga after this treaty. Both studies are valuable personal descriptions of experiences in the relations between China, Russia, and Outer Mongolia.

For the Manchurian Incident, *Ko-ming wen-hsien* (Documents of National Revolution), a series of official documents of the Kuomintang has been compiled and published by the Kuomintang Party History Commission of the Central Committee of the Nationalist Party since 1953. It devoted ten issues, Numbers 31 through 40, to Japanese aggression in Manchuria, including documents relating to the Lytton Commission. Furuya Keiji's *Chiang Tsung-t'ung mi-lu* (The Secret History of President Chiang Kai-shek) is a modern Chinese history with Chiang as the central figure. It is a well-researched work, incorporating many sections from Chiang's diary, a privilege granted by the Nationalist Party.

Japanese Aggression and the League of Nations, Volumes 1-8, is a collection of official documents from the Chinese Delegation to the League of Nations. Published by the Press Bureau of the Chinese Delegation, the papers present the Chinese point of view of multi-faceted Sino-Japanese conflict. Both Wunsz King's *China and the League of Nations: The Sino-Japanese Controversy* and Tsien Tai's *China and the Nine Powers Conference at Brussels in 1937* are concise, primary sources. Both King and Tsien participated in these meetings and assisted Koo in many ways.

The *Wellington Koo Collection* represents Koo's personal papers accumulated after 1931. Including notes and copies of official and private meetings, correspondence, telegrams, and a diary, Koo donated the entire array to Columbia University. His *Reminiscences* relied heavily upon this source. For later chapters of this study, particularly in regard to post-World War II diplomacy, Koo's documentation is essential.

Selected Bibliography

ARCHIVES, INTERVIEW, CORRESPONDENCE, AND PRIVATE PAPERS

Anderson, Roy S. *Roy S. Anderson Papers on Modern Chinese History*. In the custody of Roy S. Anderson, a nephew of Roy S. Anderson, San Diego.

Gaimushō 外務省 (Japanese Foreign Ministry). Archives of the Japanese Foreign Ministry, Tokyo, Japan, 1868–1945. Microfilmed for the Library of Congress, 1949-1951. Cecil H. Uyehara, *Checklist*, 1954.

King, Wunsz 金問泗 (Chin Wen-szu). Interview. March 24, 1967, Bethesda, Maryland.

————. Correspondence. May 26, 1966, Madison, Wisconsin; December 15, 1966, Bethesda, Maryland; March 9, 1967, Bethesda, Maryland; March 10, 1968, Bethesda, Maryland.

Koo, V. K. Wellington 顧維鈞 (Ku Wei-chün). *Wellington Koo Collection*. Special Collection, Butler Library, Columbia University.

————. Interview. November 19, 1966, New York City; November 26, 1966, New York City; August 11, 1967, New York City.

————. Correspondence. May 9, 1966, The Hague; January 27, 1967, New York City; March 14, 1968, New York City; May 2, 1968, New York City; November 12, 1968, New York City; December 23, 1968, New York City; May 19, 1969, New York City; June 16, 1969, New York City; July 1, 1969, New York City; September 23, 1969, New York City.

————. *Reminiscences of Wellington Koo*. An autobiography of some 11,000 typed pages, 1976.

Tong, Te-kong 唐德剛 (T'ang Te-kang). Interview. November 15, 1966, New York City.

Waichiaopu 外交部 (Ministry of Foreign Affairs). Archives of the Chinese Foreign Ministry, 1862-1927. Entrusted to the Institute of Modern History, Academia Sinica, Taiwan, Republic of China.

MATERIALS IN ORIENTAL LANGUAGES

Official Documents and Publications

Cheng-fu kung-pao 政府公報 (Government Gazette). Peking: Yin-chu-chü, 1912-1928.

Gaimushō 外務省 (Japanese Foreign Ministry) (comp.). *Dai Nihon gaiko bunsho* 大日本外交文書 (Documents of Japanese Foreign Affairs). 45 vols. Tokyo: Gaimushō, 1936-1956.

————. *Nihon gaikō nenpyō narabi ni shuyō bunsho, 1840-1945* 日本外交年報及主要文書 (Chronological Tables and Major Documents Pertaining to Japan's Foreign Relations). 2 vols. Tokyo: Nihon Kokusai Rengō Kyōkai, 1955.

Lo Chia-lun 羅家倫 (comp.). *Ko-ming wen-hsien* 革命文獻 (Documents on National Revolution). 40 *chi*. Taipei: Tang-shih Shih-liao Pien-tsuan Wei-yüan-hui, 1958-1967. New series to 79th *chi* in 1981.

Waichiaopu 外交部 (Ministry of Foreign Affairs) (ed.). *Lu-an Chung-Jih lien-ho wei-yüan-hui hui-i-lu ti-i-pu* 魯案中日聯合委員會會議錄第一部 (Conference Minutes of the Joint Sino-Japanese Commission on the Shantung Case, Part One); *Ti-erh-pu* 第二部 (Part Two). 2 vols. Annex: Shan-tung hsüan-an hsi-mu hsieh-ting 山東懸案細目協定 (Detailed Agreements on the Unsettled Question of Shantung). Peking: Waichiaopu, no date.

————. *Chung O hui-i ts'an-k'ao wen-chien* 中俄會議參考文件 (Documents for Reference on Sino-Russian Conference). Peking: Waichiaopu, no date.

————. *Treaties between the Republic of China and Foreign States, 1927-1961* (中外條約輯編). Taipei: Commercial Press, 1963.

————. *Wai-chiao kung-pao* 外交公報 (Foreign Affairs Gazette). Peking: Waichiaopu, 1921-1928.

————. *Wai-chiao wen-tu* 外交文牘 (Diplomatic Documents). Peking: Waichiaopu, 1920-1923.

This collection of documents includes the following subtitles: Hsiu-kai shui-tse an 修改稅則案 (Tariff Revision, 1912-1915); Ts'an-chan an 參戰案 (Participation in the War); Chung-Jih chün-shih hsieh-ting an 中日軍事協定案 (Sino-Japanese Military Agreements); Chung-Te hsieh-yüeh chi fu-chien 中德協約及附件 (The Sino-German Agreement and Annex); Hua-sheng-tun hui-i an 華盛頓會議案 (Washington Conference).

Wang Yen-wei 王彥威 and Wang Liang 王亮 (eds.). *Ch'ing-chi wai-chiao shih-liao* 清季外交史料 (Diplomatic Documents of the Ch'ing Dynasty, Kuang-hsü and Hsüan-t'ung's Reigns). Taipei: Wen-hai shu-chü, 1964.

Primary Sources

Chang Chih-tung 張之洞. *Chang Wen-hsiang-kung ch'üan-chi* 張文襄公全集 (The Complete Works of Chang Chih-tung). 231 books. Taipei: Wen-hai shu-chü, 1963.

Chang Kuo-t'ao 張國燾. "Wo-te hui-i" 我的回憶 (Memoir of Chang Kuo-t'ao). *Ming-pao yüeh-k'an* 明報月刊 (Ming-pao yu-hsien kung-szu), 1966-1969.

Ch'en Lu 陳籙. *Chih-shih pi-chi* 止室筆記 (Notes of Ch'en Lu). *Chin-tai Chung-kuo shih-liao ts'ung-k'an* 近代中國史料叢刊 (Modern China Historical Materials Series), edited by Shen Yün-lung 沈雲龍, No. 169. Taipei: Wen-hai shu-chü, no date.

Chia Shih-i 賈士毅. *Hua-hui chien-wen lu* 華會見聞錄 (Reminiscence Pertaining to the Washington Disarmament Conference). Shanghai: The Commercial Press, 1928.

Ch'in Te-ch'un 秦德純. *Hai-shih t'an-wang* 海澨談往 (Memoir of Ch'in Te-ch'un). Recorded by Institute of Modern History, Academia Sinica, Taipei. No place, no publisher, no date.

Furuya Keiji 古屋奎二. *Chiang Tsung-t'ung mi-lu* 蔣總統秘錄 (The Secret History of President Chiang Kai-shek), I-XV. Translated by the Central Daily News. Taipei: Central Daily News, 1974-1978.

Ho Szu-yüan 何思源. "Hua-sheng-tun hui-i chung Shan-tung wen-t'i chih ching-kuo"

華盛頓會議中山東問題之經過 (The Story of the Shantung Question at the Washington Conference). *Tung-fang tsa-chih*, XIX:2 (January 1922), pp. 54-65.

Hsü Ching-ch'eng 許景澄. *Hsü Wen-su-kung i-shu* 許文肅公遺書 (Papers of the Late Hsü Ching-ch'eng). Taipei: I-wen Press, 1964.

Hsü Shih-ying 許士英. *Hsü Shih-ying hui-i lu* 許士英回憶錄 (Memoir of Hsü Shih-ying). Taipei: Jen-chien-shih yüeh-k'an she, 1966.

Korostovets, Ivan J. *Von Cinggis Khan zur Sowjetrepublik* 從成吉思汗到蘇維埃共和國 (From Chinggis Khan to Soviet Republic). Berlin, 1926. Translated into Chinese as *K'u-lun t'iao-yüeh chih shih-mo* 庫倫條約之始末 (The Complete Story of the Russo-Mongolian Treaty at K'u-lun). Translated by Wang Kuang-ch'i 王光祈. Shanghai: Chung-hua shu-chü, 1930.

Kung Te-po 龔德柏. *Kung Te-po hui-i lu* 龔德柏回憶錄 (Memoir of Kung Te-po). Taipei: The Author, 1967.

Liu Ju-ming 劉汝明. *Liu Ju-ming hui-i lu* 劉汝明回憶錄 (Memoir of Liu Ju-ming). Taipei: Chuan-chi wen-hsüeh tsa-chih she, 1966.

Lo Chia-lun 羅家倫. "Wo tui-yü Chung-kuo tsai Hua-sheng-tun hui-i chih kuan-ch'a" 我對於中國在華盛頓會議之觀察 (My Observations on China at the Washington Conference). *Tung-fang tsa-chih*, XIX:2 (January 1922), pp. 12-54.

Morishima Morito 森島守人. *Imbō, ansatsu, guntō: ichi gaikōkan no kaiso* 陰謀，暗殺，軍刀：一外交官の回想 (Conspiracies, Assassinations, Sabers: Reminiscences of a Diplomat). Tokyo: Iwanami Shoten, 1957.

Pi Kuei-fang 畢桂芳. *Wai-Meng chiao-she shih-mo chi* 外蒙交涉始末記 (The Complete Story of Negotiations on Outer Mongolia). Taipei: Wen-hai shu-chü, no date.

Shen Yün-lung 沈雲龍 (ed.). *Chin-tai Chung-kuo shih-liao ts'ung-k'an* 近代中國史料叢刊 (Modern China Historical Materials Series). Taipei: Wen-hai shu-chü, 1966- .

Shidehara Kijūrō 幣原喜重郎. *Gaikō gojūnen* 外交五十年 (Fifty Years of Diplomacy). Tokyo: Yomiuri Shimbunsha, 1951.

Shigemitsu Mamoru 重光葵. *Shōwa no dōran* 昭和の動亂 (The Shōwa Upheavals). 2 vols. Tokyo: Chuō Kōronsha, 1952.

Sze, Sao-Ke Alfred 施肇基 (Shih Chao-chi). *Shih Chao-chi tsao-nien hui-i lu* 施肇基早年回憶錄 (Reminiscences of His Early Years as Told to Anming Fu). Taipei: Chuan-chi wen-hsüeh tsa-chih she, 1967.

Ts'ao Ju-ling 曹汝霖. *I-sheng chih hui-i* 一生之回憶 (Memoir of Ts'ao Ju-lin). Hong Kong: Ch'un-ch'iu tsa-chih she, 1966.

Ts'en Hsüeh-lü 岑學呂. *San-shui Liang Yen-sun hsien-sheng nien-p'u* 三水梁燕孫先生年譜 (Chronological Biography of Liang Shih-i). 2 vols. Taipei: Wen-hsing Books, 1962.

Tso Shun-sheng 左舜生. *Chin san-shih nien chien-wen tsa-chi* 近三十年見聞雜記 (A Record of Miscellany in the Past Thirty Years). Hong Kong: Tzu-yu ch'u-pan-she, 1952.

Tung Hsien-kuang. 董顯光. *Chiang Tsung-t'ung chuan* 蔣總統傳 (A Biography of President Chiang Kai-shek). Rev. ed. Taipei: Chung-hua wen-hua ch'u-pan shih-yeh wei-yüan hui, 1952.

T'ung Chih-jen 童志仁. "Tsai-chi Hua-sheng-tun hui-i chung Shan-tung wen-ti chih ching-kuo" 再記華盛頓會議中山東問題之經過 (The Problem of Shantung at the Washington Conference, the Latter Part). *Tung-fang tsa-chih*, XIX:9 (May 1922), pp. 81-87.

Wang, Chengting T. 王正廷 (Wang Cheng-t'ing). *Wang Cheng-t'ing chin yen lu* 王正廷近言錄 (The Recent Speeches of Chengting T. Wang). Shanghai: Hsien-tai shu-chü, 1933. Wang's memoir has been published recently.

Wang Yün-sheng 王芸生 (comp.). *Liu-shih-nien-lai Chung-kuo yü Jih-pen* 六十年來中國與日本 (China and Japan during the Past Sixty Years). 6 vols. Tientsin: Ta-kung Pao,

1932–1933.

Weng T'ung-ho 翁同龢. *Weng Wen-kung-kung jih-chi* 翁文恭公日記 (Diary of Weng T'ung-ho). 40 *ts'e*. 1925.

Wu Hsiang-hsiang 吳相湘 (ed.). *Chung-kuo hsien-tai-shih ts'ung-k'an* 中國現代史叢刋 (Modern Chinese History Series). Taipei: Cheng-chung shu-chü, 1961.

Yoshizawa Kenkichi 芳澤謙吉. *Gaikō rokujūnen* 外交六十年 (Sixty Years of Diplomacy). Tokyo: Jiyū Ajiasha, 1958.

Books and Articles

Chang Chung-fu 張忠紱. *Chung-hua min-kuo wai-chiao shih* 中華民國外交史(Diplomatic History of the Republic of China). Vol. 1. Taipei: Cheng-chung shu-chü, 1961.

Ch'en Chih-mai 陳之邁. *Chiang T'ing-fu ti chih-shih yü sheng-p'ing* 蔣廷黻的志事與生平 (The Life of Chiang T'ing-fu). Taipei: Chuan-chi wen-hsüeh tsa-chih she, 1966.

Ch'en Ch'ung-tsu 陳崇祖. *Wai-Meng chin-shih shih* 外蒙近世史 (Modern History of Outer Mongolia). Taipei: Wen-hai shu-chü, 1964.

Ch'en Hsi-chang 陳錫璋. *Pei-yang ts'ang-sang shih-hua* 北洋滄桑史話 (Story of Great Changes of the Peiyang Government). Tainan, Taiwan: The Author, 1967.

Ch'ien T'ai 錢泰. *Chung-kuo pu-p'ing-teng t'iao-yüeh chih yüan-ch'i chi ch'i fei-ch'u chih ching-kuo* 中國不平等條約之緣起及其廢除之經過 (The Origin and Abolition of the Unequal Treaties of China). Taipei: Kuo-fang yen-chiu she, 1961.

Chou Keng-sheng 周鯁生. *Chieh-fang yün-tung chung chih tui-wai wen-t'i* 解放運動中之對外問題 (Problems of Foreign Affairs during the Liberation Movement). Shanghai: T'ai-p'ing-yang shu-chü, 1927.

————. "Chung O kuan-hsi lun" 中俄關係論 (On the Relations between China and Russia). *Tung-fang tsa-chih*, XXI:1 (January 1924).

————. *Ko-ming wai-chiao lun* 革命外交論 (A Discourse on the Revolutionary Diplomacy). Shanghai: T'ai-p'ing-yang shu-chü, 1928.

Fu Ch'i-hsüeh 傅啟學. *Chung-kuo wai-chiao shih* 中國外交史 (A Diplomatic History of China). Taipei: San-min shu-chü, 1966.

Ho Han-wen 何漢文. *Chung O wai-chiao shih* 中俄外交史 (A Diplomatic History between China and Russia). Shanghai: Chung-hua shu-chü, 1935.

Hsia T'ien 夏天. *Chung-kuo wai-chiao-shih chi wai-chiao wen-t'i* 中國外交史及外交問題 (Chinese Diplomatic History and Diplomatic Problems). Shanghai: Kuang-hua shu-chü, 1932.

Huang Wu-chih 黃武智. *Kuo-chi fa-yüan fa-kuan Ku Wei-chün chih ke-pieh i-chien yü fan-tui i-chien, 1957-67* 國際法院法官顧維鈞之個別意見與反對意見 (Judge V. K. Wellington Koo's Individual and Minority Opinions at the International Court of Justice). Taipei: The Soochow University and Chung-kuo hsüeh-shu chiang-chu wei-yüan hui, 1974.

Kao Tien-chün 高殿均. *Chung-kuo wai-chiao shih* 中國外交史 (The Diplomatic History of China). Taipei: P'a-mi-erh shu-tien, 1952.

King, Wunsz 金問泗 (Chin Wen-szu). *Ts'ung Pa-li ho-hui tao Kuo-lien* 從巴黎和會到國聯 (From Paris Peace Conference to the League of Nations). Taipei: Chuan-chi wen-hsüeh tsa-chih she, 1967.

Liang Ching-tun 梁敬錞. *Chiu-i-pa shih-pien shih-shu* 九一八事變史述 (The Manchurian Affair). New York: Center of Asian Studies, St. John's University, 1965.

————. *Tsai Hua ling-shih ts'ai-p'an-ch'üan lun* 在華領事裁判權論 (A Discourse on the Consular Jurisdiction in China). Shanghai: The Commercial Press, 1930.

Liu Yen 劉彥. *Chung-kuo wai-chiao shih* 中國外交史 (A Diplomatic History of China), supplemented by Li Fang-ch'en 李方晨. Taipei: San-min shu-chü, 1962.

————. *Ou-chan ch'i-chien Chung-Jih chiao-she shih* 歐戰期間中日交涉史 (A History of Sino-Japanese Negotiations during the European War). Shanghai: The Author, 1921.

————. *Pei ch'in-hai chih Chung-kuo* 被侵害之中國 (The Encroached China). Shanghai: T'ai-p'ing-yang shu-tien, 1932.

Lo Kuang 羅光. *Lu Cheng-hsiang chuan* 陸徵祥傳 (Biography of Lou Tseng-tsiang). Taipei: Commercial Press, 1967.

Sun Hsiao-lou 孫曉樓 and Chao I-nien 趙頤年. *Ling-shih ts'ai-p'an ch'üan wen-t'i* 領事裁判權問題 (On the Consular Jurisdiction). Shanghai: The Commercial Press, no date.

T'an T'ien-k'ai 譚天凱. *Shan-tung wen-t'i shih-mo* 山東問題始末 (A Complete Account of the Shantung Question). Shanghai: The Commercial Press, 1935.

Tseng Yu-hao 曾友豪. *Chung-kuo wai-chiao shih* 中國外交史 (Chinese Diplomatic History). Shanghai: The Commercial Press, 1926.

Wai-chiao yen-chiu so 外交研究所 (ed.). *Chung-kuo chin-tai wai-chiao kai-yao* 中國近代外交概要 (A Concise Diplomatic History of Modern China). Peiping: Wai-chiao yen-chiu so, 1929.

Wang, Chengting T. 王正廷 (Wang Cheng-t'ing). *Chung-kuo chin-tai wai-chiao shih* 中國近代外交史 (A Diplomatic History of Modern China). Nanking: Wai-chiao yen-chiu so, 1928.

Wang Yü-chün 王聿均. *Chung-Su wai-chiao ti hsü-mu: Ts'ung Yu-lin tao Yüeh-fei* 中蘇外交的序幕：從優林到越飛 (The Beginning of Sino-Soviet Diplomacy: From Yurin to Joffe). Taipei: Institute of Modern History, Academia Sinica, 1963.

Wen Kung-chih 文公直 (ed.). *Chung-O wen-t'i chih ch'üan-pu yen-chiu* 中俄問題之全部研究 (A Complete Study on Sino-Russian Problems). Shanghai: I-hsin shu-she, 1929.

Wu Chün-ju 吳君如. *Chih-shih Chung-kuo wai-chiao shih* 近世中國外交史 (A Diplomatic History of Modern China). Shanghai: Shen-chou kuo-kuang she, 1932.

Wu Han-t'ao 吳瀚濤. *Tung-pei yü Jih-pen chih fa ti kuan-hsi* 東北與日本之法的關係 (A Legal Study: Japan's Acts of Treaty Violation and Encroachment upon the Sovereign Rights of China in the Northeastern Provinces). In *Tung-pei wen-ti yen-chiu-hui ts'ung-shu* 東北問題研究會叢書 (The Northeastern Affairs Research Institute Series), edited by Wang Cho-jan 王卓然. Peiping: The Institute, 1932.

Wu P'ei-fu chuan 吳佩孚傳 (Biography of Wu P'ei-fu). Compiled by editors of the Chung-hua shu-chü. Taipei: Chung-hua shu-chü, 1957.

Wu Hsiang-hsiang 吳相湘. *O-ti ch'in-liao Chung-kuo shih* 俄帝侵略中國史 (History of Russian Imperialists' Aggression in China). Taipei: Kuo-li pien-i kuan, 1964.

Newspapers and Periodicals

Chuan-chi wen-hsüeh 傳記文學 (Biographical Literature). Taipei: Chuan-chi wen-hsüeh she, 1963- .

Gaikō Jihō 外交時報 (Revue Diplomatique). Tokyo: Gaikō Jihō Sha, 1898-1938.

Hsiang Tao 嚮導 (Guide Weekly). 201 issues. Shanghai: Hsiang-tao chou-pao she, 1924.

Hsien-tai p'ing-lun 現代評論 (The Contemporary Review). Peking: Hsien-tai ping-lun she, 1924-1928.

Hua-kuo yüeh-k'an 華國月刊 (Hua-kuo Monthly). Shanghai: Hua-kuo yüeh-k'an she, 1923-1926.

Kuo-wen chou-pao 國聞週報 (Kuowen Weekly). Tientsin: Ta-kung Pao she, 1924-1937.

Ming-pao yüeh-k'an 明報月刊 (Ming-pao Monthly). Hong Kong: Ming-pao yu-hsien kung-szu, 1966- .

Ta-kung pao 大公報 (Ta-kung Daily). Tientsin.

Tung-fang tsa-chih 東方雜誌 (The Eastern Miscellany). Shanghai: The Commercial Press, 1904-1948.

Wai-chiao 外交 (Foreign Affairs Monthly). Peiping: Wai-chiao yüeh-pao she, 1932.

World Journal 世界日報. New York and San Francisco: World Journal Inc., 1976- .

The Yi-shih Pao 益世報. Tientsin.

References

Brunnert, H. S. and V. V. Hagelstrom. *Present Day Political Organization of China.* Revised by N. Th. Kolessoff and translated from Russian by A. Beltchenko and E. E. Moran, 1911. Taipei: World Book Co., no date of reprint.

Ch'ing-mo tui-wai chiao-she t'iao-yüeh chi, Kuang-hsü t'iao-yüeh 清末對外交涉條約輯：光緒條約 (Treaties between China and Foreign States in the Latter Part of the Ch'ing Dynasty, Kuang-hsü's Reign). Taipei: Kuo-feng Press, 1963.

Chung-kuo ts'an-chia chih kuo-chi kung-yüeh hui-pien 中國參加之國際公約彙編 (A Compendium of International Treaties to Which China Adheres). Shanghai: The Commercial Press, 1937.

Chung-wai t'iao-yüeh hui-pien 中外條約彙編 (Treaties between China and Foreign States, 1687-1932). Taipei: Wen-hai shu-chü, 1964.

Division of Archives and Materials, Ministry of Foreign Affairs (ed.). *Chung-kuo wai-chiao chi-kuan li-jen shou-chang hsien-ming nien-piao* 中國外交機關歷任首長銜名年表 (Table of the Names and Titles of the Successive Heads of the Organ of Foreign Affairs of China). Taipei: Commercial Press, 1967.

Kao Yin-tsu 高蔭祖. *Chung-hua min-kuo ta-shih chi* 中華民國大事記 (The Important Issues of the Republic of China). Taipei: The World Book Co., 1957.

A List of the Various Cliques among Members of Central Committee Elected by the Sixth Congress of the Kuomintang (Confidential for reference only). It was prepared by the Communist intelligence for confidential purposes in August 1945. It was translated into English by the Committee on International and Regional Studies of Harvard University and was distributed in February 1948.

Wu Chün-ts'ai 吳俊才 (ed.). *Chung-Kung jen-ming lu* 中共人名錄 (A Name List of the Chinese Communists). Taipei: Kuo-chi kuan-hsi yen-chiu so, 1967.

Wu P'ei-fu hsien-sheng nien-p'u 吳佩孚先生年譜 (The Chronological Biography of Mr. Wu P'ei-fu). No place, no publisher, no date. (Copy kept by East Asiatic Library of the University of California, Berkeley.)

Yang Chia-lo 楊家駱. *Chia-wu i-lai Chung-Jih chün-shih wai-chiao ta-shih chi-yao, 1894-1937* 甲午以來中日軍事外交大事記要 (Essential Military and Diplomatic Issues between China and Japan Since the Sino-Japanese War). Changsha: The Commercial Press, 1941.

Yin Shou-sung 尹壽松 (ed.). *Chung-Jih tiao-yüeh hui-tsuan* 中日條約彙纂 (Compendium of Sino-Japanese Treaties). Shanghai: The Commercial Press, 1924.

MATERIAL IN WESTERN LANGUAGES

Government Documents and Publications

Butler, Rohan and E. L. Woodward (eds.). *Documents on British Foreign Policy, 1919-1939*. London: H. M. Stationery Office, 1960.

China. Ministry of Communications. *Railway Loan Agreements of China.* Compiled by Chin-chun Wang, T. T. Linn, and E. W. Chang. 2 vols. Peking: Railway Department, Ministry of Communications, 1922.

————. Ministry of Railways. *Statistics of Chinese National Railways, 10th-18th, 1924-1932.* 9 vols. Nanking: Ministry of Railways, 1925-1933.

Chinese Delegation to the League of Nations. *Japanese Aggression and the League of Nations, 1937-1940*, I-VIII. Geneva: Press Bureau of the Chinese Delegation, 1937-1940.

Commission on Extraterritoriality. *Report of the Commission on Extraterritoriality in China, Peking, September 16, 1926. Being the Report to the Government of the Commission Appointed in Pursuance to Resolution I of the Conference on the Limitation of Armaments*. Washington: Government Printing Office, 1926.

Conversations between Chinese and Japanese Representatives (to Conference on Limitation of Armament) in regard to the Shantung question, Treaty for settlement of outstanding questions relative to Shantung (and) agreed terms of understanding recorded in the minutes of the Japanese and Chinese Delegations concerning the conclusion of the treaty for the settlement of outstanding questions relative to Shantung; minutes prepared by the Japanese Delegation (Document catalogue, Vol. 16, p. 2088). Washington: Government Printing Office, 1922. 396 pp.

International Military Tribunal Far East, International Prosecution Section. Proceedings, Exhibits, Rejected Documents, as held by the Harvard Law School, Cambridge and the University of California, Berkeley, California.

Koo, V. K. Wellington. *A Statement of the Views of the Chinese Government on the Report of the Commission of Enquiry of the League of Nations*. Geneva: Chinese Delegation to the League of Nations, December 1932.

Oakes, Augustus H. (comp. and ed.). *British and Foreign State Papers, 1891-1906*. London: Her Majesty's Stationery Office, 1841-19 .

U. S. Department of State. *Conference on the Limitation of Armament, Washington, November 12, 1921-February 6, 1922*. Washington: Government Printing Office, 1922.

————. *Conference on the Limitation of Armament: Subcommittees, Washington, November 12, 1921-February 6, 1922.* Washington: Government Printing Office, 1922.

————. *Documents on German Foreign Policy, 1918-1945*. Washington: Government Printing Office, 1957-1960.

————. *National Archives Microfilm Publications Microcopy No. 329. Records of the Department of State Relating to Internal Affairs of China, 1910-1929.* Reel No. 1-227.

————. *Papers Relating to the Foreign Relations of the United States*. Washington: Government Printing Office, 1911-1928.

————. *Papers Relating to the Foreign Relations of the United States: The Lansing Papers, 1914-1920*. 2 vols. Washington: Government Printing Office, 1940.

————. *Papers Relating to the Foreign Relations of the United States: The Paris*

Peace Conference, 1919. 13 vols. Washington: Government Printing Office, 1942.

U. S. Senate. *Senate Documents of the United States, 67th Congress, Second Session, 1921-1922*, No. 126. Washington: Government Printing Office, 1922.

Primary Sources

Baker, Ray Stannard. *Woodrow Wilson and World Settlement.* 3 vols. New York: Doubleday, Page and Co., 1923.

Carnegie Endowment for International Peace. *The Sino-Japanese Negotiations of 1915: Japanese and Chinese Official Statement.* Washington: The Endowment, 1921.

Carnegie Endowment for International Peace, Division of International Law. *China Treaties and Agreements, 1919-1929.* Washington: The Endowment, 1929.

Clyde, Paul Hibbert (ed.). *United States Policy toward China: Diplomatic and Public Documents, 1839-1939.* New York: Russell and Russell, 1964.

Degras, Jane (ed.). *Soviet Documents on Foreign Policy.* 3 vols. London: Oxford University Press, 1951-1953.

Eudin, Xenia Joukoff and Robert C. North. *Soviet Russia and the East, 1920-1927: A Documentary Survey.* Stanford: Stanford University Press, 1964.

House, Edward M. *The Intimate Papers of Colonel House: The Ending of the War.* Edited by Charles Seymour. Boston: Houghton Mifflin Company, 1928.

King, Wunsz. *China and the League of Nations: The Sino-Japanese Controversy.* New York: St. John's University Press, 1965.

Koo, Hui-lan (Ku Huang Hui-lan). *Hui-lan Koo: An Autobiography as Told to Mary Van Rensselaer Thayer.* New York: Dial Press, 1943.

———— with Isabella Taves. *No Feast Lasts Forever.* New York: The New York Times Book Co., 1975.

Koo, V. K. Wellington (Ku Wei-chün). *Memoranda Presented to the Lytton Commission.* 2 vols. New York: Chinese Cultural Society, 1932-1933.

————. "The Real China." *Annals of the American Academy of Political and Social Science*, No. 294 (1954), pp. 71-82.

————. *The Status of Aliens in China.* New York: Columbia University, 1912.

Lansing, Robert. *The Peace Negotiations: A Personal Narrative.* Boston: Houghton Mifflin Co., 1921.

Lloyd George, David. *Memoirs of the Peace Conference.* New Haven: Yale University Press, 1939.

MacMurray, John V. A. (comp. and ed.). *Treaties and Agreements with and Concerning China, 1894-1919.* 2 vols. New York: Oxford University Press, 1921.

Maki, John M. *Selected Documents: Far Eastern International Relations (1689-1951).* Seattle: University of Washington Press, 1957.

The Shantung Question: A Statement of China's Claim Together with Important Documents Submitted to the Peace Conference in Paris. San Francisco: Chinese National Welfare Society in America, 1919.

Stimson, Henry L. *The Far Eastern Crisis: Recollections and Observations.* New York: Harper and Brothers, 1936.

———— and McGeorge Bundy. *On Active Service in Peace and War.* New York: Harper and Brothers, 1948.

Sze, Sao-Ke Alfred (Shih Chao-chi). "What China Asks of the Powers." *Chinese Student Monthly*, 1927, pp. 7-12.

Tsien Tai. *China and the Nine Powers Conference at Brussels in 1937*. New York: St. John's University Press, 1964.

Wang, Chengting T. (Wang Cheng-t'ing). "Democratic China: An Address Delivered by His Excellency Dr. C. T. Wang before the Philadelphia Board of Trade," October 21, 1937. Philadelphia: no publisher, 1937.

———. *Japan's Aggression upon China*. Boston: no publisher, 1937.

———. *Selected Statements and Addresses of His Excellency Dr. Cheng-t'ing Wang Concerning the Sino-Japanese Conflict*. No place, no publisher, 1938.

Wilbur, C. Martin and Julie Lien-ying How (eds.). *Documents on Communism, Nationalism, and Soviet Advisers in China, 1918-1927: Papers Seized in the 1927 Peking Raid*. New York: Columbia University Press, 1956.

Willoughby, Westel W. *China at the Conference*. Baltimore: The Johns Hopkins University Press, 1922.

———. *The Sino-Japanese Controversy and the League of Nations*. Baltimore: The Johns Hopkins University Press, 1935.

Witte, Sergei. *The Memoirs of Count Witte*. Translated by Abraham Yarmolinsky. New York: Howard Fertig, 1967.

Yen, W. W. *East-West Kaleidoscope 1877-1944: An Autobiography*. New York: St. John's University Press, 1974.

Books and Articles

Abbott, James Francis. *Japanese Expansion and American Policies*. New York: Macmillan Co., 1916.

Asada, Sadao. "Japan's Special Interests and the Washington Conference, 1921-1922." *American Historical Review*, No. 1 (October 1961), p. 62.

Bailey, Thomas A. *Woodrow Wilson and the Lost Peace*. Chicago: Quadrangle Books, 1963.

Baker, Ray Stannard. *What Wilson Did at Paris*. New York: Doubleday, Page and Co., 1919.

Bashford, James W. *China: An Interpretation*. New York: The Abingdon Press, 1919.

Borg, Dorothy. *American Policy and the Chinese Revolution, 1925-1928*. New York: Institute of Pacific Relations, 1947.

Brandt, Conrad. *Stalin's Failure in China, 1924-1927*. Cambridge: Harvard University Press, 1958.

Brown, Delmer M. *Nationalism in Japan*. Berkeley: University of California Press, 1955.

Brown, Sidney DeVere. "Shidehara Kijūrō: The Diplomacy of the Yen." In *Diplomats in Crisis: United States-Chinese-Japanese Relations, 1919-1941*, edited by R. D. Burns and E. M. Bennett. Santa Barbara, California: ABC-Clio Press, 1974.

Buehrig, Edward H. (ed.). *Wilson's Foreign Policy in Perspective*. Bloomington, Indiana: Indiana University Press, 1957.

———. *Woodrow Wilson and the Balance of Power*. Bloomington, Indiana: Indiana University Press, 1955.

Ch'en, Jerome. *Mao and the Chinese Revolution*. New York: Oxford University Press, 1967.

———. *Yüan Shih-k'ai, 1859-1916*. Stanford: Stanford University Press, 1961.

Cheng, Tien-fong. *A History of Sino-Russian Relations*. Washington: Public Affairs Press, 1957.

Chiang Chung-cheng (Chiang Kai-shek). *Soviet Russia in China: A Summary-up at Seventy*. New York: Farrar, Straus and Cudahy, 1957.

Chow Tse-tsung (Chou Ts'e-tsung). *The May Fourth Movement: Intellectual Revolution in Modèrn China*. Cambridge: Harvard University Press, 1960.

Clubb, O. Edmund. *Twentieth Century China*. New York: Columbia University Press, 1964.

Coons, Arthur Gardiner. *The Foreign Public Debt of China*. Philadelphia: University of Pennsylvania Press, 1930.

Dallin, David J. *Soviet Russia and the Far East*. New Haven: Yale University Press, 1948.

Dulles, Foster Phea. *China and America*. Princeton: Princeton University Press, 1946.

Fairbank, John King. *The United States and China*. Cambridge: Harvard University Press, 1958.

Fifield, Russell H. *Woodrow Wilson and the Far East: The Diplomacy of the Shantung Question*. Hamden, Connecticut: Archon Books, 1965.

Fishel, Wesley R. *The End of Extraterritoriality in China*. Berkeley: University of California Press, 1952.

Friters, Gerard M. *Outer Mongolia and Its International Position*. Baltimore: The Johns Hopkins University Press, 1949.

Garthof, Raymond L. *Sino-Soviet Military Relations*. New York: Frederick A. Praeger, 1966.

Gilbert, Rodney. *What's Wrong with China*? London: J. Murray, 1926.

Gillin, Donald G. *Portrait of a Warlord: Yen Hsi-shan in Shanshi Province, 1911-1949*. Princeton: Princeton University Press, 1966.

Godshall, Wilson Leon. *Tsingtao Under Three Flags*. Shanghai: The Commercial Press, 1929.

Griswold, A. Whitney. *The Far Eastern Policy of the United States*. New York: Harcourt, Brace & Co., 1938.

Herz, John H. *Political Realism and Political Idealism: A Study in Theories and Realities*. Chicago: The University of Chicago Press, 1951.

Hill, C. *The Doctrine of Rebus Sic Stantibus in International Law*. Columbia: University of Missouri Press, 1934.

Hoover, Herbert. *The Ordeal of Woodrow Wilson*. New York: McGraw-Hill Book Company, 1951.

Houn, Franklin W. *Central Government of China, 1912-1928*. Madison: University of Wisconsin Press, 1957.

Hsia Chin-lin. *Studies in Chinese Diplomatic History*. Shanghai: The Commercial Press, 1922.

Hsü, Shu-hsi. *China and Her Political Entity* (A Study of China's Foreign Relations with Reference to Korea, Manchuria, and Mongolia). London: Oxford University Press, 1926.

———. *An Introduction to Sino-Foreign Relations*. Shanghai: Kelly and Walsh, 1941.

———. *Japan and the Third Powers*. Shanghai: Kelly and Walsh, 1941.

Hsüeh, Chün-tu. *Huang Hsing and the Chinese Revolution*. Stanford: Stanford University Press, 1961.

Huang Sung-k'ang. *Lu Hsün and the New Culture Movement of Modern China*. Amsterdam: Djambatan, 1957.

Iriye, Akira. *After Imperialism: The Search for a New Order in the Far East: 1921-1931*. Cambridge: Harvard University Press, 1965.

Israel, John. *Student Nationalism in China, 1927-1937*. Stanford: Stanford University Press, 1966.

Kajima, Morinosuke. *A Brief Diplomatic History of Modern Japan*. Rutland, Vermont:

Charles E. Tuttle, 1965.

———. *The Emergence of Japan as a World Power, 1895-1925*. Rutland, Vermont: Charles E. Tuttle, 1968.

Kane, Albert E. *China, the Powers and the Washington Conference*. Shanghai: The Commercial Press, 1937.

Kawakami, K. K. *Japan and World Peace*. New York: The Macmillan Co., 1919.

———. *Japan's Pacific Policy: Especially in Relation to China, the Far East, and the Washington Conference*. New York: E. P. Dutton and Company, 1922.

King, Wunsz (Chin Wen-szu). *China at the Paris Peace Conference in 1919*. New York: St. John's University Press, 1961.

———. *China at the Washington Conference, 1921-1922*. New York: St. John's University Press, 1963.

Kirby, E. Stuart (ed.). *Contemporary China*. Hong Kong: Hong Kong University Press, 1955.

La Fargue, Thomas Edward. *China and the World War*. Stanford: Stanford University Press, 1937.

Lattimore, Owen. *Manchuria: Cradle of Conflict*. New York: The Macmillan Company, 1932.

———. *The Mongols of Manchuria: Their Tribal Division, Geographical Distribution, Historical Relations with Manchus and Chinese and Present Political Problems*. New York: The John Day Company, 1934.

———. *Nationalism and Revolution in Mongolia*. New York: Oxford University Press, 1955.

———. *Studies in Frontier History, Collected Papers, '1928-1958*. London: Oxford University Press, 1962.

Leng Shao-chuan and Norman D. Palmer. *Sun Yat-sen and Communism*. Published under the auspices of the Foreign Policy Research Institute at the University of Pennsylvania. New York: Frederick A. Praeger, 1960.

Levenson, Joseph R. *Liang Ch'i-ch'ao and the Mind of Modern China*. Cambridge: Harvard University Press, 1953.

Levi, Werner. *Modern China's Foreign Policy*. Minneapolis: University of Minnesota Press, 1953.

Li Chien-nung. *The Political History of China, 1840-1928*. Translated by Teng Ssu-yü and Jeremy Ingalls. Princeton: Van Nostrand, 1956.

Link, Arthur S. *Wilson the Diplomatist: A Look at His Major Foreign Policies*. Baltimore: The Johns Hopkins University Press, 1957.

Ma Ho-t'ien. *Chinese Agent in Mongolia*. Translated by John de Francis. Baltimore: The Johns Hopkins University Press, 1949.

MacNair, Harley Farnsworth. *China in Revolution*. Chicago: The University of Chicago Press, 1931.

———. *China's International Relations and Other Essays*. Shanghai: The Commercial Press, 1926.

Meisner, Maurice. *Li Ta-ch'ao and the Origin of Chinese Marxism*. Cambridge: Harvard University Press, 1967.

Millard, Thomas Franklin Fairfax. *China, Where It Is Today and Why*. New York: Harcourt, Brace & Co., 1928.

Morse, Hosea Ballou. *The International Relations of the Chinese Empire*. 3 vols. Taipei: Wen-hsin shu-tien, no date.

Norton, Henry Kittredge. *China and the Powers*. New York: The John Day Company, 1927.

Notter, Harley. *The Origins of the Foreign Policy of Woodrow Wilson*. Baltimore: The Johns Hopkins University Press, 1937.

Pollard, Robert R. *China's Foreign Relations, 1917-1931*. New York: The Macmillan Company, 1933.

Scalapino, Robert A. *Democracy and the Party Movement in Prewar Japan: The Failure of the First Attempt*. Berkeley: University of California Press, 1962.

Schiffrin, Harold Z. *Sun Yat-sen and the Origins of the Chinese Revolution*. Berkeley: University of California Press, 1968.

Sharman, Lyon. *Sun Yat-sen: His Life and Its Meaning: A Critical Biography*. Hamden, Connecticut: Archon Books, 1965.

Shepherd, Charles R. *The Case Against Japan*. New York: Daniel Ryerson, 1938.

Sheridan, James E. *Chinese Warlord: The Career of Feng Yü-hsiang*. Stanford: Stanford University Press, 1952.

Smith, Rev. George. *Consular Cities of China*. New York: Harper and Brothers, 1847.

Sze, Tsung-yu. *China and the Most-Favored-Nation Clause*. New York: Fleming H. Revell, 1925.

Takeuchi, Tatsuji. *War and Diplomacy in the Japanese Empire*. New York: Doubleday, Doran and Co., 1935.

Tang, Peter S. H. *Russian and Soviet Policy in Manchuria and Outer Mongolia, 1911-1931*. Durham, North Carolina: Duke University Press, 1959.

Tung, William L. *V. K. Wellington Koo and China's Wartime Diplomacy*. New York: St. John's University Press, 1977.

Wei, Henry. *China and Soviet Russia*. Princeton: D. Van Nostrand, 1956.

Weigh, Ken-shen. *Russo-Chinese Diplomacy*. Shanghai: The Commercial Press, 1928.

Whiting, Allen S. *Soviet Policies in China, 1917-1924*. New York: Columbia University Press, 1954.

Whyte, Sir Frederick. *China and Foreign Powers: An Historical Review of Their Relations*. New York: Oxford University Press, 1927.

Williams, Edward Thomas. *China: Yesterday and Today*. New York: Thomas Y. Crowell, 1927.

Willoughby, Westel W. *China at the Conference*. Baltimore: The Johns Hopkins University Press, 1922.

———. *Foreign Rights and Interests in China*. 2 vols. Reprint; Taipei: Ch'eng-wen Publishing Co., 1966.

Wood, G. Zay. *The Twenty-One Demands: Japan versus China*. New York: Fleming H. Revell, 1921.

Wright, Stanley Fowler. *China's Struggle for Tariff Autonomy, 1843-1938*. Shanghai: Kelly and Walsh, 1938.

Wu, Aitchen K. *China and the Soviet Union: A Study of Sino-Soviet Relations*. New York: The John Day Co., 1950.

Yakhontoff, Victor A. *Russia and the Soviet Union in the Far East*. London: G. Allen and Unwin, 1932.

Yanaga, Chitoshi. *Japan Since Perry*. New York: McGraw-Hill Book Co., 1949.

Yang, C. Walter. *The International Relations of Manchuria*. Chicago: The University of Chicago Press, 1929.

Unpublished Materials

Buss, Claude Albert. "The Relation of Tariff Autonomy to the Political Situation in China." Unpublished Ph.D. dissertation, University of Pennsylvania, 1927.

Dean, Britten. "Sino-Japanese Relations in the 1920's." Unpublished Ph.D. dissertation, Columbia University, 1966.

Fan, Carole C. "Description and Interpretation of the Geographic Distribution of Leadership in China, 1875-1937." Unpublished Ph.D. dissertation, University of California, Los Angeles, 1964.

Yang, Alexander. "The Twenty-One Demands." Unpublished Ph.D. dissertation, The East Asian Institute, Columbia University, 1964.

Newspapers and Periodicals

China Year Book, Tientsin.
The Far Eastern Times, Peking.
New York Times, New York.
The North China Daily News, Peking.
The North China Herald, Shanghai.
The North China Star, Tientsin.
Peking and Tientsin Times, Tientsin.

References

Boorman, Howard L. (ed.). *Biographical Dictionary of Republican China*. 4 vols. New York: Columbia University Press, 1967-1970. Vol. 5 was added in later years.

————. *Men and Politics in Modern China: Preliminary 50 Biographies*. New York: Columbia University Press, 1960.

Burt, A. R., J. B. Powell, and Carl Crow. *Biographies of Prominent Chinese*. Shanghai: Biographical Publishing Company, 1925.

Carnegie Endowment for International Peace, Division of International Law. *Shantung: Treaties and Agreements*. Washington: The Endowment, 1921.

Fairbank, John King and Kwang-ching Liu. *Modern China: A Bibliographical Guide to Chinese Works, 1898-1937*. Cambridge: Harvard University Press, 1961.

Hucker, Charles O. *China: A Critical Bibliography*. Tucson: The University of Arizona Press, 1962.

Kuo Ting-yee (comp.) and James W. Morely (ed.). *Sino-Japanese Relations, 1862-1927: A Checklist of the Chinese Foreign Ministry Archives*. New York: The East Asian Institute, Columbia University Press, 1965.

Lust, John (comp.). *Index Sinicus: A Catalogue of Articles Relating to China in Periodicals and Other Collective Publications, 1920-1955*. Cambridge, England: W. Heffer & Sons, 1964.

MacMurray, John V. A. *Treaties and Agreements with and concerning China, 1894-1919*. 2 vols. New York: Oxford University Press, 1921.

The Maritime Customs (comp.). *Treaties, Conventions, etc., between China and Foreign States*. 2 vols. Shanghai: Statistical Department of the Inspectorate General of Customs, 1917.

Yüan Tung-li (comp.). *China in Western Literature: A Continuation of Cordier's Bibliotheca Sinica*. New Haven, Connecticut: Far Eastern Publications, Yale University Press, 1958.